Contents

Textbook Of Instrumental Methods Of Analysis: Principles And Techniques

Ms. K. Pranusha, M.Pharm.

Assistant Professor,

Department of Pharmaceutical Chemistry,

GET School of Pharmacy,

Rajahmundry 533296, Andhra Pradesh, India

Dr. Lagu Surendra Babu, M.Pharm., Ph.D.

Assistant Professor,

Pharmaceutical Chemistry Division,

Adikavi Nannaya University College of Pharmaceutical Sciences,

Tadepalligudem 534101, Andhra Pradesh, India

Dr. Nammi Usha Rani, M.Pharm., Ph.D.

Professor,

Maharajah's College of Pharmacy,

Vizianagaram Dist., Pincode: 535002, Andhra Pradesh, India

Published by Notion Press

Notion Press, Inc.

800, West El Camino Real #180,

California, USA 94040

Notion Press Media Pvt Ltd

#7, Red Cross Road,

Egmore, Chennai, Tamil Nadu 600008

Email ID: publish@notionpress.com

Phone Number: +91 44 46315631

CHAPTERS

- **12.1 Introduction and Theory of GC**

  - Principles of Gas Chromatography
  - Gas-Liquid Partitioning

- **12.2 Instrumentation of GC**

  - Carrier Gas, Injector, Column, Detector
  - Temperature Programming

- **12.3 Applications of GC**

  - Analysis of Volatile Compounds
  - Pharmaceutical and Environmental Applications

Chapter 13: High-Performance Liquid Chromatography (HPLC)

- **13.1 Introduction and Theory of HPLC**

  - Principles of HPLC
  - Modes of Separation: Normal and Reverse Phase

- **13.2 Instrumentation of HPLC**

  - Pumps, Injectors, Columns, Detectors

- **13.3 Applications of HPLC**

  - Drug Analysis and Purity Testing
  - Bioavailability Studies

Chapter 14: Ion Exchange Chromatography

- **14.1 Introduction to Ion Exchange Chromatography**

  - Classification and Types of Ion Exchange Resins
  - Properties and Mechanism of Ion Exchange

- **16.3 Applications of Affinity Chromatography**

  - Purification of Antibodies
  - Enzyme Isolation

Authors

K. Pranusha

Dr. Lagu Surendra Babu

Dr. N. Usha Rani

CHAPTER ONE

UV-Visible Spectroscopy

1.1 Electronic Transitions

Overview of Electronic Transitions

In UV-visible spectroscopy, **electronic transitions** refer to the movement of electrons between different energy levels within a molecule when it absorbs light in the ultraviolet (UV) or visible spectrum. These transitions occur because the energy provided by the absorbed light matches the difference in energy between two electronic states of the molecule. When a molecule absorbs UV or visible light, one of its electrons is excited from a lower-energy orbital to a higher-energy orbital. The specific wavelengths of light absorbed correspond to the energy required for these transitions, which is unique to each type of molecule.

The most common electronic transitions observed in UV-visible spectroscopy are those involving π (pi) and σ (sigma) bonds. **π-π^* transitions** occur when an electron in a bonding π orbital is excited to an anti-bonding π^* orbital. These transitions are typically observed in molecules with conjugated double bonds, where the π electrons are more easily excited. **n-π^* transitions** involve the excitation of a non-bonding electron (n) to a π^* orbital and are often seen in molecules containing lone pairs of electrons, such as carbonyl compounds. **σ-σ^*** transitions, on the other hand, are less common in UV-visible spectroscopy because they require higher energy and typically occur in the far UV region.

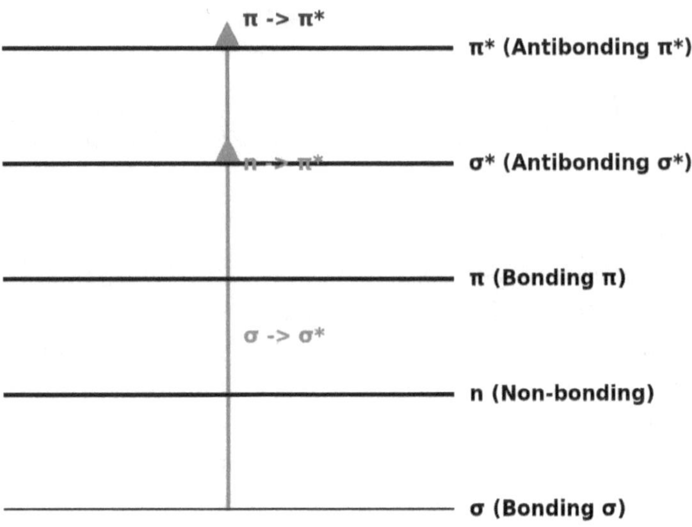

Here is the energy level diagram that illustrates different electronic transitions such as $\pi \to \pi^*$, $n \to \pi^*$, and $\sigma \to \sigma^*$. This visual representation helps in understanding how electrons transition between molecular orbitals when they absorb energy, which is fundamental to UV-Visible spectroscopy

Interpretation of the Diagram

1. **Energy Levels:**

   - The horizontal lines represent different energy levels corresponding to different molecular orbitals.
   - From bottom to top, these energy levels are:

     - **σ (Bonding σ):** The lowest energy bonding orbital.
     - **n (Non-bonding):** The orbital that does not participate in bonding, typically associated with lone pairs of electrons.
     - **π (Bonding π):** The bonding orbital formed by the sideways overlap of p-orbitals.

- π *(Antibonding π):*** The antibonding orbital corresponding to the π bonding orbital.
- σ *(Antibonding σ):*** The antibonding orbital corresponding to the σ bonding orbital.

2. **Electronic Transitions:**

- $\sigma \to \sigma^*$:

  - This transition involves an electron moving from the bonding σ orbital to the antibonding σ^* orbital.
  - This transition typically requires high energy, found in the far UV region (vacuum UV).

- $n \to \pi^*$:

  - This transition involves an electron from a non-bonding orbital (n) moving to an antibonding π^* orbital.
  - This transition is characteristic of unsaturated molecules with lone pairs and generally occurs in the UV region.

- $\pi \to \pi^*$:

  - This transition involves an electron moving from a bonding π orbital to an antibonding π^* orbital.
  - This is common in conjugated systems (like alkenes and aromatic compounds) and occurs in the UV-visible region.

Chromophores and Auxochromes

In the context of UV-visible spectroscopy, **chromophores** and **auxochromes** play a critical role in determining the absorption characteristics of molecules. A **chromophore** is a part of a molecule responsible for its color, specifically the portion that absorbs UV or visible light, leading to an electronic transition. When a chromophore absorbs light, it causes an electron within the molecule to transition from a lower energy level to a higher energy level. The energy absorbed corresponds to a specific wavelength of light, which is then subtracted from the visible spectrum, giving the compound its characteristic color.

Common examples of chromophores include functional groups such as carbonyl (C=O), nitro (NO2), and azo (N=N) groups. These groups contain π-electrons or non-bonding electrons that can be excited to higher energy levels when they absorb light. The exact wavelength at which a chromophore absorbs light is influenced by the molecular structure around it, making chromophores key identifiers in the analysis of organic compounds through UV-visible spectroscopy.

Auxochromes, on the other hand, are groups of atoms attached to the chromophore that do not themselves absorb UV or visible light but influence the absorption properties of the chromophore. An auxochrome can either shift the absorption wavelength (usually toward the longer wavelength or red region) or increase the intensity of absorption. This phenomenon is known as a **bathochromic shift** or **hyperchromic effect**, respectively. Common auxochromes include hydroxyl (-OH), amino (-NH2), and methyl (-CH3) groups. When these groups are attached to a chromophore, they can alter the electron distribution within the molecule, thereby modifying the energy required for electronic transitions.

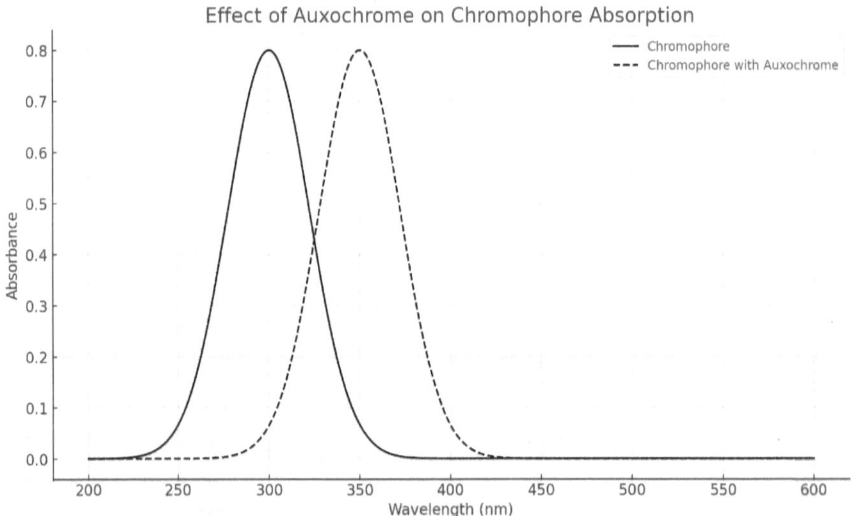

Here is the diagram showing the effect of an auxochrome on the absorption of a chromophore:

Chromophore: The solid line represents the original absorption spectrum of the chromophore.

Chromophore with Auxochrome: The dashed line shows how the presence of an auxochrome shifts the absorption maximum to a longer wavelength, indicating a bathochromic shift (red shift).

This diagram illustrates how auxochromes can alter the absorption properties of chromophores

1.2 Spectral Shifts

Bathochromic, Hypsochromic, Hyperchromic, and Hypochromic Shifts

In UV-visible spectroscopy, **spectral shifts** refer to changes in the absorption wavelength or intensity of a compound's electronic transitions due to structural modifications or changes in the environment. These shifts are critical for understanding how different factors influence the absorption characteristics of molecules.

A **bathochromic shift**, also known as a red shift, occurs when the absorption maximum of a molecule moves to a longer wavelength (toward the red end of the spectrum). This shift typically results from structural changes in the molecule, such as conjugation or the introduction of auxochromes like hydroxyl or amino groups. Bathochromic shifts indicate that less energy is required for electronic transitions, often due to increased electron delocalization within the molecule.

In contrast, a **hypsochromic shift**, also known as a blue shift, occurs when the absorption maximum moves to a shorter wavelength (toward the blue end of the spectrum). This shift suggests that more energy is required for electronic transitions, which can result from the removal of conjugation or the presence of electron-withdrawing groups like nitro or carbonyl groups. Hypsochromic shifts are common when the electronic environment of the chromophore becomes more restricted.

Hyperchromic shifts refer to an increase in the intensity of absorption, meaning that more light is absorbed at the absorption maximum. This effect often occurs when there is an increase in the number of absorbing species, such as when the concentration of the solution is increased or when an auxochrome enhances the overall electron density in the chromophore. The result is a more intense absorption band.

On the other hand, **hypochromic shifts** indicate a decrease in the intensity of absorption, meaning that less light is absorbed at the absorption maximum. This effect can occur due to dilution, aggregation of molecules, or structural changes that reduce the effectiveness of the chromophore in absorbing light. Hypochromic shifts often signal a reduction in the number of absorbing species or a decrease in the overall electron density around the chromophore.

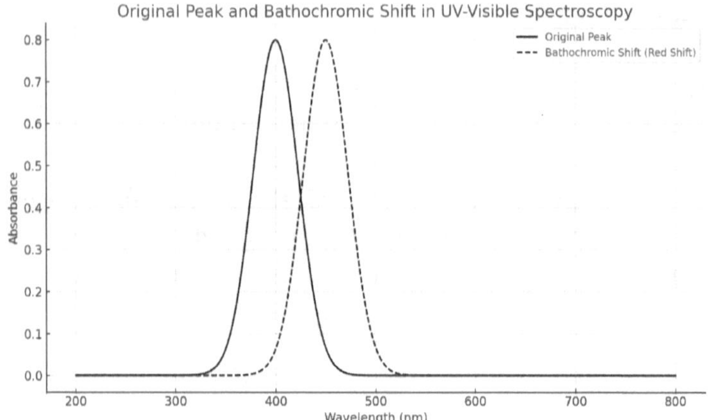

Bathochromic Shift (Red Shift): The peak shifts to a longer wavelength

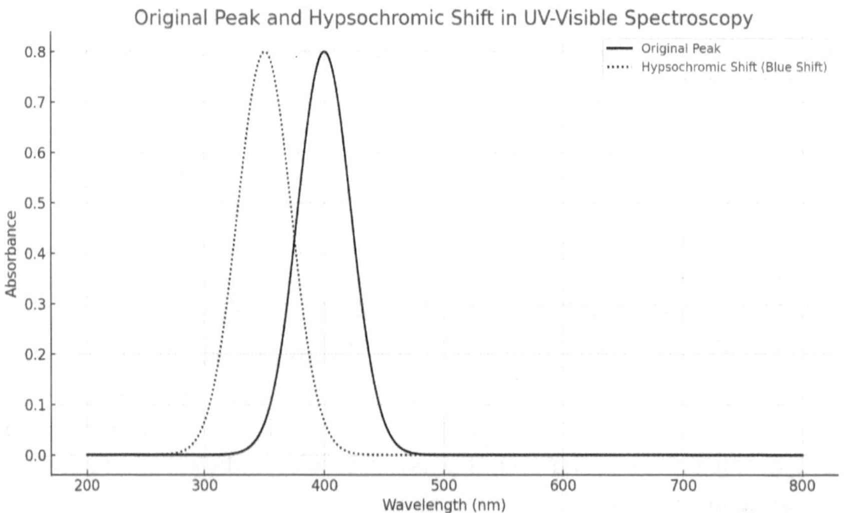

Hypsochromic Shift (Blue Shift): The peak shifts to a shorter wavelength (blue)

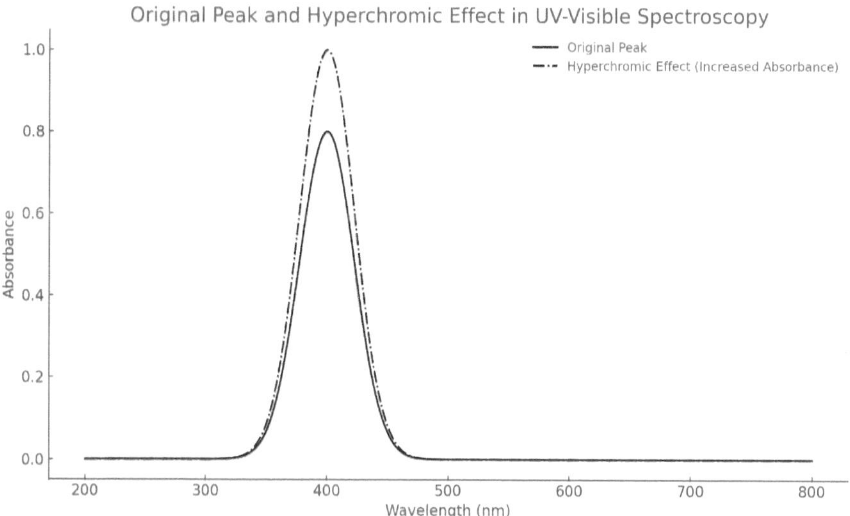

Hyperchromic Effect: An increase in absorbance without a change in wavelength

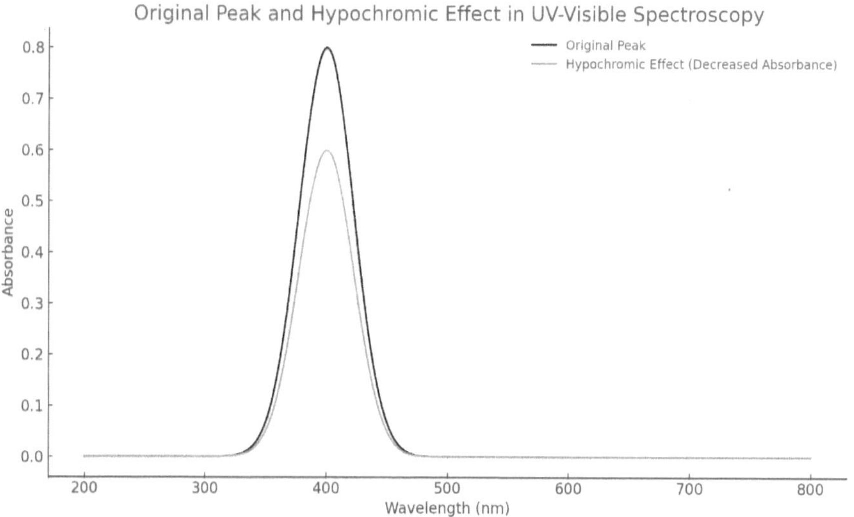

Hypochromic Effect: A decrease in absorbance without a change in wavelength

Solvent Effect on Absorption Spectra

The **solvent effect on absorption spectra** is a crucial aspect of UV-visible spectroscopy, as the choice of solvent can significantly influence the absorption characteristics of a molecule. When a solute is dissolved in a solvent, the interactions between the solute molecules and the solvent molecules can alter the energy levels of the electronic states, leading to changes in the absorption spectra.

One of the primary ways solvents affect absorption spectra is through changes in **polarity**. Polar solvents, such as water or ethanol, can stabilize different electronic states of the solute to varying degrees. This stabilization occurs because polar solvents interact strongly with polar or charged groups in the solute molecule. For instance, if the excited state of a molecule is more polar than the ground state, a polar solvent will stabilize the excited state more, leading to a decrease in the energy gap between the ground and excited states. This effect often results in a **bathochromic shift** (red shift) in the absorption maximum, meaning the absorption occurs at a longer wavelength.

Conversely, in non-polar solvents, such as hexane or toluene, the lack of strong solvent-solute interactions can lead to different effects. If the ground state of the molecule is more polar than the excited state, non-polar solvents may stabilize the ground state more effectively, leading to an increase in the energy gap between the states. This scenario often causes a **hypsochromic shift** (blue shift) in the absorption maximum, meaning the absorption occurs at a shorter wavelength.

In addition to affecting the wavelength of absorption, solvents can also influence the **intensity** of absorption bands. The nature of the solvent can either enhance or diminish the probability of electronic transitions, leading to **hyperchromic** (increase in intensity) or **hypochromic** (decrease in intensity) effects. For example, hydrogen bonding between the solute and a protic solvent like water can either increase or decrease absorption intensity depending on how it alters the electronic environment of the chromophore.

1.3 Beer and Lambert's Law

Derivation of the Law

Beer and Lambert's Law is a fundamental principle in UV-Visible spectroscopy that relates the absorbance of light by a sample to the concentration of the absorbing species in the sample. This law can be derived by considering the basic interactions between light and matter.

Basic Principles

- **Absorbance (A):** The amount of light absorbed by the sample.
- **Incident Light (I^0):** The intensity of light entering the sample.
- **Transmitted Light (I):** The intensity of light passing through the sample.
- **Path Length (l):** The distance the light travels through the sample.
- **Concentration (c):** The concentration of the absorbing species in the sample.
- **Molar Absorptivity (ε):** A constant that represents how strongly the species absorbs light at a given wavelength.

Derivation Steps

1. **Consider a thin layer of the sample:**

   - Let a thin layer of thickness dx of the sample solution absorb a small fraction of the incident light I^0.

Light Attenuation:

- The decrease in the intensity of light dI as it passes through the thin layer is proportional to the intensity of the incident light I, the concentration of the absorbing species c, and the thickness dx.
- Mathematically, this can be expressed as:

$$dI = -k \cdot I \cdot c \cdot dx$$

Here, k is a proportionality constant.

3. **Integrating Over the Path Length:**

   - To find the total decrease in light intensity over the entire path length `1`, we integrate the equation from `x = 0` to `x = 1`:

$$\int_{I_0}^{I} \frac{dI}{I} = -k \cdot c \cdot \int_{0}^{l} dx$$

   - Solving the integrals:

$$\ln\left(\frac{I}{I_0}\right) = -k \cdot c \cdot l$$

4. **Relating to Absorbance:**

   - The absorbance `A` is defined as:

$$A = \log_{10}\left(\frac{I_0}{I}\right)$$

   - Since natural logarithms can be converted to base-10 logarithms by multiplying by `2.303`:

$$A = \epsilon \cdot c \cdot l$$

   - Here, `ε = k / 2.303` is the molar absorptivity, a constant that depends on the substance and the wavelength of light.

The final form of Beer-Lambert's Law is:

A=ε·c·l

This equation shows that the absorbance A is directly proportional to the concentration c of the absorbing species, the path length l, and the molar absorptivity ε. This law is widely used in UV-Visible spectroscopy to determine the concentration of a substance in a solution by measuring the absorbance of light at a specific wavelength.

Deviations from Beer-Lambert Law

While Beer-Lambert's Law provides a straightforward relationship between absorbance, concentration, and path length, there are certain conditions under which deviations from this law occur. These deviations can be classified into **real deviations, chemical deviations, and instrumental deviations.**

Real deviations arise when the assumptions underlying Beer-Lambert's Law are not met, particularly at very high concentrations. At high concentrations, solute molecules are so close to each other that interactions between them can alter their absorption characteristics. This can lead to non-linear relationships between absorbance and concentration, causing deviations from the law.

Chemical deviations occur when the absorbing species undergoes a chemical change at different concentrations. For example, in cases where the solute associates or dissociates, or where the pH of the solution changes, the absorption characteristics can change, leading to deviations from Beer-Lambert's Law. In such scenarios, the relationship between absorbance and concentration is no longer linear.

Instrumental deviations stem from limitations or inaccuracies in the measurement instruments. These can include factors such as stray light, polychromatic radiation, or detector sensitivity. Stray light refers to light that reaches the detector without passing through the sample, which can lead to lower than expected absorbance readings. Polychromatic radiation occurs when the light source is not monochromatic, meaning it contains a range of wavelengths rather than a single wavelength. This can lead to inaccuracies because the molar absorptivity ϵ varies with wavelength.

1.4 Instrumentation

1.4.1 Sources of Radiation

In UV-visible spectroscopy, the **source of radiation** is a critical component of the instrumentation, as it provides the light needed to excite the electrons in the sample. The selection of an appropriate light source is essential for accurate and reliable spectroscopic measurements, as it directly influences the quality and range of the data obtained.

For **UV spectroscopy**, the most commonly used sources of radiation are **deuterium** and **hydrogen lamps**. These lamps emit continuous radiation in the UV region, typically covering wavelengths from 160 nm to 400 nm. The deuterium lamp is preferred due to its stable output and broad spectrum, making it suitable for most UV-visible spectroscopic applications. The hydrogen lamp is similar in function but is less commonly used due to the superior performance of the deuterium lamp.

In the **visible region**, typically ranging from 400 nm to 700 nm, **tungsten filament lamps** are commonly used. These lamps produce a continuous spectrum of visible light and are known for their high intensity and stability. Tungsten lamps emit light over a wide range of wavelengths, making them ideal for visible spectroscopy. They are also relatively inexpensive and have a long operational life, contributing to their widespread use in spectrometers.

For applications requiring light in both the UV and visible regions, **xenon arc lamps** are often employed. Xenon lamps emit a broad spectrum of light that spans from the UV through the visible and into the near-infrared region. These lamps are highly intense and provide a continuous spectrum, making them suitable for a wide range of spectroscopic analyses. However, they are more expensive and require more complex handling compared to deuterium or tungsten lamps.

In addition to these common sources, **LEDs** (light-emitting diodes) are increasingly being used in modern spectrometers. LEDs are available in specific wavelengths and are highly efficient, compact, and have a long operational life. They are particularly useful in portable and miniaturized spectrometers, where size and power consumption are critical considerations.

The choice of radiation source in UV-visible spectroscopy depends on the specific requirements of the analysis, including the wavelength range of interest, the intensity needed, and the stability of the light output. Proper selection and maintenance of the radiation source are essential for obtaining accurate and reproducible results in spectroscopic measurements.

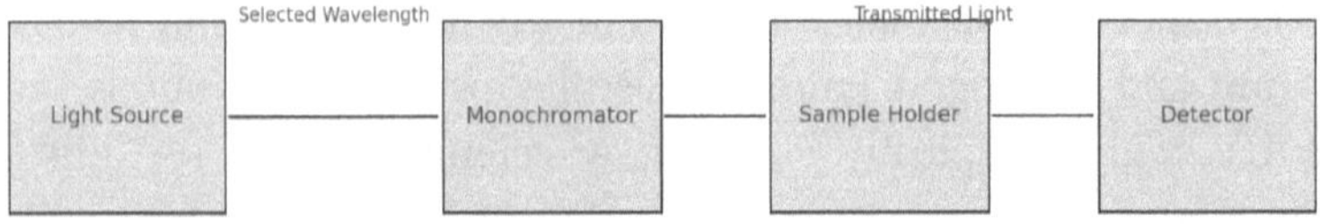

Basic components of UV-Visible spectroscopy instrumentation:Light Source: The origin of the radiation used for the analysis.Monochromator: Selects a specific wavelength from the light source.Sample Holder: Where the sample is placed for measurement.Detector: Measures the intensity of light after it passes through the sample.

1.4.2 Wavelength Selectors

Wavelength selectors are crucial components in UV-visible spectroscopy, as they determine the specific wavelengths of light that are allowed to pass through the sample. The accuracy and precision of a spectroscopic measurement largely depend on the effectiveness of the wavelength selector in isolating the desired wavelength while excluding others. There are two primary types of wavelength selectors used in spectrometers: **monochromators** and **filters**.

Monochromators are optical devices that disperse light into its component wavelengths and allow the selection of a narrow band of wavelengths for analysis. They typically consist of a prism or diffraction grating combined with a slit system. The diffraction grating or prism disperses the incoming light into its spectrum, and the slits are used to isolate the desired wavelength. The grating can be rotated to change the angle at which light is dispersed, thereby allowing different wavelengths to be selected. Monochromators are highly precise and are commonly used in applications where accurate wavelength selection is critical.

Here is the diagram showing the diffraction grating wavelength selector. It illustrates how incident light is diffracted at different angles, resulting in a spectrum of diffracted light. This is a key concept in understanding how wavelength selection is achieved in spectroscopic instruments.

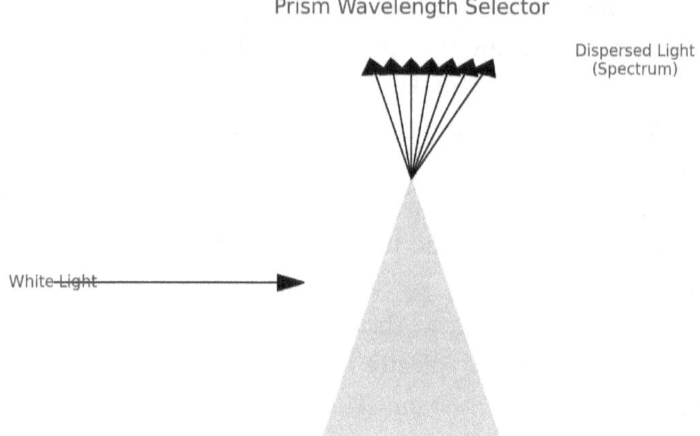

Here is the diagram showing the prism wavelength selector. It illustrates how white light enters the prism and is dispersed into a spectrum of different wavelengths. This diagram is useful for understanding the basic principles of how prisms are used in spectroscopy to separate light into its component wavelengths

Filters are simpler devices that allow only specific wavelengths of light to pass through while blocking others. There are two main types of filters: **absorption filters** and **interference filters**. Absorption filters work by absorbing unwanted wavelengths and transmitting the desired wavelength range. These filters are usually made from colored glass or other materials that selectively absorb certain wavelengths. Interference filters, on the other hand, use the principle of interference to reflect unwanted wavelengths while transmitting a narrow band of wavelengths. Interference filters provide higher precision than absorption filters and are often used in situations where a specific wavelength range is required.

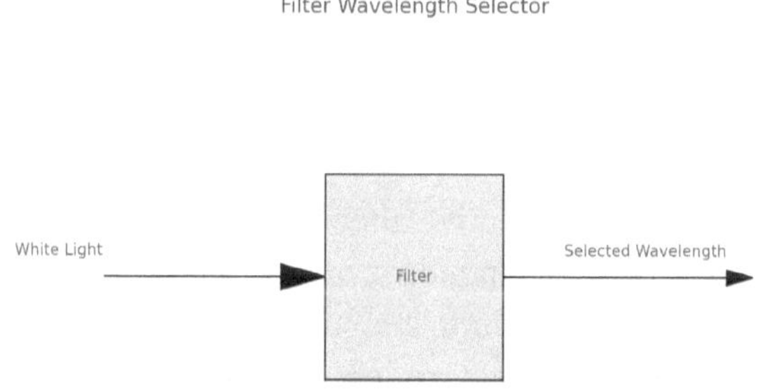

Here is the diagram showing the filter wavelength selector. It illustrates how white light enters the filter, and only the selected wavelength passes through, while other wavelengths are blocked. This clear visual representation helps in understanding the basic principle of filtering specific wavelengths in spectroscopy

Both monochromators and filters are essential in ensuring that only the desired wavelength reaches the sample, thereby reducing noise and improving the accuracy of the measurements. The choice between a monochromator and a filter depends on the requirements of the analysis, with monochromators offering greater flexibility and precision, while filters are typically more robust and cost-effective.

1.4.3 Sample Cells

Sample cells are an integral part of UV-visible spectroscopy, as they hold the sample solution that is being analyzed. The material and design of the sample cell are crucial, as they must allow the passage of the selected wavelengths of light without introducing significant absorption or scattering.

The most common materials used for sample cells are **quartz, glass, and plastic. Quartz** cells, also known as cuvettes, are widely used in UV spectroscopy because quartz is transparent to both UV and visible light, typically covering a wavelength range from 160 nm to 3000 nm. This makes quartz cells ideal for analyses that require accurate measurements in the UV region. However, quartz cells are relatively expensive and require careful handling due to their fragility.

Glass cells are suitable for measurements in the visible region, generally from 350 nm to 2000 nm. They are less expensive than quartz cells and are commonly used in routine analyses where only visible light measurements are needed. However, glass absorbs UV light below 350 nm, making it unsuitable for UV spectroscopy.

Plastic cells offer a cost-effective alternative and are available for both UV and visible spectroscopy, depending on the type of plastic used. Plastic cells are disposable, which eliminates the risk of cross-contamination between samples. However, they are less durable and can absorb certain wavelengths of light, making them less reliable for precise measurements compared to quartz or glass cells.

The **path length** of the sample cell is another important consideration, as it directly influences the absorbance measured according to Beer-Lambert's Law. Standard path lengths are typically 1 cm, but cells with longer or shorter path lengths are available for specific applications. The path length must be consistent and precisely known to ensure accurate quantitative measurements.

In addition to the material and path length, the shape and volume of the sample cell are also important. Standard cells are rectangular with a square cross-section, but specialized cells with cylindrical shapes or microvolume cells are used for specific applications where sample volume is limited.

1.4.4 Detectors

In UV-visible spectroscopy, **detectors** are essential components that convert the light passing through the sample into an electrical signal, which can then be measured and analyzed. The effectiveness and sensitivity of the detector play a crucial role in the overall performance of the spectrometer. Different types of detectors are used depending on the specific requirements of the analysis, including **photo tubes, photomultiplier tubes, photo voltaic cells**, and **silicon photodiodes**.

Photo Tube

A **photo tube** is a simple and early type of detector used in spectroscopy. It consists of a vacuum tube with a photosensitive cathode and an anode. When light strikes the cathode, it emits electrons due to the photoelectric effect. These electrons are then attracted to the anode, creating a current that is proportional to the intensity of the light. Photo tubes are reliable and provide a linear response to light intensity over a certain range. However, they are not as sensitive as other modern detectors and are primarily used in applications where high sensitivity is not critical.

Photomultiplier Tube

The **photomultiplier tube (PMT)** is one of the most sensitive detectors used in UV-visible spectroscopy. It operates on a principle similar to that of the photo tube but with significant amplification of the signal. The PMT contains a photosensitive cathode that emits electrons when struck by light. These electrons are then multiplied through a series of dynodes, each of which amplifies the signal by releasing additional electrons. The result is a highly amplified current that is proportional to the intensity of the incoming light. PMTs are capable of detecting very low levels of light and are widely used in applications requiring high sensitivity, such as low-concentration analyses or weakly absorbing samples. However, they are more expensive and require more precise control of operating conditions.

Photo Voltaic Cell

A **photo voltaic cell** is another type of detector that converts light into an electrical signal. Unlike the photo tube and PMT, which operate based on the photoelectric effect, a photovoltaic cell generates a voltage when light is absorbed by a semiconductor material. This voltage is proportional to the intensity of the light. Photovoltaic cells are simple, robust, and do not require an external power source, making them suitable for portable or field instruments. However, their sensitivity and response time are generally lower than those of photomultiplier tubes, limiting their use in applications where high sensitivity is required.

Silicon Photodiode

The **silicon photodiode** is a widely used detector in modern spectrometers due to its high sensitivity, fast response time, and compact size. It operates by converting light into an electrical current when photons are absorbed by the silicon material, creating electron-hole pairs. The resulting current is proportional to the intensity of the light. Silicon photodiodes are highly versatile and can be used across a broad range of wavelengths, including UV, visible, and near-infrared regions. They are also more stable and require less maintenance compared to photomultiplier tubes, making them ideal for routine analytical applications. Additionally, silicon photodiodes are relatively inexpensive and can be integrated into array detectors for simultaneous multi-wavelength detection.

1.5 Applications of UV-Visible Spectroscopy

Spectrophotometric Titrations

Spectrophotometric titrations are a significant application of UV-visible spectroscopy, combining the principles of titration with spectroscopic analysis to determine the concentration of an analyte in a solution. Unlike traditional titrations, which rely on visual indicators to signal the endpoint, spectrophotometric titrations use changes in the absorbance of light at a specific wavelength to monitor the progress of the reaction. This method offers higher sensitivity, accuracy, and the ability to analyze colored and colorless solutions alike.

In a spectrophotometric titration, the absorbance of the solution is measured at various points during the addition of the titrant. The absorbance is directly related to the concentration of the species in the solution, as per Beer-Lambert's Law. By plotting absorbance against the volume of titrant added, a titration curve is obtained, which allows for the precise determination of the endpoint. The point at which the absorbance changes most sharply corresponds to the equivalence point of the titration, indicating that the reaction between the analyte and the titrant is complete.

One of the primary advantages of spectrophotometric titrations is the ability to analyze reactions that involve species with distinct absorbance characteristics. For instance, if the product of the titration has a different absorbance than the reactants, the progress of the titration can be easily monitored by measuring the absorbance at a wavelength where the product absorbs strongly. This method is particularly useful for complexometric titrations, redox titrations, and acid-base titrations where traditional indicators may not be effective or where precise endpoint detection is required.

Spectrophotometric titrations are widely used in pharmaceutical analysis to determine the concentration of active ingredients in drugs, the purity of substances, and the stoichiometry of reactions. They are also employed in environmental analysis, biochemistry, and clinical laboratories, where accurate and sensitive determination of analytes is crucial. The technique's ability to provide real-time monitoring and its applicability to a wide range of chemical reactions make it an invaluable tool in both research and routine analysis.

Single Component Analysis

Single component analysis is one of the fundamental applications of UV-visible spectroscopy, used to determine the concentration of a single analyte in a sample solution. This technique is particularly valuable in situations where the analyte exhibits a distinct absorption peak in the UV or visible spectrum, allowing for accurate and direct quantification based on its absorbance.

In single component analysis, the absorbance of the solution is measured at a specific wavelength where the analyte has maximum absorption. According to Beer-Lambert's Law, the absorbance (A) is directly proportional to the concentration (c) of the analyte, provided that the path length (l) and molar absorptivity (ϵ) are known. The concentration of the analyte can thus be calculated using the equation:

$A = \epsilon \cdot c \cdot l$

To perform a single component analysis, a calibration curve is typically constructed by measuring the absorbance of standard solutions with known concentrations of the analyte. The resulting plot of absorbance versus concentration is used to determine the concentration of the unknown sample by interpolating its absorbance on the calibration curve. This method is straightforward, highly accurate, and applicable to a wide range of substances, provided that the analyte does not interact with other components in the solution in a way that affects its absorption characteristics.

Single component analysis is widely used in various fields, including pharmaceuticals, where it is employed to determine the concentration of active pharmaceutical ingredients (APIs) in formulations. It is also commonly used in environmental monitoring to measure the concentration of pollutants, in food and beverage industries for quality control, and in clinical laboratories to quantify biomolecules such as proteins and nucleic acids.

One of the main advantages of single component analysis is its simplicity and speed. The method does not require extensive sample preparation, and results can be obtained quickly, making it ideal for routine analysis. However, it is important to ensure that the analyte is the only species absorbing at the chosen wavelength, as the presence of other absorbing species can lead to errors in quantification.

Multi-Component Analysis

Multi-component analysis in UV-visible spectroscopy is an advanced technique used to simultaneously determine the concentrations of two or more analytes present in a mixture. This method is particularly useful in situations where the components of the mixture have overlapping absorption spectra, making it challenging to analyze each component separately. By applying mathematical methods and using the absorbance data at multiple wavelengths, multi-component analysis allows for the accurate quantification of each component in the mixture.

In multi-component analysis, the absorbance of the sample mixture is measured at several selected wavelengths, where each component has significant but different absorbance. The total absorbance at each wavelength is a sum of the absorbances due to each individual component, as described by the extended Beer-Lambert's Law:

$$A_\lambda = \epsilon_{1\lambda} \cdot c_1 \cdot l + \epsilon_{2\lambda} \cdot c_2 \cdot l + \ldots + \epsilon_{n\lambda} \cdot c_n \cdot l$$

Here, A_λ is the total absorbance at wavelength λ, $\epsilon_{1\lambda}, \epsilon_{2\lambda}, \ldots$ are the molar absorptivities of the components at that wavelength, $c_1, c_2, \ldots$ are the concentrations of the components, and l is the path length.

To solve for the concentrations ($c_1, c_2, \ldots c_1, c_2, \ldots$) of the components, a set of simultaneous linear equations is generated using the absorbance data at different wavelengths. These equations can then be solved using mathematical techniques such as matrix algebra or least squares fitting, which allow for the determination of the concentrations of each component in the mixture.

Multi-component analysis is widely used in pharmaceutical analysis, where it is essential to determine the concentration of active ingredients in complex formulations containing multiple components. It is also valuable in environmental analysis, where mixtures of pollutants need to be quantified, and in food and beverage industries, where multi-component analysis helps in assessing the composition of products.

The key advantage of multi-component analysis is its ability to accurately quantify multiple analytes in a single measurement, even in the presence of overlapping spectra. This reduces the need for time-consuming separation techniques and allows for faster analysis of complex mixtures. However, successful multi-component analysis requires careful selection of wavelengths, accurate measurement of absorbance, and appropriate mathematical processing of the data.

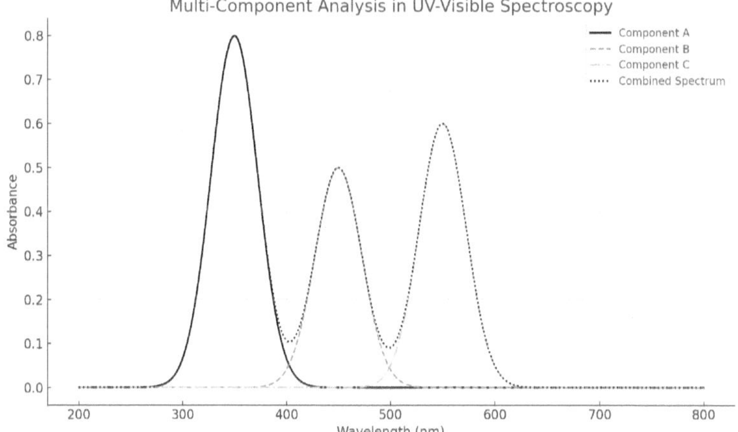

Multi-Component Analysis in UV-Visible Spectroscopy
Component A
Component B
Component C
Combined Spectrum
Absorbance
Wavelength (nm)

CHAPTER TWO

Fluorimetry

2.1 Theory and Concepts

Singlet, Doublet, and Triplet Electronic States

In fluorimetry, understanding the **electronic states** of molecules is crucial, as these states determine the behavior of molecules when they interact with light. The terms **singlet, doublet,** and **triplet states** refer to specific configurations of electron spins in a molecule, which play a vital role in the processes of absorption, emission, and fluorescence.

A **singlet electronic state** occurs when all the electrons in a molecule are paired, meaning their spins are opposite and cancel each other out. In this state, the molecule's total spin quantum number is zero. The singlet ground state is the most stable and common state for most molecules. When a molecule in its singlet ground state absorbs a photon, it may be excited to a higher energy singlet state. In this excited singlet state, the molecule retains paired electron spins, and it can return to the ground state by emitting a photon, a process known as **fluorescence**. Fluorescence typically occurs very rapidly, within nanoseconds, and involves the release of energy in the form of light as the molecule returns to its lower energy state.

A **doublet electronic state** is less common and typically occurs in molecules with an unpaired electron, such as free radicals. In a doublet state, the total spin quantum number is 1/2, indicating that one electron has no paired counterpart. Doublet states are often associated with highly reactive species and play a significant role in certain types of photochemical reactions, though they are not commonly encountered in conventional fluorimetry.

The **triplet electronic state** arises when two electrons in a molecule have parallel spins, meaning they do not cancel each other out. In this state, the total spin quantum number is 1. The triplet state is usually lower in energy than the corresponding singlet excited state due to the rules of quantum mechanics, which favor the stabilization of parallel spins. A molecule in an excited singlet state can undergo **intersystem crossing** to transition into a triplet state, where it may become "trapped" because returning to the singlet ground state is forbidden by quantum mechanical selection rules. However, this transition can still occur, albeit more slowly, through a process called **phosphorescence**, where light emission is delayed, often lasting from microseconds to seconds.

Understanding these electronic states is essential in fluorimetry because the nature of these states influences how molecules interact with light and how they emit light after excitation. Fluorescence, which involves singlet-singlet transitions, is generally a fast process and is the primary focus of fluorimetric techniques. Phosphorescence, involving triplet-singlet transitions, is slower and can provide additional information about the molecular environment and dynamics.

Internal and External Conversions

Internal and external conversions are important non-radiative processes in fluorimetry, where excited molecules dissipate energy without emitting light. These processes occur after a molecule absorbs energy and enters an excited state but before it can return to the ground state by emitting fluorescence or phosphorescence.

Internal conversion is a process where an excited molecule transfers energy from a higher electronic state to a lower one within the same molecule, without emitting radiation. This process occurs very rapidly, often in femtoseconds to picoseconds. Internal conversion usually takes place between two singlet states, where the molecule undergoes a transition from a higher excited singlet state to a lower excited singlet state. The excess energy is typically dissipated as heat through vibrations within the molecule. This process is crucial in determining the quantum yield of fluorescence, as a significant portion of the energy absorbed by the molecule may be lost through internal conversion rather than being emitted as light.

On the other hand, **external conversion** involves the transfer of energy from an excited molecule to its surrounding environment, leading to the deactivation of the excited state without emission of light. This process occurs through interactions between the excited molecule and other molecules or solvents around it, often resulting in the dissipation of energy as heat. External conversion depends on the nature of the environment, such as the solvent type, temperature, and concentration of quenchers in the solution. The efficiency of external conversion can significantly reduce the fluorescence intensity of a molecule, making it an important factor in fluorimetric analysis.

Both internal and external conversions are key factors in determining the fate of an excited molecule. They compete with radiative processes like fluorescence and phosphorescence, influencing the overall efficiency of light emission. Understanding these processes is essential for optimizing fluorimetric techniques, as they help explain why certain molecules exhibit strong fluorescence while others do not, even when they absorb the same amount of light. By minimizing external conversion, for example, through careful choice of solvents or conditions, the fluorescence yield can be enhanced, leading to more accurate and sensitive measurements in fluorimetry.

2.2 Factors Affecting Fluorescence

Factors Influencing Fluorescence Intensity

The intensity of fluorescence emitted by a molecule is influenced by several factors that determine how efficiently the molecule absorbs and re-emits light. Understanding these factors is crucial for optimizing fluorimetric analysis and ensuring accurate, reliable results.

One of the primary factors affecting fluorescence intensity is the **nature of the molecule** itself. The presence of certain functional groups, such as aromatic rings and conjugated double bonds, enhances a molecule's ability to fluoresce because these structures allow for efficient absorption of light and subsequent emission. Molecules with rigid structures tend to fluoresce more strongly because they limit non-radiative decay processes, such as internal conversion and vibrational relaxation, thereby retaining more energy for emission.

Concentration of the fluorescent molecule also plays a significant role. At low concentrations, the fluorescence intensity generally increases linearly with concentration, as more molecules are available to absorb and emit light. However, at higher concentrations, a phenomenon known as **concentration quenching** can occur, where the intensity decreases despite increasing concentration. This quenching is often due to interactions between closely packed molecules, which can lead to non-radiative energy transfer or reabsorption of emitted light.

Solvent effects are another critical factor influencing fluorescence intensity. The polarity of the solvent can impact the electronic states of the fluorescent molecule, either stabilizing or destabilizing the excited state.

Polar solvents, for instance, may quench fluorescence by stabilizing the excited state, leading to increased non-radiative decay. Additionally, the presence of impurities or quenching agents in the solvent can lead to reduced fluorescence intensity by facilitating external conversion processes.

pH is an important factor for molecules that contain ionizable groups. Changes in pH can alter the ionization state of the molecule, affecting its electronic structure and, consequently, its fluorescence properties. For example, certain molecules may fluoresce strongly in their protonated form but show little or no fluorescence when deprotonated, or vice versa.

Temperature can influence fluorescence intensity as well. Higher temperatures typically increase the rate of non-radiative processes, such as internal conversion and external conversion, leading to reduced fluorescence intensity. This is because increased thermal energy promotes molecular vibrations that facilitate energy loss without light emission.

Oxygen and other quenching agents can also significantly reduce fluorescence intensity. Oxygen, in particular, is a well-known quencher of fluorescence, as it can interact with the excited state of the molecule, leading to energy transfer without the emission of light. This process, known as dynamic quenching, is often a concern in biological and environmental fluorescence studies, where oxygen is present in significant amounts.

Finally, **instrumental factors**, such as the intensity and stability of the excitation source, the sensitivity of the detector, and the geometry of the sample cell, can all affect the measured fluorescence intensity. Ensuring that these factors are properly controlled is essential for obtaining accurate and reproducible fluorescence measurements.

Quenching Mechanisms

Quenching mechanisms refer to the processes by which the fluorescence of a molecule is diminished or completely suppressed. These mechanisms are important to understand because they can significantly affect the results of fluorimetric analyses. There are several types of quenching mechanisms, each involving different interactions between the fluorescent molecule (fluorophore) and its environment.

One of the most common quenching mechanisms is **collisional quenching**, also known as **dynamic quenching**. In this process, the excited fluorophore collides with a quencher molecule while in its excited state. The energy from the excited state is transferred to the quencher, and the fluorophore returns to the ground state without emitting a photon. Oxygen is a well-known quencher that often participates in collisional quenching due to its ability to accept energy from excited states. The efficiency of collisional quenching increases with temperature and concentration of the quencher, as these factors increase the likelihood of collisions.

Another significant mechanism is **static quenching**, which occurs when the fluorophore forms a non-fluorescent complex with the quencher in the ground state, before excitation occurs. This complex formation prevents the fluorophore from being excited and thus reduces fluorescence intensity. Static quenching is independent of temperature because it involves the formation of a stable complex rather than a dynamic process of energy transfer. The presence of static quenching can often be identified by changes in the absorption spectrum of the fluorophore, as the complex may have different absorption characteristics than the free fluorophore.

Resonance energy transfer (RET), also known as **Förster resonance energy transfer (FRET)**, is another quenching mechanism that involves the non-radiative transfer of energy from an excited fluorophore (donor) to a nearby acceptor molecule. The efficiency of FRET depends on the distance between the donor and acceptor, the overlap between the donor's emission spectrum and the acceptor's absorption spectrum, and the relative orientation of their dipoles. FRET is widely used in biological studies to investigate molecular interactions and distances at the nanoscale.

Intersystem crossing leading to **triplet state quenching** is a mechanism where the excited singlet state of the fluorophore undergoes a transition to a triplet state. The triplet state is usually lower in energy and longer-lived than the singlet state. Molecules in the triplet state can be quenched by oxygen or other triplet quenchers, leading to a reduction in fluorescence. This type of quenching is particularly relevant in molecules with heavy atoms, where intersystem crossing is more likely.

Concentration quenching occurs when the concentration of the fluorophore is so high that interactions between fluorophores lead to quenching. This can happen through mechanisms such as excimer or exciplex formation, where an excited fluorophore interacts with another fluorophore in the ground state, forming a non-fluorescent complex. As the concentration of fluorophores increases, these interactions become more frequent, leading to a decrease in fluorescence intensity.

Finally, **pH-induced quenching** can occur when changes in the pH of the solution alter the ionization state of the fluorophore, affecting its ability to fluoresce. Certain fluorophores are sensitive to pH changes and may either increase or decrease in fluorescence intensity depending on the pH of the environment. This is particularly important in biological systems where pH can vary significantly.

2.3 Instrumentation

Overview of Fluorimetry Instruments

Fluorimetry instruments are specialized devices designed to measure the fluorescence emitted by a sample when it is exposed to light, typically in the ultraviolet or visible spectrum. These instruments are essential in a wide range of scientific and industrial applications, including biochemical analysis, environmental monitoring, and pharmaceutical research. The fundamental components of fluorimetry instruments work together to excite the sample, detect the emitted fluorescence, and quantify it with high precision.

At the heart of a fluorimetry instrument is the **excitation source**. This source provides the light required to excite the electrons in the sample molecules. Common excitation sources include **xenon arc lamps, mercury vapor lamps**, and **LEDs** (light-emitting diodes). Xenon arc lamps are widely used because of their broad spectrum and high intensity, making them suitable for exciting a wide range of fluorophores. LEDs are increasingly popular due to their energy efficiency, long lifespan, and ability to provide specific wavelengths of light with high precision.

Once the sample is illuminated, the emitted fluorescence is collected and passed through a **wavelength selector**, which isolates the specific wavelengths of interest. The wavelength selector can be a **monochromator** or an **optical filter**. Monochromators use diffraction gratings to disperse the light and allow the selection of a narrow wavelength range. Filters, on the other hand, selectively transmit certain wavelengths while blocking others. The choice between a monochromator and a filter depends on the required precision and the nature of the sample being analyzed.

The isolated fluorescence is then directed to the **detector**, which converts the light into an electrical signal. Several types of detectors are used in fluorimetry, including **photomultiplier tubes (PMTs), photodiodes**, and **charge-coupled devices (CCDs)**. PMTs are highly sensitive and capable of detecting very low levels of light, making them ideal for applications requiring high sensitivity. Photodiodes are robust and offer a wide dynamic range, while CCDs provide the ability to detect fluorescence at multiple wavelengths simultaneously, making them useful for imaging applications.

In addition to these core components, modern fluorimetry instruments often include advanced features such as **automated sample handling systems** and **data analysis software**. Automated systems allow for high-throughput analysis, where multiple samples can be processed in quick succession with minimal manual intervention. Data analysis software provides tools for interpreting the fluorescence data, including calibration, quantification, and statistical analysis.

The design and configuration of fluorimetry instruments can vary depending on the specific application. For example, **spectrofluorometers** are used for detailed spectral analysis, where the entire fluorescence spectrum of a sample is recorded. **Fluorescence microscopes** combine fluorimetry with optical microscopy to visualize and measure fluorescence in biological samples at high spatial resolution. **Flow cytometers** are specialized instruments that measure the fluorescence of cells or particles in a fluid stream, often used in immunology and cell biology.

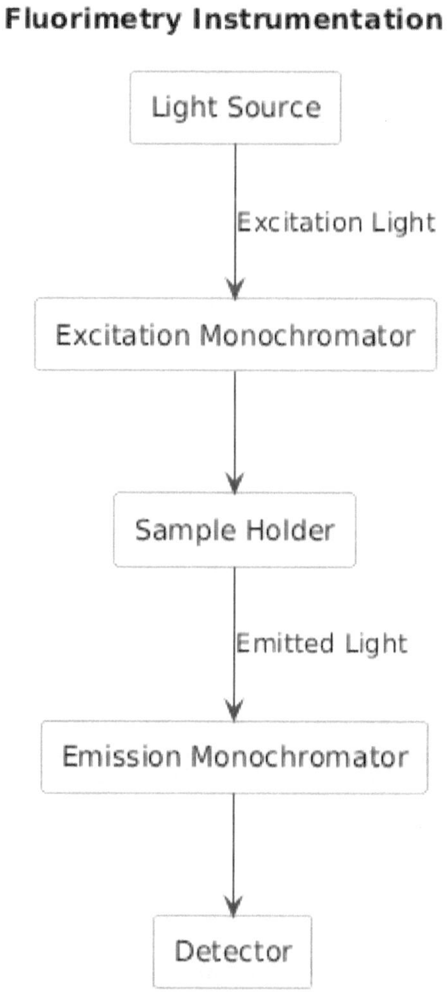

Fluorimetry Instrumentation

Fluorimetry Instrumentation

Detectors and Filters

In fluorimetry, **detectors and filters** are critical components that work together to ensure accurate measurement of fluorescence signals. Each plays a specific role in the process of capturing and analyzing the light emitted by the sample, contributing to the overall precision and reliability of the fluorimetric analysis.

Detectors in fluorimetry are responsible for converting the emitted light into an electrical signal that can be measured and quantified. The choice of detector depends on the sensitivity required and the specific application of the analysis.

One of the most commonly used detectors is the **photomultiplier tube (PMT)**. PMTs are highly sensitive devices that can detect very low levels of light, making them ideal for applications where fluorescence signals are weak. They work by amplifying the small number of photons they receive, converting them into a measurable current through a series of dynodes that multiply the electrons produced by the initial photon impact. This high sensitivity makes PMTs suitable for detecting fluorescence in dilute samples or in applications requiring precise quantification of low-intensity signals.

Another widely used detector is the **photodiode**, which is less sensitive than the PMT but offers a wide dynamic range and robustness. Photodiodes convert incoming photons directly into an electrical current, with the amount of current produced being proportional to the intensity of the light. They are often used in applications where the fluorescence signals are relatively strong and where the robustness and stability of the detector are more critical than extreme sensitivity.

Charge-coupled devices (CCDs) are also employed as detectors in certain fluorimetry applications, particularly where multi-wavelength detection or imaging is required. CCDs consist of an array of light-sensitive elements that can simultaneously detect fluorescence at different wavelengths, making them useful in applications such as fluorescence microscopy or spectral imaging. They provide high spatial resolution and are capable of detecting low levels of light, though they are generally more expensive and complex than PMTs and photodiodes.

Filters are equally important in fluorimetry as they selectively allow certain wavelengths of light to pass through while blocking others. This ensures that the detected signal corresponds only to the specific fluorescence emission of interest, reducing background noise and improving the accuracy of the measurement.

Excitation filters are used to isolate the desired wavelength of light that will excite the fluorophore in the sample. By blocking unwanted wavelengths, these filters ensure that the excitation light is precisely matched to the absorption characteristics of the fluorophore, optimizing the efficiency of the excitation process.

Emission filters play a crucial role in selecting the specific wavelength of light emitted by the fluorophore that reaches the detector. After the sample fluoresces, the emission filter blocks any scattered excitation light and transmits only the wavelengths corresponding to the fluorescence emission. This helps in minimizing interference and enhancing the signal-to-noise ratio, leading to more accurate and reliable fluorescence measurements.

Bandpass filters and **long-pass filters** are common types of filters used in fluorimetry. **Bandpass filters** allow only a specific range of wavelengths to pass through, making them ideal for selecting precise excitation or emission wavelengths. **Long-pass filters**, on the other hand, allow all wavelengths longer than a specified cutoff to pass through while blocking shorter wavelengths, which is useful in eliminating unwanted shorter wavelength light.

2.4 Applications of Fluorimetry

Pharmaceutical Analysis

Fluorimetry plays a crucial role in **pharmaceutical analysis**, offering a highly sensitive and specific method for the quantification and characterization of various pharmaceutical compounds. One of the primary applications of fluorimetry in this field is the **quantitative determination of active pharmaceutical ingredients (APIs)** in drug formulations. Many APIs possess intrinsic fluorescence or can be derivatized to produce fluorescent products, enabling precise measurement at very low concentrations. This capability is particularly useful in quality control, where ensuring the correct dosage of an API is critical for the efficacy and safety of pharmaceutical products.

Additionally, fluorimetry is employed in the **analysis of drug impurities and degradation products**. Even small amounts of impurities can significantly affect the safety and efficacy of a drug, making their detection and quantification essential. Fluorimetry's high sensitivity allows for the detection of these impurities at trace levels, which might be undetectable by other analytical methods. This makes fluorimetry an invaluable tool in stability studies and during the shelf-life evaluation of pharmaceutical products.

Fluorimetry is also used in the **study of drug interactions with biological macromolecules** such as proteins and nucleic acids. By monitoring the changes in fluorescence intensity or wavelength shifts, researchers can gain insights into the binding affinities, reaction kinetics, and conformational changes of drugs when they interact with their targets. This application is critical in drug discovery and development, where understanding these interactions is key to designing effective and safe therapeutics.

Environmental Monitoring

In the field of **environmental monitoring**, fluorimetry is widely used for the detection and quantification of pollutants and contaminants in water, soil, and air. One of the significant applications is the **monitoring of polycyclic aromatic hydrocarbons (PAHs)**, which are common environmental pollutants that exhibit strong fluorescence. Fluorimetry allows for the rapid and sensitive detection of PAHs in environmental samples, even at very low concentrations. This capability is essential for assessing environmental pollution levels and for ensuring compliance with regulatory standards.

Fluorimetry is also used in the **analysis of heavy metals** in environmental samples. Certain metal ions, such as zinc, cadmium, and lead, can quench or enhance the fluorescence of specific probes or chelating agents, allowing for their detection and quantification. This application is particularly important in monitoring water quality, as the presence of heavy metals poses significant risks to both human health and the environment.

Another important application of fluorimetry in environmental monitoring is the **detection of organic pollutants**, such as pesticides, herbicides, and industrial chemicals. Many of these compounds can be either naturally fluorescent or can be made fluorescent through chemical derivatization. Fluorimetry enables the detection of these pollutants in water and soil samples at trace levels, facilitating early warning and remediation efforts.

In addition, fluorimetry is employed in the **monitoring of natural water bodies,** where it is used to measure the concentration of dissolved organic matter (DOM), chlorophyll, and other biological indicators of water quality. By analyzing the fluorescence characteristics of these substances, environmental scientists can assess the health of aquatic ecosystems, detect algal blooms, and monitor the impact of human activities on natural water resources.

CHAPTER THREE

Infrared Spectroscopy (IR)

3.1 Introduction to IR Spectroscopy

Fundamental Modes of Vibrations in Polyatomic Molecules

Infrared (IR) spectroscopy is a powerful analytical technique used to study the vibrational modes of molecules. When molecules absorb infrared radiation, their atoms undergo various vibrational motions, which can be detected and analyzed to provide detailed information about the molecular structure. These vibrational modes are fundamental to understanding how molecules interact with IR light and are classified into different types based on the movement of atoms within the molecule.

In **polyatomic molecules**, which consist of three or more atoms, the atoms can vibrate in several distinct ways. The number of fundamental vibrational modes for a non-linear polyatomic molecule is given by the formula $3N-6$, where N is the number of atoms in the molecule. For linear molecules, the formula is $3N-5$. These modes can be broadly categorized into **stretching** and **bending** vibrations.

Stretching vibrations involve changes in the bond lengths between atoms. There are two main types of stretching vibrations: **symmetric stretching** and **asymmetric stretching**. In symmetric stretching, the bonds between atoms lengthen or shorten simultaneously in a coordinated manner, while in asymmetric stretching, one bond lengthens while the other shortens. Stretching vibrations typically occur at higher frequencies compared to bending vibrations because more energy is required to change bond lengths.

Bending vibrations, on the other hand, involve changes in the angles between bonds or the movement of atoms relative to each other without altering bond lengths. Bending vibrations can be further classified into several types, including **scissoring, rocking, wagging,** and **twisting**.

- **Scissoring** involves the movement of two atoms toward and away from each other in a plane, similar to the motion of a pair of scissors.
- **Rocking** occurs when two atoms move in the same direction within a plane, causing the angle between bonds to change.
- **Wagging** involves the out-of-plane movement of two atoms, where they move in opposite directions perpendicular to the plane.
- **Twisting** refers to the rotation of one part of the molecule relative to another around a bond axis.

Each of these vibrational modes corresponds to a specific frequency of IR radiation, which is absorbed by the molecule. By analyzing the IR spectrum, which shows the absorption of different frequencies of IR light, scientists can identify the presence of specific functional groups and infer details about the molecular structure.

Factors Affecting Vibrations

In infrared (IR) spectroscopy, the vibrational frequencies of molecules are influenced by several factors that determine how the atoms within a molecule move relative to each other when exposed to infrared radiation. Understanding these factors is crucial for interpreting IR spectra accurately and for using this technique to identify molecular structures and functional groups.

One of the primary factors affecting molecular vibrations is the **mass of the atoms** involved in the vibration. According to the principles of vibrational mechanics, heavier atoms vibrate at lower frequencies compared to lighter atoms when bonded to the same atom. For example, a carbon-hydrogen (C-H) bond, where hydrogen is a light atom, will vibrate at a higher frequency than a carbon-chlorine (C-Cl) bond, where chlorine is much heavier. This relationship between atomic mass and vibrational frequency is fundamental in predicting and understanding the positions of absorption bands in an IR spectrum.

Another significant factor is the **bond strength** or the force constant of the bond. Stronger bonds, such as double and triple bonds, have higher force constants and therefore vibrate at higher frequencies compared to single bonds. For instance, the C≡C triple bond vibrates at a higher frequency than the C=C double bond, which in turn vibrates at a higher frequency than the C-C single bond. This correlation between bond strength and vibrational frequency allows IR spectroscopy to distinguish between different types of bonds within a molecule.

Molecular geometry and **symmetry** also play a crucial role in determining the vibrational characteristics of a molecule. Molecules with higher symmetry often have fewer IR-active vibrational modes because symmetric vibrations may not lead to a change in the dipole moment of the molecule, which is necessary for IR absorption. Conversely, in less symmetrical molecules, more vibrations are IR-active, leading to a more complex spectrum. The geometry of the molecule also affects how the vibrations are coupled, particularly in larger molecules where interactions between different vibrational modes can shift frequencies or split absorption bands.

The **environment of the molecule**, including intermolecular interactions such as hydrogen bonding, can significantly affect vibrational frequencies. Hydrogen bonding, for example, tends to lower the vibrational frequency of the bond involved in the interaction because it effectively weakens the bond, making it easier to stretch. This effect is commonly observed in the broadening and shifting of the O-H and N-H stretching vibrations in IR spectra when these groups are involved in hydrogen bonding.

Concentration and **state of matter** (solid, liquid, or gas) of the sample also influence the vibrational frequencies observed in IR spectroscopy. In solids and liquids, molecules are closely packed, and intermolecular forces such as Van der Waals forces or hydrogen bonds can alter vibrational frequencies compared to those in the gas phase, where such interactions are minimal. Similarly, concentration can lead to interactions between identical molecules (such as in dimer formation), causing shifts in vibrational frequencies.

Temperature is another factor that can affect molecular vibrations. As temperature increases, the kinetic energy of the molecules increases, leading to more significant vibrational energy levels being populated. This can cause slight shifts in vibrational frequencies and changes in the intensity of absorption bands, as well as broadening of the spectral lines.

3.2 Instrumentation

3.2.1 Sources of Radiation

In infrared (IR) spectroscopy, the **source of radiation** is a critical component of the instrumentation, as it provides the infrared light required to excite the vibrational modes of the molecules being analyzed. The quality, intensity, and stability of the radiation source directly impact the accuracy and reliability of the spectroscopic measurements.

The most commonly used sources of radiation in IR spectroscopy are **thermal emitters**, which produce broad-spectrum infrared radiation by heating a material to a high temperature. These sources emit continuous radiation across a wide range of IR wavelengths, making them ideal for general-purpose IR spectroscopy.

One of the most widely used thermal emitters is the **Globar source**, which is made of silicon carbide (SiC). When electrically heated to temperatures around 1000 to 1650°C, the Globar source emits infrared radiation across the mid-infrared region (approximately 2.5 to 25 micrometers). This source is preferred for its stability and strong output over a broad range of wavelengths, making it suitable for many types of IR spectroscopy, including the analysis of organic and inorganic compounds.

Another common thermal emitter is the **Nernst glower**, which is composed of a ceramic material, typically a mixture of oxides such as zirconium oxide (ZrO_2), yttrium oxide (Y_2O_3), and thorium oxide (ThO_2). The Nernst glower is heated to around 1200 to 2000°C, producing a continuous spectrum in the mid-infrared region. Unlike the Globar, the Nernst glower requires a preheating phase because it is not electrically conductive at room temperature. However, once it reaches its operating temperature, it provides a stable and intense source of infrared radiation.

The **incandescent lamp** is another radiation source used in some IR spectrometers, particularly for near-infrared (NIR) applications. These lamps, similar to the filament in a standard light bulb, typically consist of a tungsten filament that is heated to temperatures between 1500 and 3000°C. The radiation emitted by an incandescent lamp covers the near-infrared region (approximately 0.7 to 2.5 micrometers) and is useful for applications that require analysis of overtone and combination bands, often found in organic compounds and polymers.

For far-infrared spectroscopy, which covers wavelengths longer than 25 micrometers, **mercury arc lamps** or **high-pressure mercury lamps** are commonly used. These sources produce strong radiation in the far-infrared region, making them suitable for studying low-frequency vibrations, such as those associated with heavier atoms and metal-ligand bonds in coordination complexes.

In addition to these traditional thermal emitters, **laser sources** have become increasingly important in IR spectroscopy, particularly for applications requiring high precision and intensity at specific wavelengths. The **carbon dioxide (CO_2) laser** is one of the most common laser sources used in IR spectroscopy. It emits highly monochromatic radiation in the mid-infrared region, typically around 10.6 micrometers. Laser sources are particularly useful in techniques such as Fourier-transform infrared (FTIR) spectroscopy, where they provide a highly stable and intense source of IR radiation for high-resolution measurements.

3.2.2 Wavelength Selectors

Wavelength selectors are essential components in infrared (IR) spectroscopy, as they determine which specific wavelengths of infrared radiation are allowed to reach the detector after interacting with the sample. The ability to isolate and analyze specific wavelengths is crucial for accurately identifying the vibrational modes of molecules and for obtaining detailed IR spectra.

There are two primary types of wavelength selectors used in IR spectroscopy: **monochromators** and **filters**.

Monochromators are optical devices that disperse light into its component wavelengths and allow the selection of a narrow band of wavelengths for analysis. The most common type of monochromator used in IR spectroscopy is the **grating monochromator**. This device uses a diffraction grating, which is a surface with many closely spaced grooves, to disperse the incoming infrared light into its spectrum. By rotating the grating, different wavelengths of light can be directed through a slit and onto the detector. Grating monochromators are highly versatile and can cover a broad range of wavelengths, from the near-infrared to the far-infrared regions. They are particularly valuable in dispersive IR spectrometers, where precise wavelength selection is necessary for scanning across the spectrum.

Another type of monochromator used in some IR spectrometers is the **prism monochromator**. Prisms are made from materials like sodium chloride (NaCl) or potassium bromide (KBr), which are transparent in the IR region. When infrared light passes through the prism, it is refracted, and different wavelengths are dispersed at different angles. By adjusting the position of the prism, specific wavelengths can be selected and passed through a slit to the detector. Although less common than grating monochromators, prism monochromators are still used in certain applications, particularly where high throughput and simplicity are desired.

Filters are another type of wavelength selector used in IR spectroscopy. **Interference filters** and **absorption filters** are the most common.

Interference filters work on the principle of constructive and destructive interference. They consist of multiple thin layers of dielectric material with different refractive indices. By carefully designing the thickness of these layers, the filter allows only a narrow band of wavelengths to pass through while reflecting or absorbing the rest. Interference filters are highly effective at isolating specific wavelengths and are often used in applications where precise wavelength selection is required, such as in narrowband infrared detection.

Absorption filters operate by selectively absorbing certain wavelengths of light while allowing others to pass through. These filters are typically made from materials that have specific absorption characteristics in the IR region. For example, a filter made from a particular salt may absorb light in the mid-infrared region while transmitting light in the near-infrared region. Absorption filters are simpler and less expensive than interference filters but are generally less precise in terms of wavelength selection.

In modern IR spectroscopy, particularly in **Fourier-transform infrared (FTIR)** spectrometers, **interferometers** are used instead of traditional wavelength selectors like monochromators and filters. The most common type of interferometer used is the **Michelson interferometer**. It works by splitting a beam of infrared light into two paths using a beamsplitter. One beam travels a fixed distance, while the other is reflected off a movable mirror. The two beams are then recombined, creating an interference pattern that depends on the difference in path lengths. By varying the mirror position, the interferometer effectively measures all wavelengths simultaneously, allowing for rapid data collection and high-resolution spectra after Fourier transformation.

3.2.3 Detectors

Golay Cell

The **Golay cell** is a type of detector used in infrared (IR) spectroscopy, particularly in the far-infrared region where other detectors may be less effective. It is named after Marcel J.E. Golay, who developed the cell in the 1940s. The Golay cell is a **pneumatic detector** that operates based on the principle of gas expansion in response to absorbed infrared radiation, making it a sensitive and accurate detector for IR spectroscopy.

The basic structure of a Golay cell consists of a small, sealed chamber filled with a gas, typically xenon or air, and a flexible diaphragm or mirror. The walls of the chamber are designed to absorb infrared radiation. When infrared light enters the cell, it is absorbed by the gas or the absorbing material on the walls, causing the gas inside the chamber to heat up and expand. This expansion increases the pressure within the chamber, which, in turn, causes the diaphragm to flex or the mirror to move.

The movement of the diaphragm or mirror is detected and converted into an electrical signal, which is proportional to the intensity of the infrared radiation absorbed by the cell. This signal is then used to measure the amount of IR radiation reaching the detector, allowing for the analysis of the sample.

One of the key advantages of the Golay cell is its high sensitivity to low levels of infrared radiation, particularly in the far-infrared region (wavelengths longer than about 50 micrometers). This makes it an excellent choice for applications where detecting weak IR signals is critical, such as in the analysis of gases or in situations where only a small amount of IR radiation is available.

Another advantage of the Golay cell is its relatively fast response time, which allows for real-time monitoring of changes in infrared radiation. This is particularly useful in dynamic experiments where the IR signal may vary rapidly.

However, the Golay cell also has some limitations. It is sensitive to mechanical vibrations and external temperature changes, which can affect the accuracy of the measurements. Additionally, the Golay cell is more complex and fragile compared to other types of detectors, such as thermocouples or pyroelectric detectors, making it less suitable for rugged or field applications.

Bolometer

The **bolometer** is another type of detector used in infrared (IR) spectroscopy, known for its ability to measure very small amounts of radiant energy, particularly in the mid- to far-infrared regions. The bolometer was invented by Samuel Pierpont Langley in 1880 and has since become an essential tool in various fields, including spectroscopy, astronomy, and thermal imaging.

A bolometer operates on the principle of temperature change in response to absorbed radiation. It consists of a thermally sensitive material that changes its electrical resistance when it absorbs infrared radiation. This material is often made from metals such as platinum or semiconductors like vanadium oxide, which have a significant temperature coefficient of resistance—meaning their resistance changes markedly with temperature.

The basic structure of a bolometer includes a thin film or strip of the thermally sensitive material mounted on a substrate with low thermal conductivity. This design ensures that the absorbed infrared radiation heats the material without significant heat loss to the surroundings. When the IR radiation strikes the bolometer, it causes a slight temperature increase in the material, leading to a change in its electrical resistance. This change is measured using a Wheatstone bridge or a similar circuit, and the resulting electrical signal is proportional to the intensity of the absorbed radiation.

Advantages of the Bolometer:

1. **High Sensitivity:** Bolometers are extremely sensitive to small changes in temperature, making them capable of detecting very low levels of infrared radiation. This sensitivity is particularly useful in applications where detecting weak IR signals is essential.
2. **Broad Spectral Response:** Bolometers can detect a wide range of infrared wavelengths, from the mid-infrared to the far-infrared regions, making them versatile detectors for various applications.
3. **Wide Dynamic Range:** They can measure a broad range of radiation intensities, from very weak to relatively strong signals, without requiring significant adjustments to the instrument.

Limitations of the Bolometer:

1. **Slow Response Time:** One of the primary limitations of bolometers is their relatively slow response time compared to other IR detectors, such as pyroelectric detectors. This slow response is due to the time it takes for the material to absorb radiation, change temperature, and subsequently alter its resistance. As a result, bolometers are not ideal for applications requiring rapid measurements or real-time monitoring.
2. **Temperature Sensitivity:** Bolometers are sensitive to external temperature changes, which can introduce noise or drift in the measurements. This sensitivity necessitates careful temperature control and calibration to ensure accurate results.
3. **Complex Cooling Requirements:** In some high-sensitivity applications, bolometers need to be cooled to cryogenic temperatures to reduce thermal noise and improve sensitivity. This cooling adds complexity and cost to the system.

Applications of Bolometers:

- In infrared spectroscopy, bolometers are used in specialized instruments where high sensitivity to low-level IR radiation is required, such as in the analysis of trace gases or weakly absorbing samples.
- In astronomy, bolometers are widely used to detect infrared radiation from celestial objects, helping astronomers study phenomena that are not visible in other parts of the electromagnetic spectrum.
- In thermal imaging, bolometers are used in infrared cameras to detect heat patterns and create thermal images, which are valuable in various fields, including medical diagnostics, building inspections, and military applications.

Thermocouple

A **thermocouple** is a widely used detector in infrared (IR) spectroscopy and other thermal measurement applications. It operates based on the **Seebeck effect**, where a voltage is generated in response to a temperature difference between two different metals or semiconductors. This voltage can then be correlated with the amount of infrared radiation absorbed by the thermocouple, making it a useful tool for detecting and measuring infrared radiation.

A thermocouple consists of two dissimilar metals or alloys that are joined at one end, forming a junction. When this junction is exposed to infrared radiation, it absorbs the energy and heats up, creating a temperature difference between the heated junction (the "hot junction") and a reference junction (the "cold junction") that remains at a known, usually cooler temperature. The temperature difference between these two junctions generates a small voltage, which is proportional to the temperature difference and, consequently, to the intensity of the absorbed infrared radiation.

Advantages of Thermocouples:

1. **Broad Spectral Response:** Thermocouples are sensitive to a wide range of wavelengths in the infrared region, making them versatile detectors for various IR spectroscopy applications.
2. **Simplicity and Durability:** Thermocouples are relatively simple devices with no moving parts, which makes them durable and reliable even in harsh environments. They are also easy to fabricate and integrate into

various spectroscopic instruments.

3. **Wide Temperature Range:** Thermocouples can measure a broad range of temperatures, from very low to extremely high, depending on the materials used. This makes them suitable for applications that require temperature measurements under various conditions.

Limitations of Thermocouples:

1. **Lower Sensitivity:** Compared to other IR detectors like bolometers or photodetectors, thermocouples generally have lower sensitivity to small changes in infrared radiation. This makes them less suitable for applications requiring high sensitivity and precision, such as detecting very weak IR signals.
2. **Slow Response Time:** Thermocouples have a relatively slow response time, which can be a disadvantage in applications requiring real-time monitoring or rapid measurements.
3. **Need for Calibration:** The voltage generated by a thermocouple is typically small, often in the microvolt range, and requires careful calibration to ensure accurate temperature readings. The calibration process must account for the specific materials used and the temperature range of the application.

Applications of Thermocouples in IR Spectroscopy:

- Thermocouples are commonly used in IR spectrometers for general-purpose temperature measurements and as simple, cost-effective detectors for infrared radiation in industrial and laboratory settings.
- They are often used in combination with other types of detectors in multi-sensor systems, where their broad spectral response and durability are advantageous.
- In applications such as gas analysis, thermocouples can be used to measure the temperature changes associated with IR absorption by gases, providing valuable data for identifying and quantifying gas components.

How Thermocouples are Used in IR Spectroscopy:

- In an IR spectrometer, the thermocouple is typically placed where it can absorb IR radiation that has passed through or been reflected by the sample. As the sample absorbs specific wavelengths of IR light, corresponding changes in temperature at the thermocouple junction produce a voltage signal. This signal is then processed and analyzed to generate an IR spectrum, which reveals the molecular composition and structure of the sample.

Thermistor

A **thermistor** is a type of temperature-sensitive resistor used as a detector in infrared (IR) spectroscopy and various thermal measurement applications. Unlike thermocouples, which generate a voltage based on temperature differences, thermistors operate by changing their electrical resistance in response to temperature changes. This property makes them useful for detecting infrared radiation, as the absorbed IR radiation leads to a temperature increase, which in turn alters the thermistor's resistance.

Thermistors are made from semiconductor materials, typically metal oxides like manganese oxide or nickel oxide, that have a high temperature coefficient of resistance. There are two main types of thermistors:

- **Negative Temperature Coefficient (NTC) Thermistors**: In NTC thermistors, the resistance decreases as the temperature increases. This behavior is commonly used in temperature measurement and control systems.
- **Positive Temperature Coefficient (PTC) Thermistors**: In PTC thermistors, the resistance increases with rising temperature. These are often used in applications requiring current limiting or overcurrent protection.

Advantages of Thermistors:

1. **High Sensitivity:** Thermistors are highly sensitive to small changes in temperature, making them capable of detecting minute amounts of infrared radiation.
2. **Wide Range of Temperatures:** They can operate over a broad range of temperatures, providing flexibility in various applications.
3. **Compact and Inexpensive:** Thermistors are small, easy to manufacture, and relatively inexpensive, making them accessible for a wide range of

applications.

Limitations of Thermistors:

1. **Non-Linear Response:** Thermistors have a non-linear response to temperature changes, which can complicate the calibration and interpretation of results.
2. **Slower Response Time:** Compared to other types of detectors, thermistors may have slower response times, limiting their use in applications that require rapid measurements.
3. **Limited Use in High Temperatures:** While thermistors are sensitive, they may not be suitable for extremely high-temperature applications due to the potential for material degradation.

Applications of Thermistors in IR Spectroscopy:

- Thermistors are often used in IR spectroscopy for detecting temperature changes induced by infrared radiation. They are particularly useful in applications where compact size and high sensitivity are required.
- They are also used in combination with other detectors in multi-sensor systems, where their temperature sensitivity complements other detection methods.

Pyroelectric Detector

A **pyroelectric detector** is a highly sensitive device used in infrared (IR) spectroscopy that operates based on the pyroelectric effect. This effect occurs in certain materials, known as pyroelectric materials, which generate a temporary voltage when they undergo a change in temperature. Pyroelectric detectors are particularly useful for detecting changes in infrared radiation, making them ideal for applications requiring fast response times and high sensitivity.

Pyroelectric materials are typically crystalline materials such as triglycine sulfate (TGS), lithium tantalate ($LiTaO_3$), or lead zirconate titanate (PZT). These materials possess a spontaneous polarization that changes with temperature. When infrared radiation strikes the pyroelectric material, it causes a rapid temperature change, leading to a change in polarization and the generation of an electrical signal.

Advantages of Pyroelectric Detectors:

1. **High Sensitivity:** Pyroelectric detectors are extremely sensitive to changes in infrared radiation, making them capable of detecting very weak IR signals.
2. **Fast Response Time:** These detectors respond quickly to changes in IR radiation, allowing for real-time monitoring and fast measurements.
3. **Broad Spectral Range:** Pyroelectric detectors can operate across a wide range of IR wavelengths, making them versatile for various applications.

Limitations of Pyroelectric Detectors:

1. **Need for Modulated Signal:** Pyroelectric detectors are sensitive to changes in radiation rather than steady-state radiation, so they often require the IR source to be modulated (pulsed) to produce a measurable signal.
2. **Temperature Sensitivity:** These detectors can be sensitive to ambient temperature changes, which may require careful control of the environment or additional compensation methods.
3. **Complexity and Cost:** Pyroelectric detectors are more complex and expensive compared to simpler detectors like thermocouples or thermistors, limiting their use to specialized applications.

Applications of Pyroelectric Detectors in IR Spectroscopy:

- Pyroelectric detectors are widely used in Fourier-transform infrared (FTIR) spectrometers due to their fast response time and high sensitivity, which are essential for capturing the rapid changes in IR intensity during interferometric measurements.
- They are also used in applications such as gas analysis, thermal imaging, and security systems, where quick detection of infrared radiation is crucial.

3.3 Applications of IR Spectroscopy
Identification of Functional Groups

One of the most important applications of infrared (IR) spectroscopy is the **identification of functional groups** within a molecule. Functional groups are specific groupings of atoms within molecules that have distinct chemical properties and reactivity. Each functional group absorbs infrared radiation at characteristic frequencies, leading to unique absorption bands in the IR spectrum. By analyzing these absorption bands, chemists can identify the presence and nature of functional groups in an unknown compound, providing crucial information about its molecular structure.

In IR spectroscopy, the absorption of infrared radiation causes the atoms in a molecule to vibrate. Different types of vibrations, such as stretching and bending, occur at specific frequencies that depend on the mass of the atoms, the bond strength, and the molecular environment. These vibrations are associated with specific functional groups, and the resulting absorption bands appear at characteristic wavenumbers (measured in cm^-1) in the IR spectrum.

Common Functional Groups and Their IR Absorption Bands:

1. **Hydroxyl Group (–OH):** The O-H stretching vibration is typically observed as a broad, strong absorption band around 3200-3600 cm^-1. This broadness is often due to hydrogen bonding, especially in alcohols and carboxylic acids. In the case of carboxylic acids, the O-H stretch appears even broader and may overlap with the C=O stretch.

2. **Carbonyl Group (C=O):** The C=O stretching vibration produces a strong, sharp absorption band around 1650-1750 cm^-1. The exact position can vary depending on the specific type of carbonyl-containing compound, such as aldehydes, ketones, carboxylic acids, esters, or amides. For instance, aldehydes and ketones typically show C=O absorption near 1720-1740 cm^-1, while esters absorb slightly lower, around 1735-1750 cm^-1.

3. **Amines (–NH2, –NHR, –NR2):** The N-H stretching vibrations for primary and secondary amines appear as one or two bands in the region of 3300-3500 cm^-1. Primary amines (–NH2) usually exhibit two N-H stretching bands due to symmetric and asymmetric stretching. Secondary amines (–NHR) show a single band in this region.

4. **Alkyl Groups (–CH3, –CH2–, –CH–):** C-H stretching vibrations in alkanes typically appear just below 3000 cm^-1 (2850-2960 cm^-1). Methyl (–CH3) and methylene (–CH2–) groups can also show bending vibrations in the fingerprint region, around 1350-1470 cm^-1.

5. **Alkenes (C=C) and Aromatics:** The C=C stretching vibration in alkenes generally appears near 1620-1680 cm^-1. In aromatic compounds, C=C stretching in the benzene ring typically produces multiple absorption bands between 1450-1600 cm^-1, known as the aromatic ring vibrations. Additionally, the C-H stretching vibrations in aromatics occur just above

3000 cm^-1.

6. **Nitro Group (–NO2):** Nitro groups show two strong absorption bands due to asymmetric and symmetric N-O stretching vibrations, typically around 1500-1600 cm^-1 and 1300-1400 cm^-1, respectively.

7. **Ethers (C–O–C):** The C-O stretching vibration in ethers appears as a band in the region of 1050-1150 cm^-1. This band is usually strong and can be used to identify the presence of an ether linkage in the molecule.

8. **Carboxylic Acids (–COOH):** Carboxylic acids show a strong, broad O-H stretch around 2500-3000 cm^-1, often overlapping with the C-H stretching region. The C=O stretch appears around 1700-1725 cm^-1, and there may also be a C-O stretch around 1210-1320 cm^-1.

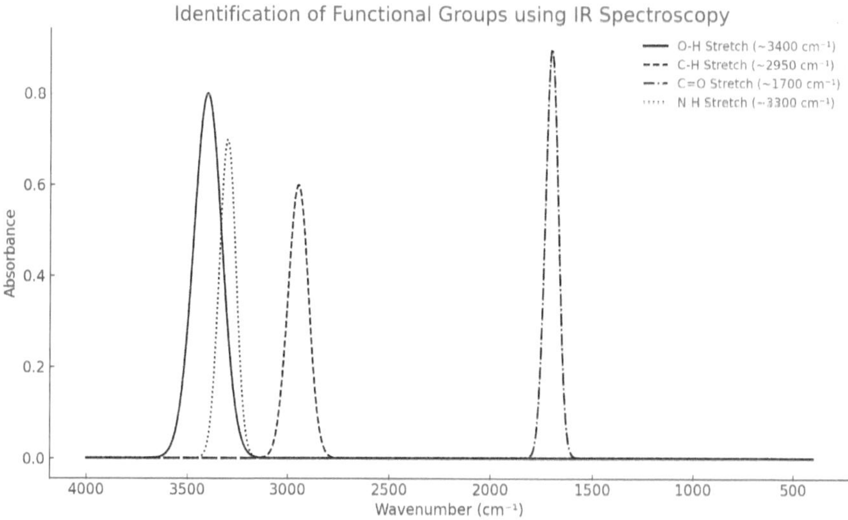

Here is the diagram illustrating the identification of functional groups using IR spectroscopy:

O-H Stretch (~3400 cm⁻¹): A broad and strong peak characteristic of alcohols and carboxylic acids.

C-H Stretch (~2950 cm⁻¹): A sharp peak commonly associated with alkanes.

C=O Stretch (~1700 cm⁻¹): A strong and sharp peak indicative of carbonyl groups found in aldehydes, ketones, carboxylic acids, and esters.

N-H Stretch (~3300 cm⁻¹): A peak typically found in amines and amides.

Practical Application: In practice, a chemist uses an IR spectrum to identify functional groups by matching the observed absorption bands with known characteristic wavenumbers. For instance, if an unknown compound shows a strong absorption band at 1720 cm^-1, it is likely that the molecule contains a carbonyl group. If additional bands are observed around 3200-3600 cm^-1, an O-H group might also be present, suggesting the compound could be a carboxylic acid or an alcohol. By analyzing the entire spectrum, chemists can piece together the functional groups present, leading to a clearer understanding of the molecule's structure.

Drug Analysis

Infrared (IR) spectroscopy is a powerful analytical tool used extensively in **drug analysis** to identify and characterize pharmaceutical compounds. Its ability to provide detailed information about the molecular structure of drugs makes it indispensable in both research and quality control within the pharmaceutical industry.

One of the primary applications of IR spectroscopy in drug analysis is the **identification of active pharmaceutical ingredients (APIs)**. Each API has a unique IR spectrum, often referred to as its molecular "fingerprint," which can be used to confirm the identity of the compound. By comparing the IR spectrum of a sample with a reference spectrum of the known API, analysts can verify the presence and purity of the drug in a formulation. This is particularly important for ensuring that the correct API is present in the right quantity and that there are no contaminants or degradation products.

IR spectroscopy is also used in the **characterization of drug excipients**—substances other than the active ingredient that are included in pharmaceutical formulations to aid in the manufacturing process, protect, support, or enhance stability, or assist in drug delivery. Excipients, such as binders, fillers, preservatives, and disintegrants, each have distinct IR absorption bands that can be analyzed to ensure they are correctly included in the formulation. The ability to monitor both APIs and excipients helps ensure the overall quality and consistency of pharmaceutical products.

Polymorphism is another area where IR spectroscopy plays a crucial role in drug analysis. Polymorphism refers to the ability of a substance to exist in more than one crystalline form, which can significantly impact the drug's solubility, stability, and bioavailability. IR spectroscopy can distinguish between different polymorphs by detecting subtle differences in the vibrational frequencies of the molecules. This capability is essential in the pharmaceutical industry, where controlling the polymorphic form of an API can affect the efficacy and safety of the drug.

IR spectroscopy is also employed in **monitoring drug degradation** and **stability studies**. Over time, drugs can degrade due to exposure to light, heat, moisture, or other environmental factors, leading to the formation of degradation products that may be less effective or potentially harmful. By analyzing the IR spectrum of a drug over time, analysts can identify any changes in the molecular structure that indicate degradation. This information is crucial for determining the shelf life of pharmaceutical products and for ensuring they remain safe and effective throughout their intended use.

In addition to qualitative analysis, IR spectroscopy can also be used for **quantitative analysis** of drugs. By measuring the intensity of specific absorption bands corresponding to the functional groups of the API, it is possible to quantify the concentration of the drug in a sample. This application is particularly useful in quality control laboratories, where ensuring the correct dosage of a drug in a formulation is critical.

Furthermore, IR spectroscopy is employed in the **detection of counterfeit drugs**. Counterfeit pharmaceuticals pose a significant risk to public health, as they may contain incorrect ingredients, improper dosages, or harmful substances. By comparing the IR spectrum of a suspect drug with that of a genuine product, analysts can quickly identify discrepancies that indicate the presence of counterfeit drugs. This rapid and non-destructive method is an effective tool in the fight against pharmaceutical counterfeiting.

CHAPTER FOUR

Flame Photometry

4.1 Principle of Flame Photometry

Flame Emission and Its Relevance

Flame photometry, also known as flame atomic emission spectrometry (FAES), is an analytical technique used to detect and quantify the concentration of certain metal ions, particularly alkali and alkaline earth metals, based on their characteristic emission of light when excited in a flame. The principle behind flame photometry relies on the ability of these metal ions to emit light at specific wavelengths when they are heated in a flame, a process known as **flame emission.**

Flame Emission and Its Relevance in Flame Photometry

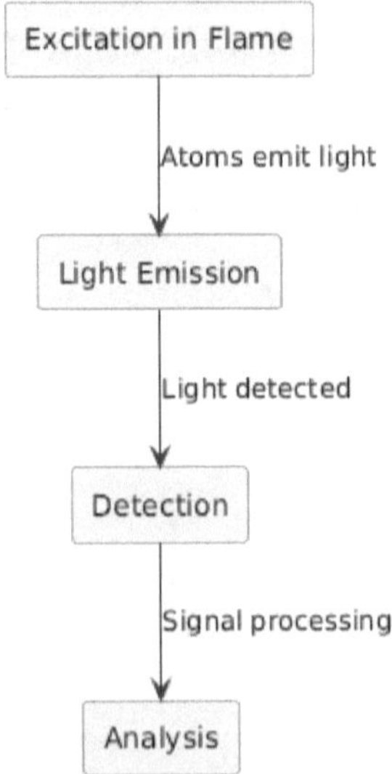

Flame emission occurs when a sample containing metal ions is introduced into a flame. The high temperature of the flame provides enough energy to excite the outer electrons of the metal atoms to higher energy levels. When these excited electrons return to their ground state, they release energy in the form of light. The wavelength of the emitted light is specific to each element, corresponding to the difference in energy between the excited state and the ground state of the atom. For example, sodium emits a bright yellow light at a wavelength of approximately 589 nm, while potassium emits a violet light at around 766 nm.

The intensity of the emitted light is directly proportional to the concentration of the metal ion in the sample. This relationship forms the basis of quantitative analysis in flame photometry. By measuring the intensity of the light at the specific wavelength corresponding to the metal of interest, it is possible to determine the concentration of that metal in the sample with a high degree of accuracy.

Relevance of Flame Emission in Analytical Chemistry:

Flame photometry is particularly relevant in the analysis of biological samples, environmental monitoring, and the quality control of various industrial products. It is widely used to measure the concentrations of elements like sodium, potassium, calcium, lithium, and magnesium, which are essential in clinical diagnostics for assessing electrolyte balance in the human body. For instance, the measurement of sodium and potassium levels in blood serum is critical in diagnosing and managing conditions such as electrolyte imbalances, dehydration, and kidney function disorders.

In environmental science, flame photometry is used to monitor the levels of metal ions in water, soil, and plant materials, helping to assess the impact of pollution and the availability of essential nutrients. In agriculture, the technique is used to analyze soil and plant samples to determine nutrient content and guide fertilization practices.

The simplicity, speed, and cost-effectiveness of flame photometry make it an attractive method for routine analysis in laboratories. Unlike more complex techniques such as atomic absorption spectroscopy (AAS) or inductively coupled plasma optical emission spectrometry (ICP-OES), flame photometry does not require extensive sample preparation or expensive equipment, making it accessible for a wide range of applications.

However, it is important to note that flame photometry has its limitations. It is primarily suited for the analysis of alkali and alkaline earth metals, as these elements are easily excited in a flame and produce strong, characteristic emissions. The technique is less effective for detecting metals that require higher excitation energies or those that do not emit light in the visible spectrum. Additionally, the presence of other elements in the sample can cause spectral interference, affecting the accuracy of the results.

Interferences in Flame Photometry

In flame photometry, **interferences** are factors that can affect the accuracy and precision of the measurement of metal ion concentrations. These interferences can arise from various sources, including the sample matrix, the flame conditions, and the presence of other elements. Understanding and mitigating these interferences is crucial for obtaining reliable results in flame photometric analysis.

1. Spectral Interference:

Spectral interference occurs when the emission spectrum of one element overlaps with the emission spectrum of the element of interest. This overlap can cause inaccurate readings, as the detector may pick up light from both elements, leading to an overestimation or underestimation of the concentration of the target element. For example, in the case of sodium and lithium, both emit light in the yellow region of the spectrum, which can cause overlap and interfere with the measurement. To reduce spectral interference, filters or monochromators are used to isolate the specific wavelength of the element being measured, ensuring that the detected light corresponds only to that element.

2. Chemical Interference:

Chemical interference occurs when other chemical species in the sample affect the absorption or emission of the target element. This type of interference can happen in several ways:

- **Ionization Interference:** At high flame temperatures, certain elements may ionize rather than emit light, reducing the intensity of the emission and leading to inaccurate readings. Ionization interference is common with elements like potassium and calcium. Adding ionization suppressants, such as cesium or sodium, can help reduce this interference by providing a more stable environment for the target element.

- **Formation of Refractory Compounds:** Some elements can form stable, non-volatile compounds in the flame, such as oxides or phosphates, which do not easily dissociate and emit light. This reduces the number of free atoms available for excitation and emission, leading to lower signal intensity. For example, calcium can form calcium phosphate, which is not easily excited in the flame. Adjusting the flame conditions or using releasing agents can help break down these refractory compounds and reduce chemical interference.

3. Physical Interference:

Physical interference arises from variations in the physical properties of the sample, such as viscosity, surface tension, or density, which can affect the nebulization process and the transport of the sample into the flame. These factors can lead to inconsistencies in the sample introduction, resulting in fluctuations in the emission intensity. For example, a sample with high viscosity may produce larger droplets during nebulization, leading to incomplete vaporization and lower emission signals. To minimize physical interference, it is essential to standardize the sample preparation process, including dilution, and use internal standards to correct for any variations.

4. Matrix Interference:

Matrix interference occurs when the overall composition of the sample affects the measurement of the target element. The presence of other ions, solvents, or organic materials can alter the flame conditions or interact with the analyte, leading to either enhancement or suppression of the signal. For example, high concentrations of sodium in a sample can suppress the emission of potassium, as both elements compete for excitation energy in the flame. Matrix interference can be addressed by using matrix-matched standards, where the standard solutions have a similar composition to the sample, or by employing the method of standard addition, which compensates for matrix effects.

5. Flame Conditions:

The temperature and composition of the flame itself can also introduce interferences in flame photometry. Variations in flame temperature can affect the excitation efficiency of the atoms, leading to inconsistent emission intensities. For example, if the flame is too cool, it may not sufficiently excite the atoms of the target element, resulting in lower signal intensity. On the other hand, a flame that is too hot may cause ionization or dissociation of the atoms, leading to inaccurate measurements. Maintaining consistent and optimal flame conditions is essential for minimizing these interferences.

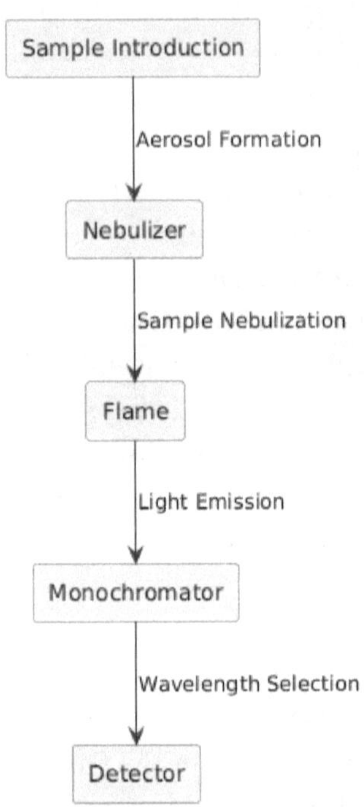

4.2 Instrumentation

Components of Flame Photometers

A **flame photometer** is an analytical instrument used to measure the concentration of specific metal ions, particularly alkali and alkaline earth metals, in a sample by detecting the light emitted when these ions are excited in a flame. The accuracy and reliability of flame photometry depend on the design and functionality of its key components. Understanding these components is essential for effectively operating the instrument and interpreting the results.

1. Flame Burner

The **flame burner** is the heart of the flame photometer, where the sample is introduced and atomized, and the metal ions are excited. The burner generates a flame by mixing a fuel gas, typically acetylene, propane, or natural gas, with an oxidant, such as air or oxygen. The flame's temperature is critical for exciting the metal ions, causing them to emit light at specific wavelengths. The design of the burner ensures that the sample is evenly dispersed into the flame as fine droplets, maximizing the efficiency of atomization and excitation. The burner must maintain a consistent and stable flame to produce accurate and reproducible results.

2. Nebulizer and Sample Introduction System

The **nebulizer** is responsible for converting the liquid sample into a fine aerosol that can be introduced into the flame. The sample introduction system typically includes a nebulizer and a spray chamber. The nebulizer uses the pressure of the oxidant gas to aspirate the liquid sample and break it into fine droplets. These droplets are then carried by the oxidant gas into the spray chamber, where larger droplets are removed, ensuring that only the finest aerosol particles reach the flame. This process is crucial for achieving consistent atomization and preventing fluctuations in the emission signal.

3. Optical System

The **optical system** in a flame photometer is designed to collect and focus the light emitted by the excited metal ions. It typically consists of lenses, mirrors, and filters that direct the light from the flame to the detector. The optical system is carefully aligned to maximize the amount of light reaching the detector while minimizing stray light and interference from other sources. The use of specific filters or monochromators in the optical system helps isolate the emission wavelength corresponding to the element of interest, ensuring accurate measurements.

4. Wavelength Selector (Monochromator or Filters)

The **wavelength selector** is a critical component that isolates the specific wavelength of light emitted by the target metal ion, ensuring that the detector only measures the relevant signal. Two main types of wavelength selectors are used in flame photometers:

- **Filters:** Optical filters are used to transmit only a narrow band of wavelengths corresponding to the emission line of the element being measured. These filters are usually interference or absorption filters tailored to specific elements like sodium, potassium, calcium, and lithium. Filters are straightforward, cost-effective, and sufficient for many routine analyses.
- **Monochromators:** In more advanced flame photometers, a monochromator may be used to precisely select and isolate the desired wavelength. Monochromators use a diffraction grating or prism to

disperse the light and select the exact wavelength required for the analysis. This allows for greater flexibility and precision, particularly when analyzing multiple elements in the same sample.

5. Detector

The **detector** is responsible for converting the light emitted by the excited atoms in the flame into an electrical signal that can be measured and analyzed. The most common detectors used in flame photometers are **photomultiplier tubes (PMTs), photodiodes,** or **photovoltaic cells:**

- **Photomultiplier Tubes (PMTs):** PMTs are highly sensitive and capable of detecting low-intensity light, making them ideal for applications where precise measurements of trace elements are required. They amplify the weak light signals produced by the sample, providing a strong electrical output for further processing.
- **Photodiodes:** Photodiodes are solid-state detectors that convert light into an electrical current. While they are less sensitive than PMTs, photodiodes are more robust, compact, and suitable for routine analyses where extreme sensitivity is not required.
- **Photovoltaic Cells:** Photovoltaic cells are also used as detectors in some flame photometers. They generate a voltage when exposed to light, with the magnitude of the voltage proportional to the intensity of the light emitted by the sample.

6. Amplifier and Readout System

The **amplifier** boosts the electrical signal generated by the detector, making it strong enough for accurate measurement and display. The **readout system** then processes the amplified signal and displays the results, typically in terms of concentration or intensity units. Modern flame photometers often feature digital displays, data logging capabilities, and interfaces for connecting to computers or other data analysis systems. The readout system may also include calibration settings and software for automatically converting the detected signal into concentration values based on standard curves.

7. Gas Control System

The **gas control system** regulates the flow of fuel and oxidant gases to the burner, ensuring that the flame remains stable and at the correct temperature throughout the analysis. Precise control of the gas mixture is essential for maintaining consistent flame conditions, which directly affect the accuracy and reproducibility of the measurements. The gas control system typically includes flow meters, pressure regulators, and safety features to prevent accidents or fluctuations in the flame.

8. Calibration System

To ensure accurate and reliable results, a flame photometer must be calibrated using standard solutions of known concentration. The **calibration system** in a flame photometer allows the user to input these standards, adjust the instrument's settings, and create calibration curves. These curves are used to determine the concentration of unknown samples based on their emission intensity. Regular calibration is essential to account for any variations in flame conditions, detector sensitivity, or sample introduction.

Monochromators and Detectors

In flame photometry, **monochromators** and **detectors** are essential components that work together to isolate and measure the specific wavelengths of light emitted by excited metal ions in a flame. These components are crucial for ensuring the accuracy and sensitivity of the analysis, as they allow the instrument to focus on the exact emission lines of the target elements and convert the emitted light into measurable electrical signals.

Monochromators

A **monochromator** is an optical device that selects and isolates a narrow band of wavelengths from the broad spectrum of light emitted by the sample in the flame. The monochromator ensures that only the light corresponding to the specific emission wavelength of the element of interest reaches the detector, minimizing interference from other wavelengths.

Key Components of a Monochromator:

1. **Entrance Slit:** The entrance slit allows light emitted from the flame to enter the monochromator. The width of the slit can be adjusted to control the amount of light entering the system, which in turn affects the resolution of the wavelength selection.

2. **Dispersive Element:** The dispersive element is the core component of the monochromator that separates the incoming light into its constituent wavelengths. The most common types of dispersive elements are:

- ○ **Diffraction Gratings:** A diffraction grating consists of a surface with closely spaced parallel lines or grooves that diffract light into its component wavelengths. By rotating the grating, different wavelengths can be directed toward the exit slit and onto the detector. Diffraction gratings are highly versatile and provide precise wavelength selection over a wide spectral range.
- ○ **Prisms:** Prisms are optical elements made of glass or quartz that refract light and separate it into its component wavelengths based on the refractive index of the material. Prisms are less commonly used than diffraction gratings but can still be effective in certain applications.

3. **Exit Slit:** The exit slit allows only the selected wavelength of light to pass through and reach the detector. The width of the exit slit also affects the resolution and intensity of the transmitted light. Narrower slits provide better resolution but may reduce the light intensity reaching the detector.

Functionality of Monochromators: In flame photometry, monochromators are used to isolate the specific emission lines of elements such as sodium (589 nm), potassium (766 nm), and calcium (422 nm). By adjusting the position of the dispersive element, the monochromator can be tuned to select the wavelength corresponding to the element of interest. This isolation is crucial for accurate quantification, as it minimizes interference from other elements or background radiation.

Detectors

The **detector** in a flame photometer is responsible for converting the isolated light from the monochromator into an electrical signal that can be measured and analyzed. The choice of detector depends on the required sensitivity, wavelength range, and application. Common types of detectors used in flame photometry include:

1. Photomultiplier Tubes (PMTs):

- **Functionality:** Photomultiplier tubes are highly sensitive detectors that can detect very low levels of light. When photons strike the photocathode inside the PMT, they emit electrons through the photoelectric effect. These electrons are then accelerated and multiplied through a series of dynodes, resulting in a strong electrical signal that is proportional to the intensity of the incoming light.

- **Advantages:** PMTs offer excellent sensitivity and are capable of detecting weak emission signals from trace elements. They are widely used in flame photometry when high precision is required.
- **Limitations:** PMTs are sensitive to mechanical vibrations and require a stable power supply. They are also more expensive and fragile compared to other detectors.

2. Photodiodes:

- **Functionality:** Photodiodes are solid-state detectors that convert incoming light into an electrical current. When photons strike the semiconductor material in the photodiode, they generate electron-hole pairs, which produce a current proportional to the light intensity.
- **Advantages:** Photodiodes are robust, compact, and offer a wide dynamic range. They are less expensive than PMTs and are suitable for routine analyses where extreme sensitivity is not required.
- **Limitations:** Photodiodes are less sensitive than PMTs, making them less suitable for detecting very low concentrations of elements.

3. Photovoltaic Cells:

- **Functionality:** Photovoltaic cells generate a voltage when exposed to light. The magnitude of the voltage is proportional to the intensity of the light. Photovoltaic cells are simpler and less expensive than PMTs and photodiodes.
- **Advantages:** Photovoltaic cells are durable, easy to use, and cost-effective. They are suitable for basic flame photometry applications.
- **Limitations:** Photovoltaic cells have lower sensitivity compared to PMTs and photodiodes, limiting their use in applications requiring high precision.

Integration of Monochromators and Detectors: In a flame photometer, the monochromator and detector work together to ensure accurate and selective measurement of the target element. The monochromator isolates the specific wavelength of interest, and the detector converts the resulting light into an electrical signal that can be quantified. This signal is then processed by the instrument's electronics and displayed as a concentration or intensity value.

4.3 Applications of Flame Photometry

Analysis of Alkali Metals

Flame photometry is a highly effective analytical technique widely used for the **analysis of alkali metals** such as sodium (Na), potassium (K), lithium (Li), and cesium (Cs). These metals are known for their strong and distinct emission lines in the visible region of the electromagnetic spectrum, making them ideal candidates for flame photometric analysis. The ability to quickly and accurately measure the concentrations of these elements has significant applications in various fields, including clinical diagnostics, agriculture, environmental monitoring, and the food industry.

1. Clinical Diagnostics:

In clinical settings, flame photometry is extensively used to measure the concentrations of sodium and potassium ions in biological fluids such as blood serum, plasma, and urine. The accurate determination of these ions is critical for diagnosing and managing electrolyte imbalances, which are associated with various medical conditions, including dehydration, kidney disease, and heart failure.

- **Sodium Analysis:** Sodium is a major extracellular ion involved in maintaining fluid balance, nerve function, and muscle contraction. In flame photometry, sodium emits a bright yellow light at a wavelength of approximately 589 nm when excited in the flame. By measuring the intensity of this emission, clinicians can determine the sodium concentration in a patient's sample, aiding in the diagnosis of conditions like hyponatremia (low sodium levels) or hypernatremia (high sodium levels).

- **Potassium Analysis:** Potassium is a crucial intracellular ion that plays a key role in nerve impulse transmission and muscle contraction. Potassium emits a violet light at around 766 nm when analyzed using flame photometry. Accurate measurement of potassium levels is essential for detecting conditions such as hypokalemia (low potassium levels) and hyperkalemia (high potassium levels), which can have severe cardiac implications if left untreated.

2. Agricultural Applications:

Flame photometry is also widely used in agriculture to assess the nutrient content of soil and plant tissues, particularly for essential alkali metals like potassium and sodium.

- **Soil Testing:** Soil fertility depends significantly on the availability of potassium, which is vital for plant growth and development. By analyzing soil samples using flame photometry, farmers and agronomists can determine the potassium levels and make informed decisions about fertilization strategies. This ensures that crops receive adequate nutrients, leading to better yields and improved crop quality.
- **Plant Tissue Analysis:** Similarly, flame photometry is employed to measure the concentration of potassium in plant tissues. This analysis helps in monitoring the nutrient uptake by plants and in diagnosing potential deficiencies or toxicities. By ensuring optimal potassium levels, farmers can enhance crop productivity and manage plant health more effectively.

3. Environmental Monitoring:

In environmental science, flame photometry is used to monitor the presence of alkali metals in natural waters, wastewater, and industrial effluents.

- **Water Quality Analysis:** Sodium and potassium are commonly present in natural water sources, and their concentrations can indicate the quality of the water. Flame photometry allows for the rapid and accurate determination of these elements, helping to assess the impact of industrial activities, agricultural runoff, or natural processes on water bodies.
- **Effluent Monitoring:** Industrial effluents often contain varying levels of alkali metals, which need to be monitored to comply with environmental regulations. Flame photometry provides a cost-effective method for routine analysis of these metals in wastewater, ensuring that discharge limits are met and reducing the environmental impact of industrial operations.

4. Food Industry:

In the food industry, flame photometry is used to analyze the sodium content in various food products. Sodium is a key component in many processed foods, and its accurate measurement is important for both quality control and regulatory compliance.

- **Sodium Content Analysis:** Monitoring sodium levels in food products is crucial for ensuring that they meet nutritional labeling requirements and for controlling the salt content, which has implications for public health. Flame photometry provides a reliable method for determining sodium concentrations in a wide range of food items, from processed meats to snack foods.

5. Pharmaceutical Applications:

In the pharmaceutical industry, flame photometry is used to analyze the content of alkali metals in drugs and pharmaceutical formulations. This ensures that the final product meets the required specifications and that the levels of these metals are within acceptable limits.

- **Quality Control:** The accurate determination of sodium, potassium, and other alkali metals in pharmaceutical products is essential for maintaining quality and ensuring patient safety. Flame photometry is a valuable tool for routine quality control testing, helping to verify the composition and purity of drug products.

Clinical and Pharmaceutical Applications

Flame photometry is widely recognized for its significant contributions to both clinical diagnostics and pharmaceutical analysis. The technique's ability to provide accurate and rapid measurements of specific metal ions, particularly alkali and alkaline earth metals, makes it an essential tool in these fields. Here's how flame photometry is applied in clinical and pharmaceutical contexts:

Clinical Applications

1. Electrolyte Balance Monitoring:

- **Sodium (Na+):** Sodium is a crucial electrolyte in the human body, involved in maintaining fluid balance, nerve transmission, and muscle function. Flame photometry is routinely used to measure sodium levels in blood serum, plasma, and urine. Accurate determination of sodium is vital for diagnosing and managing conditions like hyponatremia (low sodium levels) and hypernatremia (high sodium levels), which can result from dehydration, kidney dysfunction, or adrenal gland disorders.
- **Potassium (K+):** Potassium is another essential electrolyte, primarily found inside cells. It plays a key role in maintaining normal cell function,

nerve impulse transmission, and muscle contraction, including heart function. Flame photometry is commonly used to assess potassium levels in blood samples, helping diagnose hypokalemia (low potassium levels) or hyperkalemia (high potassium levels). These conditions can be life-threatening if not managed promptly, as they directly impact cardiac function.

2. Calcium and Magnesium Analysis:

- **Calcium (Ca2+):** Calcium is critical for bone health, blood clotting, muscle contraction, and nerve signaling. Flame photometry is employed to measure calcium levels in serum, which is crucial for diagnosing conditions such as hypercalcemia (high calcium levels) and hypocalcemia (low calcium levels). These conditions may be associated with parathyroid gland disorders, vitamin D imbalance, or chronic kidney disease.
- **Magnesium (Mg2+):** Magnesium is involved in numerous biochemical reactions, including those related to muscle and nerve function, blood glucose control, and blood pressure regulation. Measuring magnesium levels using flame photometry can help diagnose and monitor conditions such as hypomagnesemia (low magnesium levels), which can occur due to malnutrition, chronic diarrhea, or the use of certain diuretics.

3. Lithium Monitoring:

- **Therapeutic Drug Monitoring:** Lithium salts are commonly used in the treatment of bipolar disorder. Monitoring lithium levels in the blood is essential to ensure that the drug remains within its therapeutic range, as both sub-therapeutic and toxic levels can have serious implications for patient health. Flame photometry is a reliable method for determining lithium concentration, helping to optimize treatment and avoid adverse effects.

Pharmaceutical Applications
1. Quality Control of Pharmaceutical Products:

- **Active Pharmaceutical Ingredient (API) Analysis:** Flame photometry is used to analyze the content of metal ions that are part of or interact with the active pharmaceutical ingredients in drug formulations. For example, sodium and potassium salts are often included as part of the API or as excipients, and their accurate quantification is essential for ensuring product consistency and efficacy.

- **Excipients Analysis:** In addition to APIs, flame photometry is used to measure the concentration of excipients that contain alkali or alkaline earth metals. Excipients like sodium chloride, potassium chloride, or magnesium stearate are commonly used in drug formulations, and their concentrations need to be carefully controlled to ensure the stability and performance of the final product.

2. Analysis of Trace Metals in Drug Formulations:

- **Contaminant Detection:** Trace amounts of metal contaminants in pharmaceuticals can affect the safety and efficacy of the final product. Flame photometry is employed to detect and quantify these metals, ensuring that they are within acceptable limits as defined by regulatory standards. For example, trace sodium or potassium levels in parenteral drugs (injections) are closely monitored to avoid adverse reactions in patients.

3. Stability Testing:

- **Monitoring Degradation:** Flame photometry is used in stability studies to monitor the levels of metal ions over time, which can indicate the degradation of the drug or its packaging. For instance, changes in calcium or magnesium levels in a formulation could suggest interactions with the container or a breakdown of the excipient, which might compromise the drug's stability and effectiveness.

4. Development of New Formulations:

- **Excipient Compatibility Studies:** In the development of new drug formulations, flame photometry is used to study the compatibility of different excipients with the active ingredients. By analyzing the levels of metal ions in various formulations, researchers can determine the most stable and effective combinations, ensuring the optimal performance of the final product.

5. Nutritional Supplements:

- **Mineral Content Analysis:** Flame photometry is also applied in the pharmaceutical production of mineral supplements, where accurate quantification of metals like calcium, magnesium, potassium, and sodium is crucial. These supplements require precise dosing to meet health claims and regulatory requirements, and flame photometry provides a reliable method for ensuring product quality.

CHAPTER FIVE

Atomic Absorption Spectroscopy (AAS)

5.1 Principle of Atomic Absorption Spectroscopy

Atomic Absorption Mechanism

Atomic Absorption Spectroscopy (AAS) is an analytical technique used to determine the concentration of specific metal ions in a sample by measuring the amount of light absorbed by the atoms of the metal. The fundamental principle of AAS is based on the ability of ground-state atoms to absorb light at specific wavelengths. This absorption is directly related to the concentration of the metal ions in the sample, making AAS a powerful tool for quantitative analysis.

Atomic Absorption Mechanism

The atomic absorption mechanism involves several key steps:

1. Atomization:

- The first step in AAS is atomization, where the sample is introduced into a high-temperature environment, typically a flame or a graphite furnace, to convert the metal ions in the sample into free atoms. Atomization is crucial because AAS relies on the interaction of light with free atoms, not with ions or molecules.

- In flame atomization, the sample, usually in liquid form, is nebulized into a fine aerosol and introduced into the flame. The high temperature of the flame (around 2000-3000°C) evaporates the solvent and dissociates the sample into its constituent atoms.

- In graphite furnace atomization, the sample is introduced into a small graphite tube, which is electrically heated to a high temperature in a controlled manner. This method is more sensitive than flame atomization and is used for detecting very low concentrations of metals.

2. Absorption of Light:

- Once the sample is atomized, a light source, typically a hollow cathode lamp (HCL) or an electrodeless discharge lamp (EDL), emits light at specific wavelengths corresponding to the element being analyzed. Each element has a unique set of wavelengths at which it absorbs light, known as its absorption spectrum.
- As the light passes through the cloud of free atoms in the flame or graphite furnace, the atoms absorb light at their characteristic wavelengths. This absorption occurs because the energy of the incident light matches the energy difference between the ground state and an excited state of the atom. When an atom absorbs a photon of light, it is promoted from its ground state to a higher energy level (excited state).
- The amount of light absorbed by the atoms is proportional to the number of atoms present in the light path, which in turn is directly related to the concentration of the element in the sample.

3. Measurement of Absorption:

- After the light passes through the sample, the remaining light is directed to a detector, usually a photomultiplier tube (PMT) or a solid-state detector. The detector measures the intensity of the light that has not been absorbed by the sample.
- The difference between the intensity of the light emitted by the source (before it interacts with the sample) and the intensity of the light that reaches the detector (after passing through the sample) is used to calculate the amount of light absorbed by the atoms.
- This difference in light intensity is referred to as the absorbance, which is related to the concentration of the element in the sample by Beer-Lambert's law. The law states that absorbance (A) is directly proportional to the concentration (C) of the absorbing species, the path length (l) of the light through the sample, and the molar absorptivity (ε), which is a characteristic of the element being analyzed: $A=\varepsilon \cdot C \cdot l$.

4. Quantification:

- To quantify the concentration of the metal ion in the sample, a calibration curve is generated by analyzing standard solutions with known concentrations of the element. The absorbance values of these standards are plotted against their concentrations to create a calibration curve.

- The absorbance of the unknown sample is then measured and compared to the calibration curve to determine its concentration. The linearity of the calibration curve is crucial for accurate quantification, and any deviations can indicate potential issues such as matrix effects or instrumental limitations.

5. Flame vs. Graphite Furnace AAS:

- **Flame AAS** is suitable for analyzing elements present in moderate to high concentrations (typically in the parts per million range). It is a robust and rapid technique, making it ideal for routine analysis in environmental, agricultural, and industrial applications.
- **Graphite Furnace AAS** offers higher sensitivity and is capable of detecting trace elements at very low concentrations (parts per billion or lower). It is particularly useful in clinical and pharmaceutical analysis, where detecting trace amounts of metals is often required.

Types of Interferences

In Atomic Absorption Spectroscopy (AAS), **interferences** are factors that can affect the accuracy and precision of the measurement by causing errors in the detected signal. Understanding and mitigating these interferences is crucial for obtaining reliable and accurate results. The interferences in AAS can be broadly categorized into **spectral interferences**, **chemical interferences**, **ionization interferences**, and **physical interferences**.

1. Spectral Interference:

Spectral interference occurs when the absorption or emission of light by substances other than the analyte of interest overlaps with the absorption wavelength of the target element. This can lead to inaccurate readings because the detector may register additional absorbance that is not due to the analyte, causing an overestimation of its concentration.

- **Overlap of Absorption Lines:** This occurs when the emission line of the light source overlaps with the absorption line of another element present in the sample. For example, if an element in the sample has an absorption line close to that of the analyte, it can cause spectral interference.

- **Molecular Absorption:** Molecules or radicals present in the flame or graphite furnace can absorb light at the same wavelength as the analyte, leading to interference. This is common in the presence of oxides, hydroxides, or nitrates that can absorb light at the analyte's wavelength.

Mitigation: Spectral interference can often be reduced by using higher resolution monochromators to better separate overlapping lines or by selecting an alternative wavelength where the interference is less pronounced. Additionally, background correction techniques, such as deuterium lamp correction or Zeeman effect correction, can be used to account for non-analyte absorption.

2. Chemical Interference:

Chemical interference arises when other chemical species in the sample affect the absorption characteristics of the analyte by altering its atomization efficiency. This type of interference is particularly common in complex sample matrices.

- **Formation of Refractory Compounds:** Certain elements can form stable compounds in the flame or furnace that do not dissociate easily into free atoms. For example, the formation of calcium phosphate ($Ca_3(PO_4)_2$) can reduce the availability of free calcium atoms for absorption, leading to lower absorbance and an underestimation of calcium concentration.
- **Chemical Reactions in the Flame or Furnace:** Reactions such as oxidation or reduction can alter the state of the analyte, making it less likely to absorb light at the target wavelength. For instance, the presence of sulfur in the sample can lead to the formation of less volatile metal sulfides, reducing the atomization efficiency of the analyte.

Mitigation: To overcome chemical interference, chemical modifiers or releasing agents can be added to the sample. These agents react with the interfering species to prevent the formation of stable compounds. For example, adding lanthanum chloride ($LaCl_3$) can prevent the formation of calcium phosphate by forming a more stable lanthanum-phosphate complex, thus freeing up calcium atoms for detection.

3. Ionization Interference:

Ionization interference occurs when atoms in the flame or furnace ionize rather than remaining in their neutral atomic state. Since AAS relies on the absorption of light by neutral atoms, ionization reduces the number of atoms available for absorption, leading to lower absorbance and potential underestimation of the analyte concentration.

- **High Flame Temperatures:** High temperatures in the flame or furnace can cause certain elements, particularly alkali and alkaline earth metals, to ionize. For example, in the analysis of potassium (K), a significant portion of the potassium atoms may ionize at high temperatures, reducing the amount of neutral potassium available to absorb light.

Mitigation: Ionization interference can be mitigated by adding an ionization suppressor to the sample. This suppressor is typically a more easily ionized element, such as cesium or sodium, which provides a surplus of electrons in the flame, reducing the ionization of the analyte. This ensures that a higher proportion of the analyte remains in its neutral atomic state for accurate absorption measurement.

4. Physical Interference:

Physical interference is related to changes in the physical properties of the sample or the flame that affect the atomization process and the absorption signal. This type of interference includes variations in viscosity, surface tension, and sample transport efficiency.

- **Sample Nebulization Efficiency:** Inconsistent nebulization can lead to variations in the size of droplets entering the flame or furnace, affecting the atomization efficiency and, consequently, the absorbance signal. For example, a sample with high viscosity might produce larger droplets that do not completely atomize, leading to reduced signal intensity.
- **Flame Temperature and Composition:** Changes in flame temperature or composition can alter the atomization efficiency. For instance, fluctuations in the fuel-to-oxidant ratio can change the flame's temperature, affecting the excitation and ionization of atoms and leading to variations in the absorption signal.

Mitigation: Physical interferences can often be reduced by optimizing the sample preparation process, including consistent dilution and homogenization of samples, and by carefully controlling the operating conditions of the instrument, such as maintaining a stable flame temperature and consistent sample introduction rate. Using internal standards can also help correct for variations in signal due to physical interferences.

5.2 Instrumentation

Radiation Sources

In Atomic Absorption Spectroscopy (AAS), the **radiation source** is a critical component that provides the specific wavelengths of light required to excite the atoms of the element being analyzed. The choice and quality of the radiation source directly affect the accuracy, sensitivity, and precision of the analysis. The radiation source in AAS must emit light at the exact wavelengths that correspond to the absorption lines of the element of interest. The most commonly used radiation sources in AAS are **hollow cathode lamps (HCLs)** and **electrodeless discharge lamps (EDLs)**.

1. Hollow Cathode Lamps (HCLs):

Hollow cathode lamps (HCLs) are the most widely used radiation sources in AAS. They are specifically designed for each element, emitting light at the characteristic wavelengths corresponding to the absorption lines of the element being analyzed.

Structure and Operation:

- **Cathode and Anode:** The lamp consists of a cathode made from the element of interest (or an alloy containing it) and an anode, both housed in a glass tube filled with an inert gas such as neon or argon at low pressure.
- **Ionization Process:** When a high voltage is applied across the cathode and anode, the inert gas is ionized, producing positively charged gas ions. These ions are accelerated towards the cathode, where they collide with the metal atoms, sputtering them into the gas phase.
- **Emission of Light:** The sputtered metal atoms are then excited by further collisions with gas ions or electrons. As these excited atoms return to their ground state, they emit light at specific wavelengths characteristic of the element that makes up the cathode. This light is then directed through the sample in the AAS instrument.

Advantages of HCLs:

- **Element-Specific Emission:** HCLs provide highly specific wavelengths of light, which match the absorption lines of the target element, minimizing the potential for spectral interference.

- **Stable Output:** HCLs offer a stable and consistent light output, which is essential for accurate and repeatable measurements.
- **Wide Availability:** HCLs are available for a wide range of elements, making them versatile for multi-element analysis.

Limitations of HCLs:

- **Limited Lifetime:** The performance of HCLs can degrade over time, leading to reduced light intensity and potential inaccuracies in measurements.
- **Single Element Focus:** Each HCL is typically designed for a single element or a small group of elements, so different lamps may be required for multi-element analysis, which can be time-consuming to switch between.

2. Electrodeless Discharge Lamps (EDLs):

Electrodeless discharge lamps (EDLs) are another type of radiation source used in AAS, especially when higher intensity and longer lamp life are required. EDLs are often preferred for elements that require a more intense light source or where HCLs do not provide sufficient sensitivity.

Structure and Operation:

- **Gas-Filled Bulb:** EDLs consist of a small, sealed quartz or glass bulb containing a small amount of the element of interest (or its salt) and an inert gas, usually argon.
- **Microwave or Radiofrequency Excitation:** Instead of using electrodes, EDLs are excited by an external radiofrequency (RF) or microwave field. This field ionizes the gas, causing it to discharge and excite the metal atoms inside the bulb.
- **Emission of Light:** The excited atoms emit light at the characteristic wavelengths of the element as they return to their ground state. This light is then used for absorption measurement in the AAS instrument.

Advantages of EDLs:

- **Higher Intensity:** EDLs typically produce more intense light than HCLs, making them suitable for detecting elements at very low concentrations.

- **Longer Lamp Life:** EDLs tend to have a longer operational life compared to HCLs, providing consistent performance over extended periods.
- **Reduced Noise:** EDLs generally offer lower noise levels, improving the signal-to-noise ratio and the overall sensitivity of the analysis.

Limitations of EDLs:

- **Complex Setup:** EDLs require external RF or microwave generators, making the setup more complex than that of HCLs.
- **Element Specificity:** Like HCLs, EDLs are element-specific, and switching between different elements requires changing the lamp, which can be less convenient for multi-element analysis.

3. Continuous Spectrum Sources:

While HCLs and EDLs are the primary radiation sources used in AAS, **continuous spectrum sources** like deuterium lamps are sometimes used, particularly in background correction. However, continuous sources are not typically used for the primary analysis in AAS due to their lack of element specificity.

Deuterium Lamps: Deuterium lamps emit a continuous spectrum in the ultraviolet region and are primarily used for background correction to compensate for non-specific absorption and scattering by the matrix or flame.

Atomizers

In Atomic Absorption Spectroscopy (AAS), the **atomizer** is a crucial component responsible for converting the sample into free atoms, which can then absorb light at specific wavelengths corresponding to the element being analyzed. The atomization process is essential for ensuring that the sample's elements are in the correct form—neutral atoms—so they can interact with the radiation source. There are two main types of atomizers used in AAS: **flame atomizers** and **electrothermal atomizers (graphite furnace atomizers)**. Each type has its specific applications, advantages, and limitations.

1. Flame Atomizers

Flame atomization is the most common method used in AAS due to its simplicity, speed, and ability to handle a wide range of sample types. In flame AAS, the sample is typically introduced as a liquid, which is nebulized and carried into a flame where atomization occurs.

Components and Process:

- **Nebulizer:** The nebulizer converts the liquid sample into a fine aerosol. The sample solution is aspirated into the nebulizer, where it is mixed with a stream of oxidant gas (usually air or oxygen). The resulting aerosol is then carried by the gas flow into the burner head.
- **Spray Chamber:** The spray chamber allows larger droplets to be removed, ensuring that only the fine aerosol particles reach the flame. This is important for achieving consistent atomization and accurate measurements.
- **Burner Head:** The burner head directs the aerosol into the flame. The flame is created by burning a mixture of fuel gas (such as acetylene or propane) and oxidant gas (air or oxygen). The high temperature of the flame (typically around 2100-2800°C) vaporizes the solvent and decomposes the sample into free atoms.
- **Flame Types:** Different fuel-oxidant combinations produce flames of varying temperatures and characteristics:

  - **Air-Acetylene Flame:** Commonly used for most elements, providing a temperature of around 2300°C.
  - **Nitrous Oxide-Acetylene Flame:** Used for elements that require a hotter flame (up to 3000°C) for complete atomization, such as refractory metals like aluminum and calcium.

Advantages of Flame Atomizers:

- **Rapid Analysis:** Flame atomizers provide quick sample throughput, making them ideal for routine analysis of samples with moderate to high concentrations of metals.
- **Ease of Use:** The setup is straightforward, and the method requires minimal sample preparation.
- **Wide Applicability:** Flame atomization can be used for a broad range of elements, particularly alkali and alkaline earth metals.

Limitations of Flame Atomizers:

- **Lower Sensitivity:** Flame AAS is less sensitive than electrothermal atomization, making it less suitable for trace-level detection (typically in the parts per million (ppm) range).

- **Sample Consumption:** Flame atomization requires a relatively large sample volume, as much of the sample is lost during nebulization and flame interaction.

2. Electrothermal Atomizers (Graphite Furnace Atomizers)

Electrothermal atomization, commonly performed using a **graphite furnace**, offers higher sensitivity compared to flame atomization. This method is particularly suitable for trace element analysis, where detection limits in the parts per billion (ppb) range are required.

Components and Process:

- **Graphite Furnace:** The sample is introduced into a small graphite tube or cuvette, which serves as the atomization chamber. The tube is made of high-purity graphite and is electrically heated in a controlled manner.
- **Sample Introduction:** A small volume of the sample (typically 1-20 µL) is placed directly into the graphite tube using a micropipette. The sample is then dried, ashed (to remove organic material), and atomized sequentially within the furnace.
- **Temperature Control:** The graphite furnace is heated through a series of programmed temperature steps:

  - **Drying:** The sample is heated at a low temperature to evaporate the solvent without causing splattering.
  - **Ashing:** The temperature is increased to remove any organic matrix components by converting them into gases that can be vented away.
  - **Atomization:** The temperature is rapidly increased to a very high level (up to 3000°C), causing the remaining sample components to vaporize and atomize, producing free atoms for absorption measurement.

- **Inert Gas Flow:** An inert gas, such as argon, is often used to purge the graphite tube, preventing oxidation of the graphite and ensuring a stable environment for atomization.

Advantages of Electrothermal Atomizers:

- **High Sensitivity:** Graphite furnace atomization is much more sensitive than flame atomization, allowing for the detection of elements at very low concentrations (ppb range).
- **Low Sample Volume:** Only a small sample volume is required, making it suitable for precious or limited samples.
- **Reduced Interference:** The controlled environment of the graphite furnace helps to minimize chemical interferences, leading to more accurate measurements.

Limitations of Electrothermal Atomizers:

- **Slower Analysis:** The multi-step heating process is slower compared to flame atomization, resulting in longer analysis times.
- **Complex Operation:** The method requires more careful control and optimization of the heating program and is generally more complex to operate.
- **Higher Cost:** Graphite furnaces are more expensive to purchase and maintain than flame atomizers.

3. Hydride Generation and Cold Vapor Techniques

In addition to flame and electrothermal atomizers, specialized atomization techniques such as **hydride generation** and **cold vapor** methods are used for specific elements:

- **Hydride Generation:** This technique is used for elements like arsenic (As), antimony (Sb), and selenium (Se). The sample is chemically treated to form volatile hydrides, which are then introduced into a heated atomizer for detection.
- **Cold Vapor:** This technique is specifically used for mercury (Hg) analysis. Mercury is converted into its elemental vapor form by reduction, and the vapor is then passed through an absorption cell for measurement.

Detectors

In Atomic Absorption Spectroscopy (AAS), the **detector** is a critical component responsible for measuring the intensity of light that passes through the sample after some of it has been absorbed by the atoms. The detector converts the light into an electrical signal, which is then processed to determine the concentration of the element being analyzed. The effectiveness of the detector directly impacts the sensitivity, accuracy, and precision of the analysis.

There are several types of detectors used in AAS, each with its specific applications, advantages, and limitations:

1. Photomultiplier Tube (PMT)

Photomultiplier Tubes (PMTs) are the most commonly used detectors in AAS due to their high sensitivity and ability to detect low levels of light. PMTs are particularly effective in detecting the weak light signals that are typical in trace element analysis.

Structure and Function:

- **Photocathode:** The PMT consists of a photocathode, which emits electrons when struck by photons (light particles). The material of the photocathode is chosen to be responsive to the specific wavelength of light emitted by the element being analyzed.
- **Dynodes:** The emitted electrons are accelerated towards a series of dynodes within the PMT. Each dynode is set at a progressively higher voltage, and when an electron strikes a dynode, it causes the release of additional electrons. This multiplication process amplifies the initial signal.
- **Anode:** The final amplified signal is collected at the anode, where it is converted into an electrical current proportional to the light intensity. This signal is then processed and analyzed by the instrument's electronics.

Advantages of PMTs:

- **High Sensitivity:** PMTs are extremely sensitive and can detect very low light intensities, making them ideal for trace element analysis.
- **Fast Response:** They have a fast response time, allowing for rapid detection and measurement.
- **Wide Dynamic Range:** PMTs can measure a wide range of light intensities, from very low to relatively high levels.

Limitations of PMTs:

- **Temperature Sensitivity:** PMTs are sensitive to temperature variations, which can affect their performance. Proper thermal management is necessary to maintain accuracy.
- **High Voltage Requirement:** PMTs require a high voltage power supply for operation, which adds complexity and cost to the instrumentation.
- **Fragility:** PMTs are delicate and can be damaged by mechanical shock or exposure to excessive light.

2. Photodiode Array (PDA)

Photodiode Arrays (PDAs) are another type of detector used in AAS, particularly in instruments designed for simultaneous multi-element analysis. PDAs consist of multiple photodiodes arranged in an array, each capable of detecting a different wavelength of light.

Structure and Function:

- **Photodiodes:** Each photodiode in the array converts light into an electrical current, similar to how a single photodiode functions. However, in a PDA, multiple diodes are used to detect different wavelengths simultaneously.
- **Array Configuration:** The array configuration allows for the simultaneous detection of light at multiple wavelengths, enabling the analysis of several elements in one pass.

Advantages of PDAs:

- **Simultaneous Multi-Element Detection:** PDAs can detect multiple wavelengths simultaneously, making them ideal for multi-element analysis.
- **Robustness:** Photodiodes are more robust and durable compared to PMTs, making PDAs more resistant to mechanical damage and environmental conditions.
- **Compact Design:** PDAs are compact and can be integrated into smaller, more portable instruments.

Limitations of PDAs:

- **Lower Sensitivity:** PDAs are generally less sensitive than PMTs, making them less suitable for detecting very low concentrations of elements.

- **Complexity:** The data from a PDA must be processed carefully to ensure accurate wavelength discrimination, which can add complexity to the analysis.

3. Charge-Coupled Devices (CCDs)

Charge-Coupled Devices (CCDs) are high-sensitivity detectors used in some advanced AAS instruments. They are particularly useful in applications requiring high-resolution spectral analysis or imaging.

Structure and Function:

- **Pixel Array:** A CCD consists of an array of light-sensitive pixels, each capable of detecting light and generating a corresponding electrical charge. The charge produced is proportional to the light intensity.
- **Charge Transfer:** The charges from each pixel are transferred sequentially to a readout amplifier, where they are converted into a voltage signal. This signal is then digitized and processed to produce a spectrum or image.

Advantages of CCDs:

- **High Sensitivity:** CCDs are highly sensitive to low light levels, making them suitable for trace element analysis.
- **High Resolution:** They provide high spatial and spectral resolution, allowing for detailed analysis of complex spectra.
- **Imaging Capability:** CCDs can be used for imaging applications, such as in optical emission spectroscopy, where they can capture detailed spectral images.

Limitations of CCDs:

- **Cost:** CCDs are more expensive than other types of detectors, such as PMTs and PDAs.
- **Complex Operation:** The operation and data processing of CCDs are more complex, requiring advanced software and instrumentation.
- **Cooling Requirement:** CCDs often require cooling to reduce thermal noise, which adds to the complexity and cost of the system.

4. Photovoltaic Cells

Photovoltaic cells are simple detectors that generate a voltage when exposed to light. While they are less sensitive than PMTs and photodiodes, they are sometimes used in basic AAS instruments for specific applications where extreme sensitivity is not required.

Structure and Function:

- **Light Absorption:** When photons strike the photovoltaic cell, they generate electron-hole pairs within the semiconductor material, creating an electric field.
- **Voltage Generation:** The electric field causes a flow of current, generating a voltage that is proportional to the light intensity.

Advantages of Photovoltaic Cells:

- **Cost-Effective:** Photovoltaic cells are inexpensive and easy to use.
- **Durability:** They are robust and can withstand harsh environmental conditions.

Limitations of Photovoltaic Cells:

- **Low Sensitivity:** Photovoltaic cells have lower sensitivity compared to other detectors, making them less suitable for detecting trace elements.
- **Limited Dynamic Range:** They have a narrower dynamic range, which can limit their applicability in some analytical situations.

5.3 Applications of AAS

Trace Element Analysis

Atomic Absorption Spectroscopy (AAS) is widely regarded as one of the most effective techniques for **trace element analysis**, which involves the detection and quantification of elements present in very low concentrations—often at parts per million (ppm) or even parts per billion (ppb) levels. The ability of AAS to provide precise and accurate measurements of trace elements makes it an invaluable tool across various fields, including environmental monitoring, clinical diagnostics, food and beverage safety, pharmaceuticals, and industrial quality control.

1. Environmental Monitoring

Water Quality Testing:

- AAS is extensively used to monitor trace elements in water bodies, including rivers, lakes, and groundwater. The presence of heavy metals such as lead (Pb), cadmium (Cd), mercury (Hg), arsenic (As), and chromium (Cr) in water can have significant environmental and health impacts. AAS allows for the detection of these metals at very low concentrations, ensuring that water quality meets regulatory standards and is safe for human consumption and ecological health.

Soil and Sediment Analysis:

- Trace element analysis in soil and sediments is essential for assessing the impact of industrial activities, agricultural practices, and pollution on the environment. AAS is used to measure the levels of metals such as copper (Cu), zinc (Zn), nickel (Ni), and cobalt (Co) in soil samples. These measurements help in determining soil fertility, detecting contamination, and guiding remediation efforts.

Air Quality Monitoring:

- Trace metals in particulate matter (PM) present in the atmosphere can be harmful when inhaled. AAS is used to analyze air samples collected on filters to determine the concentration of metals like lead, manganese (Mn), and vanadium (V). This information is crucial for assessing air quality and implementing pollution control measures.

2. Clinical Diagnostics
Biological Sample Analysis:

- In clinical settings, AAS is employed to measure trace elements in biological samples such as blood, urine, hair, and tissues. For example:

  - **Lead Poisoning:** AAS is used to detect lead levels in blood samples, which is critical for diagnosing and treating lead poisoning, particularly in children.
  - **Zinc and Copper Deficiencies:** Zinc and copper are essential trace elements in the human body. AAS helps diagnose deficiencies or excesses of these elements by measuring their concentrations in blood or serum.

- ◦ **Mercury Exposure:** Monitoring mercury levels in biological samples using AAS is important for assessing exposure to this toxic element, which can occur through diet, occupational exposure, or environmental contamination.

Nutritional Studies:

- AAS is also used in nutritional studies to analyze the trace element content in food and biological samples, helping to understand the role of micronutrients in health and disease. This information is essential for developing dietary recommendations and fortification programs.

3. Food and Beverage Safety
Trace Metal Contamination:

- The presence of trace metals in food and beverages can pose significant health risks. AAS is used to monitor and ensure that trace metal concentrations remain within safe limits as defined by regulatory agencies. For example:

  - ◦ **Arsenic in Rice:** AAS is used to measure arsenic levels in rice and other crops, ensuring they comply with safety standards.
  - ◦ **Lead in Wine:** The analysis of lead in wine is crucial to prevent lead contamination, which can occur from soil or during the production process.
  - ◦ **Cadmium in Seafood:** AAS is employed to detect cadmium in seafood, which can accumulate in marine organisms and pose a risk to human health.

Nutrient Analysis:

- In addition to contamination analysis, AAS is used to measure essential trace elements in food products, such as iron (Fe), selenium (Se), and magnesium (Mg), to ensure that nutritional labels are accurate and that products meet nutritional standards.

4. Pharmaceutical Industry
Quality Control:

- In the pharmaceutical industry, AAS is an essential tool for ensuring the purity of raw materials and final products. Trace elements, even in small amounts, can affect the safety and efficacy of pharmaceutical products. AAS is used to detect and quantify impurities such as lead, mercury, and arsenic in drugs and active pharmaceutical ingredients (APIs).

Elemental Impurities Testing:

- Regulatory guidelines, such as those from the United States Pharmacopeia (USP) and the International Council for Harmonisation (ICH), require the testing of elemental impurities in pharmaceutical products. AAS provides the sensitivity and precision needed to comply with these stringent regulations, ensuring that products are safe for consumption.

5. Industrial Applications
Metallurgy and Alloy Analysis:

- AAS is used in the metallurgy industry to analyze trace elements in metals and alloys. Accurate measurement of trace elements is crucial for quality control and to ensure that the material properties meet the required specifications. For example, the presence of trace elements such as sulfur (S) and phosphorus (P) in steel can significantly affect its mechanical properties.

Catalyst Analysis:

- In the chemical industry, AAS is used to analyze trace metals in catalysts, which are often critical components in chemical reactions. The purity and composition of these catalysts are essential for their effectiveness and longevity, making AAS a valuable tool for catalyst quality control.

Electronics Manufacturing:

- The electronics industry requires high-purity materials to ensure the performance and reliability of electronic components. AAS is used to detect trace impurities in semiconductor materials, ensuring that the manufacturing process meets the stringent quality standards necessary for producing high-performance electronic devices.

Pharmaceutical and Environmental Applications

Atomic Absorption Spectroscopy (AAS) is a versatile analytical technique that finds extensive use in both the pharmaceutical and environmental fields due to its ability to detect and quantify trace elements with high precision and accuracy. The following sections explore the specific applications of AAS in these two critical areas.

Pharmaceutical Applications

1. Quality Control of Raw Materials and Finished Products:

- In the pharmaceutical industry, ensuring the purity and quality of raw materials and finished products is of utmost importance. Trace metal impurities, even in very low concentrations, can affect the safety, efficacy, and stability of pharmaceutical products. AAS is routinely used to detect and quantify these impurities, such as lead (Pb), mercury (Hg), arsenic (As), and cadmium (Cd), in raw materials, active pharmaceutical ingredients (APIs), and final formulations.

- **Elemental Impurities Testing:** Regulatory agencies such as the United States Pharmacopeia (USP) and the International Council for Harmonisation (ICH) have established guidelines for the permissible levels of elemental impurities in pharmaceuticals. AAS is a preferred method for complying with these guidelines, as it offers the sensitivity required to detect and quantify trace elements down to parts per billion (ppb) levels.

- **Excipients Analysis:** AAS is also used to analyze excipients, the inactive components of a pharmaceutical formulation, to ensure they do not introduce unwanted metal impurities into the final product.

2. Stability Studies:

- AAS plays a crucial role in stability studies, where pharmaceutical products are tested over time under various environmental conditions (temperature, humidity, light) to assess their shelf life and stability. Trace metal analysis is part of these studies to ensure that elemental impurities do not increase over time due to interactions between the formulation and its packaging.

- **Degradation Products:** In some cases, trace metals can catalyze the degradation of pharmaceutical compounds. AAS is used to monitor these metals and ensure that they remain within acceptable limits throughout the product's shelf life.

3. Nutritional Supplements:

- AAS is widely used in the analysis of nutritional supplements, particularly for determining the concentrations of essential trace elements such as iron (Fe), zinc (Zn), magnesium (Mg), and calcium (Ca). Accurate quantification of these elements ensures that the supplements meet their labeled claims and provides the required nutritional benefits to consumers.
- **Heavy Metal Contaminants:** In addition to measuring essential nutrients, AAS is also used to detect and quantify harmful heavy metals in supplements, ensuring they are safe for consumption.

Environmental Applications
1. Water Quality Monitoring:

- AAS is a key tool in monitoring the quality of water bodies, including rivers, lakes, groundwater, and drinking water supplies. The technique is used to detect and quantify trace metals such as lead (Pb), arsenic (As), cadmium (Cd), mercury (Hg), and chromium (Cr), which can be harmful to human health and the environment.
- **Compliance with Regulations:** Regulatory agencies, such as the Environmental Protection Agency (EPA) in the United States, set strict limits on the concentrations of toxic metals in drinking water and wastewater. AAS is routinely used to ensure compliance with these regulations, helping to protect public health and the environment.
- **Pollution Source Identification:** AAS can also be used to identify the sources of metal pollution in water bodies, whether from industrial discharges, agricultural runoff, or natural geological processes. This information is crucial for developing strategies to mitigate pollution and restore water quality.

2. Soil and Sediment Analysis:

- The analysis of soil and sediment samples for trace metals is critical for assessing environmental contamination, particularly in areas affected by industrial activities, mining operations, or agricultural practices. AAS is used to measure the concentrations of metals such as copper (Cu), zinc (Zn), nickel (Ni), and lead (Pb) in soils and sediments.
- **Agricultural Impact:** In agriculture, the presence of trace metals in soil can affect crop health and productivity. AAS helps monitor soil quality and guides the application of fertilizers and amendments to ensure optimal growing conditions.
- **Remediation Efforts:** For contaminated sites, AAS is used to assess the effectiveness of soil remediation efforts by measuring the reduction in metal concentrations over time.

3. Air Quality Monitoring:

- AAS is used in the analysis of airborne particulate matter (PM) to detect trace metals that can pose health risks when inhaled. These metals, such as lead (Pb), arsenic (As), and manganese (Mn), can originate from industrial emissions, vehicle exhaust, or natural sources.
- **Occupational Health:** In occupational settings, AAS is used to monitor air quality to ensure that workers are not exposed to harmful levels of metals, particularly in industries such as mining, smelting, and manufacturing.

4. Waste Management and Environmental Remediation:

- AAS is crucial in the analysis of waste streams, including industrial effluents, landfill leachates, and hazardous waste, to detect and quantify toxic metals before disposal or treatment. This helps prevent environmental contamination and ensures compliance with environmental regulations.
- **Site Assessment and Cleanup:** AAS is used in environmental site assessments to evaluate the extent of contamination and guide cleanup efforts. During remediation, AAS monitors the effectiveness of treatment processes, such as soil washing, chemical stabilization, or phytoremediation, in reducing metal concentrations to safe levels.

CHAPTER SIX

Nepheloturbidometry

6.1 Principle of Nepheloturbidometry

Light Scattering in Colloidal Suspensions

Nepheloturbidometry is an analytical technique used to measure the turbidity or cloudiness of a liquid sample caused by the presence of suspended particles. The principle of nepheloturbidometry is based on the scattering of light by these particles when a beam of light passes through the sample. The extent of light scattering is directly related to the concentration and size of the particles, allowing for the quantitative analysis of colloidal suspensions and other particulate matter in liquids.

Light Scattering in Colloidal Suspensions

When light passes through a colloidal suspension, it interacts with the suspended particles, which are typically in the size range of 1 to 1000 nanometers. These particles do not dissolve in the medium but remain dispersed, causing the solution to appear cloudy or turbid. The light scattering phenomenon that occurs when light encounters these particles is fundamental to nepheloturbidometry.

1. Mechanism of Light Scattering:

- **Rayleigh Scattering:** For particles much smaller than the wavelength of light (typically less than one-tenth of the wavelength), light scattering is described by Rayleigh scattering. In Rayleigh scattering, light is scattered uniformly in all directions, and the intensity of the scattered light is inversely proportional to the fourth power of the wavelength. This means that shorter wavelengths (blue light) are scattered more than longer wavelengths (red light).

- **Mie Scattering:** For particles comparable in size to the wavelength of light, Mie scattering occurs. Unlike Rayleigh scattering, Mie scattering is not strongly dependent on wavelength and can result in more complex scattering patterns. In Mie scattering, the light may be scattered in forward, backward, or sideways directions, depending on the size and refractive index of the particles.

2. Measuring Turbidity:

- **Nephelometry:** Nephelometry measures the intensity of light scattered at an angle (usually 90 degrees) to the incident light beam. This scattered light is detected and quantified, providing a measure of the turbidity of the sample. The amount of scattered light increases with the number and size of particles in the suspension, allowing for the determination of particle concentration.
- **Turbidimetry:** Turbidimetry, on the other hand, measures the decrease in intensity of the light that passes directly through the sample. As the light is scattered by the particles, less light reaches the detector positioned in line with the incident beam, and this reduction in transmitted light is used to quantify turbidity. While turbidimetry provides information on the overall light obstruction by the particles, nephelometry is more sensitive to low levels of turbidity and is often preferred for precise measurements.

3. Factors Affecting Light Scattering:

- **Particle Size and Concentration:** The size and concentration of particles in the suspension are the primary factors that influence light scattering. Larger particles and higher concentrations of particles result in more significant light scattering, increasing the measured turbidity.
- **Wavelength of Light:** The wavelength of the light source also affects scattering. Shorter wavelengths are more strongly scattered by smaller particles, which is why nephelometers often use light sources in the blue region of the spectrum to enhance sensitivity.
- **Refractive Index of Particles and Medium:** The difference in refractive index between the suspended particles and the surrounding medium affects the scattering intensity. Particles with a refractive index significantly different from that of the medium will scatter more light.

4. Applications of Nepheloturbidometry:

- **Water Quality Analysis:** Nepheloturbidometry is widely used to assess water quality by measuring the turbidity of natural waters, drinking water, and wastewater. High turbidity levels in water can indicate the presence of pollutants, microorganisms, or other contaminants, making it an essential parameter in environmental monitoring.
- **Pharmaceuticals:** In the pharmaceutical industry, nepheloturbidometry is used to measure the clarity and stability of liquid formulations, detect protein aggregation in biopharmaceuticals, and monitor the presence of particulate matter in injectable drugs.
- **Food and Beverage Industry:** The technique is also employed to monitor the turbidity of beverages like juices, beer, and wine, where clarity is a critical quality attribute. It helps in assessing the effectiveness of filtration processes and ensuring product consistency.
- **Clinical Diagnostics:** In clinical laboratories, nepheloturbidometry is used to measure the concentration of specific proteins, lipids, or other biomolecules in biological fluids by observing the formation of antigen-antibody complexes that scatter light.

5. Calibration and Standardization:

- **Calibration:** Nepheloturbidometric instruments are calibrated using standard solutions with known turbidity levels, often prepared using formazin, a polymer that forms uniform colloidal suspensions. Calibration ensures that the instrument provides accurate and consistent measurements across different samples.
- **Standard Units:** Turbidity is commonly expressed in Nephelometric Turbidity Units (NTU) or Formazin Turbidity Units (FTU), depending on the calibration standard used.

6.2 Instrumentation

Components and Configuration of Nepheloturbidometers

Nepheloturbidometers, the instruments used for measuring turbidity through light scattering, are designed with several key components that work together to ensure accurate and reliable measurements. Understanding the configuration and function of these components is essential for effectively using the instrument in various applications.

1. Light Source

The **light source** is a critical component in a nepheloturbidometer, as it provides the incident light that interacts with the particles in the sample. The choice of light source affects the sensitivity and accuracy of the measurement.

- **Tungsten Lamps:** Tungsten filament lamps are commonly used as light sources, emitting light in the visible spectrum. They are effective for general turbidity measurements but may not be as sensitive to smaller particles.
- **LEDs (Light Emitting Diodes):** LEDs are increasingly used in modern nepheloturbidometers due to their stability, long life, and ability to emit light at specific wavelengths, such as blue (around 450 nm) or near-infrared. Blue LEDs are particularly useful for enhancing sensitivity to fine particles, as shorter wavelengths are more strongly scattered by small particles.
- **Laser Diodes:** Some advanced nepheloturbidometers use laser diodes as light sources. Lasers provide a highly collimated and monochromatic beam, which can improve the precision and accuracy of turbidity measurements, especially at very low turbidity levels.

2. Sample Cell (Cuvette)

The **sample cell** or **cuvette** is the container that holds the liquid sample during measurement. It is usually made of optically clear materials, such as glass or quartz, to minimize any interference with light transmission.

- **Design and Size:** The design and size of the sample cell can vary depending on the application. For routine measurements, a standard cylindrical or square cuvette is used. The cell must be free from scratches, bubbles, or other imperfections that could scatter light and affect the accuracy of the measurements.
- **Path Length:** The path length (the distance the light travels through the sample) is an important factor that can influence the sensitivity of the measurement. Longer path lengths increase the interaction of light with particles, which can enhance sensitivity, particularly for low turbidity samples.

3. Detectors

The **detector** is responsible for measuring the intensity of light scattered by the particles in the sample. The configuration of detectors is crucial for distinguishing between nephelometry and turbidimetry.

- **Nephelometric Detector:** In nephelometry, the detector is positioned at a specific angle, typically 90 degrees, relative to the incident light beam. This detector measures the light scattered by the particles in the sample. The choice of angle is designed to maximize sensitivity to scattered light while minimizing interference from directly transmitted light.
- **Turbidimetric Detector:** For turbidimetry, a detector is placed directly in line with the incident light beam, opposite the light source. This detector measures the reduction in light intensity as it passes through the sample, providing a measure of the overall turbidity.
- **Photodiodes and Photomultiplier Tubes:** The most common types of detectors used in nepheloturbidometers are photodiodes and photomultiplier tubes (PMTs). Photodiodes are solid-state detectors that convert light into an electrical signal, offering durability and stability. PMTs, on the other hand, are more sensitive and can detect very low levels of scattered light, making them suitable for high-precision measurements.

4. Signal Processor and Readout

- **Signal Amplification:** The electrical signal generated by the detector is typically very weak and needs to be amplified before it can be accurately measured. The signal processor amplifies this signal while minimizing noise, ensuring that the measurements are precise and stable.
- **Analog-to-Digital Conversion (ADC):** In modern nepheloturbidometers, the amplified signal is converted from an analog signal to a digital one using an Analog-to-Digital Converter (ADC). This digital signal can then be processed by the instrument's microprocessor or computer for further analysis.
- **Calibration and Compensation:** The signal processor often includes calibration routines that adjust the instrument based on known standards. It may also compensate for factors such as stray light, temperature variations, and drift, which could otherwise affect the accuracy of the measurements.

- **Data Display:** The processed signal is displayed on the instrument's readout, typically as a numerical value in NTU or FTU. Many nepheloturbidometers feature digital displays that allow for easy reading and interpretation of results. Advanced models may also include graphical displays showing trends or real-time measurements.
- **Data Storage and Export:** Some nepheloturbidometers include features for storing measurement data internally or exporting it to external devices such as computers or data loggers. This is particularly useful for monitoring applications where trends over time need to be analyzed.

5. Calibration Standards

Calibration is essential for ensuring the accuracy of nepheloturbidometric measurements. Instruments are typically calibrated using standard solutions with known turbidity values.

- **Formazin Standards:** Formazin is the most commonly used standard for calibrating nepheloturbidometers because it forms a stable colloidal suspension with well-defined turbidity. Calibration solutions are prepared at various concentrations to cover the expected range of measurements.
- **Stabilized Calibration Kits:** Some instruments use pre-prepared, stabilized calibration kits that provide reliable and consistent turbidity values over time, simplifying the calibration process for routine analysis.

6. Software and Control Interface

Modern nepheloturbidometers often come equipped with sophisticated software that enhances the usability and functionality of the instrument.

- **User Interface:** The software typically includes a user-friendly interface that allows operators to easily configure the instrument, set measurement parameters, and initiate calibrations. Touchscreens or keypad controls are common in newer models.
- **Data Analysis:** Built-in software may offer data analysis tools that allow for the interpretation of turbidity measurements, such as averaging multiple readings, performing statistical analysis, or generating reports.
- **Connectivity:** Many nepheloturbidometers feature connectivity options such as USB ports, Ethernet, or wireless communication, enabling integration with laboratory information management systems (LIMS) or

remote monitoring systems.

7. Maintenance and Cleaning Systems

Proper maintenance and regular cleaning are crucial for ensuring the long-term accuracy and reliability of nepheloturbidometers.

- **Automatic Cleaning Systems:** Some advanced instruments include automatic cleaning systems that periodically clean the sample cell and optical components to prevent fouling and ensure consistent performance. These systems can use various methods, such as ultrasonic cleaning or chemical rinses.
- **User Maintenance:** Routine maintenance tasks, such as manual cleaning of the sample cell and replacement of worn components (like light sources or detectors), are also necessary. Instruments are often designed for easy access to these components, allowing users to perform maintenance without specialized tools.

CHAPTER SEVEN

Introduction to Chromatography

7.1 Basic Concepts of Chromatography

Adsorption and Partition Mechanisms

Chromatography is a powerful analytical technique used to separate, identify, and quantify components in a mixture. The basic principle of chromatography involves the differential movement of components within a mixture as they are carried by a mobile phase through a stationary phase. The separation of components occurs due to differences in their interactions with the stationary phase and their solubility in the mobile phase. Two fundamental mechanisms that govern these interactions are **adsorption** and **partition**.

Adsorption Mechanism

Adsorption chromatography is based on the principle that different compounds have varying affinities for the surface of the stationary phase. In this mechanism, the stationary phase is typically a solid material, and the mobile phase can be either a liquid or a gas. The components of the mixture adsorb onto the surface of the stationary phase to varying degrees, depending on their chemical properties.

Key Concepts of Adsorption:

- **Adsorbate and Adsorbent:** The substance that adsorbs onto the stationary phase is known as the **adsorbate**, while the stationary phase itself is referred to as the **adsorbent**. The interaction between the adsorbate and the adsorbent is usually weak and reversible, involving van der Waals forces, hydrogen bonding, or dipole-dipole interactions.
- **Retention Time:** In adsorption chromatography, components with a stronger affinity for the adsorbent will adhere more strongly to the

stationary phase and move more slowly through the column, resulting in a longer **retention time**. Conversely, components with a weaker affinity will pass through the column more quickly.

- **Elution:** The process of moving the adsorbed substances along the stationary phase by the mobile phase is known as **elution**. The rate at which a substance elutes depends on its relative affinity for the stationary phase versus the mobile phase.

Applications of Adsorption Chromatography:

- **Thin-Layer Chromatography (TLC):** In TLC, a thin layer of adsorbent material, such as silica gel or alumina, is coated on a glass, plastic, or metal plate. The sample is applied to the plate, and as the mobile phase ascends the plate, the components of the sample separate based on their adsorption to the stationary phase.
- **Column Chromatography:** In this technique, the stationary phase is packed into a column, and the sample is introduced at the top. As the mobile phase flows through the column, the components of the sample separate based on their differing adsorption to the stationary phase.

Partition Mechanism

Partition chromatography operates on a different principle, where the separation of components is based on their differential solubility in two immiscible phases: the stationary phase and the mobile phase. In this mechanism, the stationary phase is usually a liquid that is coated or immobilized on a solid support, while the mobile phase can be a liquid or a gas.

Key Concepts of Partition:

- **Distribution Coefficient (K):** The separation of components in partition chromatography is governed by their **distribution coefficient (K)**, which is the ratio of the concentration of the compound in the stationary phase to its concentration in the mobile phase. Components with a higher affinity for the stationary phase will have a higher K value and will be retained longer on the stationary phase, resulting in a longer retention time.
- **Solubility and Interaction:** The solubility of each component in the stationary and mobile phases determines its rate of migration through

the chromatographic system. Compounds that are more soluble in the stationary phase will move more slowly, while those that are more soluble in the mobile phase will move more quickly.

- **Equilibrium:** The separation process in partition chromatography involves an equilibrium between the two phases. As the mobile phase moves through the stationary phase, each component of the sample distributes itself between the two phases based on its solubility and partition coefficient.

Applications of Partition Chromatography:

- **Gas Chromatography (GC):** In gas chromatography, the stationary phase is a liquid that is coated onto the inner walls of a capillary column or packed onto a solid support. The mobile phase is an inert gas, such as helium or nitrogen. Components of the sample partition between the stationary liquid phase and the mobile gas phase, allowing for their separation.
- **Liquid-Liquid Chromatography:** This technique involves two liquid phases, where one phase is stationary and immobilized on a solid support, and the other phase is the mobile phase. The sample components separate based on their solubility in the two liquid phases.

Comparison of Adsorption and Partition Mechanisms

While both adsorption and partition mechanisms are fundamental to chromatography, they differ in how they achieve the separation of components:

- **Adsorption Chromatography:** Separation is based on the physical adherence of components to the surface of the stationary phase. It is often used when the components have different polarities or when the stationary phase is a solid.
- **Partition Chromatography:** Separation is based on the distribution of components between two liquid phases, with the stationary phase often being a liquid. This mechanism is particularly effective when separating compounds with similar polarities but different solubilities.

CHAPTER EIGHT

Adsorption and Partition Chromatography

Methodology of Column Chromatography

Column chromatography is a widely used technique in both adsorption and partition chromatography, allowing for the separation and purification of compounds based on their differential interactions with the stationary and mobile phases. The methodology of column chromatography involves several key steps, each critical to achieving efficient separation of the components in a mixture.

1. Preparation of the Column

The first step in column chromatography is the preparation of the chromatographic column, which serves as the housing for the stationary phase.

- **Choosing the Column Material:** The column is typically made of glass or plastic, with varying diameters and lengths depending on the scale of the separation. For analytical purposes, smaller columns are used, while larger columns are employed in preparative chromatography.
- **Packing the Stationary Phase:** The stationary phase, which can be a solid adsorbent (like silica gel or alumina) for adsorption chromatography or a liquid coated on a solid support for partition chromatography, is carefully packed into the column. The packing must be uniform and free of air bubbles to ensure consistent flow and effective separation. In some methods, the stationary phase is packed dry, and then the mobile phase is introduced to wet the material, while in others, the stationary phase is slurried with the mobile phase and poured into the column.

- **Wetting the Stationary Phase:** Once the stationary phase is packed, it is wetted with the mobile phase to eliminate any trapped air and to prepare the surface for interaction with the sample. The mobile phase should be the same as or compatible with the solvent in which the sample is dissolved.

2. Sample Application

After preparing the column, the sample containing the mixture of compounds to be separated is applied.

- **Sample Preparation:** The sample is typically dissolved in a small volume of solvent that is compatible with the mobile phase. It is important to ensure that the sample is fully dissolved and free of particulates to avoid clogging the column.
- **Loading the Sample:** The sample is carefully applied to the top of the column using a pipette or syringe, ensuring that it forms a narrow, concentrated band. This concentrated loading helps achieve better resolution during separation. The column is often allowed to drain slightly to ensure the sample adsorbs onto the top layer of the stationary phase before the mobile phase is added.

3. Elution Process

Elution is the process of moving the sample components through the column using the mobile phase. This step is crucial for the separation of compounds based on their differing interactions with the stationary phase.

- **Choosing the Mobile Phase:** The choice of mobile phase (or solvent) depends on the nature of the stationary phase and the compounds being separated. In adsorption chromatography, the mobile phase is usually a solvent or a mixture of solvents with varying polarities, while in partition chromatography, it might be a buffer or another liquid phase.
- **Gradient vs. Isocratic Elution:** Elution can be performed using a single solvent (isocratic elution) or by gradually changing the solvent composition (gradient elution). Gradient elution is particularly useful when separating compounds with a wide range of affinities for the stationary phase. For example, in gradient elution, a non-polar solvent might be used initially, followed by the addition of a more polar solvent to elute more strongly adsorbed compounds.

- **Flow Rate Control:** The flow rate of the mobile phase through the column is controlled to optimize the separation. Too fast a flow can lead to poor separation, while too slow a flow can make the process inefficient. The flow is typically maintained using gravity or a peristaltic pump, depending on the column's size and the required precision.

4. Collection of Fractions

As the components of the sample move through the column, they separate into distinct bands that can be collected as individual fractions.

- **Monitoring the Elution:** The progress of the separation can be monitored visually if the compounds are colored or using UV-visible spectroscopy if the compounds absorb light. Collecting small, timed fractions ensures that the separated compounds are isolated from one another.
- **Fraction Collection:** Fractions are collected in small tubes or vials as they elute from the column. The number of fractions collected depends on the resolution required and the separation of the compounds. Each fraction contains a specific compound or mixture of compounds eluted at a particular time.

5. Analysis and Recovery

After collecting the fractions, the next step is to analyze and recover the compounds of interest.

- **Analysis of Fractions:** Each fraction is analyzed using techniques such as thin-layer chromatography (TLC), high-performance liquid chromatography (HPLC), or spectroscopic methods (like UV-visible or NMR spectroscopy) to determine the composition and purity of the separated compounds.
- **Pooling and Concentration:** Fractions containing the same compound can be pooled together, and the solvent can be evaporated to concentrate the compound. The concentrated sample can then be further purified if necessary or used directly in subsequent experiments.

6. Column Regeneration

After the separation is complete, the column may need to be regenerated for future use, particularly if the stationary phase is reusable.

- **Washing the Column:** The column is washed with an appropriate solvent to remove any remaining sample components and to prepare it for the next run. In adsorption chromatography, this may involve washing with a strong solvent to remove adsorbed compounds, followed by re-equilibration with the mobile phase.
- **Storage:** If the column is to be stored for an extended period, it should be properly cleaned and filled with a storage solvent that prevents the stationary phase from drying out or degrading.

Advantages and Disadvantages of Column Chromatography

Column chromatography is a versatile and widely used technique in analytical and preparative chemistry for separating and purifying components of a mixture. While it offers several advantages that make it a valuable tool in many applications, it also has some limitations. Understanding these advantages and disadvantages can help in determining when and how to best utilize column chromatography for specific tasks.

Advantages of Column Chromatography

1. Versatility:

- **Wide Range of Applications:** Column chromatography can be used to separate a broad spectrum of compounds, from small organic molecules to large biomolecules like proteins and nucleic acids. It is applicable in various fields such as pharmaceuticals, environmental science, biochemistry, and materials science.
- **Adaptability:** The technique can be adapted to suit different separation needs by varying the type of stationary and mobile phases, the column size, and the elution method. This flexibility makes it suitable for both analytical and preparative purposes.

2. Scalability:

- **From Analytical to Preparative Scale:** Column chromatography can be easily scaled from small analytical columns used in laboratory research to large preparative columns used in industrial processes. This makes it a valuable tool for both small-scale purification and large-scale production.

3. High Resolution:

- **Effective Separation:** Column chromatography offers high resolution, allowing for the effective separation of complex mixtures into individual components. The ability to control the flow rate, gradient, and other parameters enables precise separation of closely related compounds.

4. Simple and Accessible:

- **Ease of Use:** The basic setup for column chromatography is relatively simple and does not require sophisticated instrumentation. This makes it accessible to a wide range of users, from students in educational laboratories to researchers in advanced industrial settings.
- **Cost-Effective:** The technique can be cost-effective, especially for routine separations, as it requires relatively inexpensive materials like silica gel, alumina, and basic solvents.

5. Reusability:

- **Regeneration of Columns:** Many stationary phases used in column chromatography can be regenerated and reused multiple times, which reduces the cost of materials and makes the technique more sustainable.

Disadvantages of Column Chromatography
1. Time-Consuming:

- **Slow Separation Process:** Column chromatography can be a time-consuming process, especially when dealing with large volumes of sample or complex mixtures. The need for careful loading, slow elution, and fraction collection can extend the duration of the experiment significantly.
- **Labor-Intensive:** The process often requires manual intervention, such as monitoring the elution, collecting fractions, and analyzing samples, which can be labor-intensive and prone to human error.

2. Limited Automation:

- **Lack of Automation:** While some advanced chromatography techniques (like HPLC) are highly automated, traditional column chromatography typically lacks automation, which can limit its efficiency and throughput, particularly in high-throughput settings.

3. Sample Dilution:

- **Dilution of Fractions:** The elution process can lead to significant dilution of the separated components, requiring further concentration steps before the compounds can be used or analyzed. This can be particularly problematic when dealing with small quantities of material or when the target compound is in low concentration.

4. Solvent Consumption:

- **High Solvent Usage:** Column chromatography often requires large volumes of solvent for the elution process, especially in gradient elution methods. This can be expensive and environmentally unfriendly, as it generates significant amounts of solvent waste that must be properly disposed of.

5. Potential for Decomposition:

- **Decomposition of Sensitive Compounds:** Some compounds may be sensitive to the conditions used in column chromatography, such as prolonged exposure to certain solvents, high temperatures, or the stationary phase. This can lead to decomposition or loss of activity, particularly in the case of labile biological molecules.

6. Band Broadening:

- **Band Broadening Effects:** As the sample components travel through the column, they can experience band broadening, where the separation between components decreases due to diffusion and other factors. This can reduce the resolution of the separation, making it more difficult to isolate closely related compounds.

Applications of Column Chromatography in Drug Purification

Column chromatography plays a pivotal role in the pharmaceutical industry, particularly in the purification of drugs and active pharmaceutical ingredients (APIs). The ability of column chromatography to separate and purify complex mixtures with high precision makes it an invaluable tool in drug development, manufacturing, and quality control. Below are some of the key applications of column chromatography in drug purification.

1. Purification of Active Pharmaceutical Ingredients (APIs)
Separation of Impurities:

- During the synthesis of active pharmaceutical ingredients (APIs), various by-products, unreacted starting materials, and intermediates may be present. Column chromatography is used to separate these impurities from the desired API, ensuring that the final product meets the stringent purity requirements set by regulatory authorities.
- **Gradient Elution for Complex Mixtures:** In cases where the API and impurities have similar chemical properties, gradient elution can be employed to achieve effective separation. By gradually changing the polarity or composition of the mobile phase, it is possible to selectively elute different components of the mixture, thereby isolating the pure API.

Crystallization and Precipitation Aid:

- After column chromatography, the purified API can be further crystallized or precipitated to enhance purity and yield. The use of column chromatography as a pre-purification step can significantly improve the efficiency of these downstream processes.

2. Isolation of Natural Products and Bioactive Compounds
Extraction of Plant-Based Drugs:

- Many drugs are derived from natural products, such as plant extracts. Column chromatography is used to isolate and purify bioactive compounds from these complex mixtures. For example, alkaloids, flavonoids, terpenoids, and other secondary metabolites can be separated based on their adsorption or partition behavior in the column.
- **Fractionation of Extracts:** Column chromatography allows for the fractionation of plant extracts into different components, which can then be tested for biological activity. This is crucial in the discovery of new drugs, where identifying and isolating the active component from a natural source is the first step in drug development.

Purification of Antibiotics and Anticancer Agents:

- Antibiotics and anticancer agents often require purification from fermentation broths or biological extracts. Column chromatography is used to isolate these drugs from complex biological matrices, removing proteins, lipids, and other unwanted components.

3. Chiral Separation of Enantiomers
Separation of Chiral Compounds:

- Many drugs contain chiral centers, meaning they can exist as two or more enantiomers with different biological activities. It is often necessary to separate these enantiomers to obtain a pure, active form of the drug. Column chromatography, particularly with chiral stationary phases, is a key technique for achieving this separation.
- **Enantiomeric Purity:** The purification of enantiomers using column chromatography ensures that only the desired isomer is present in the final product, which is essential for both efficacy and safety. This application is particularly important in the development of drugs where one enantiomer may be therapeutically active while the other could be inactive or even harmful.

4. Removal of Organic Solvents and Residual Catalysts
Solvent Removal:

- In the synthesis of drugs, organic solvents are often used as reaction media. Column chromatography can be used to remove residual solvents from the final API, ensuring that the drug product meets safety standards for residual solvent levels.
- **Catalyst Removal:** Catalysts used in chemical reactions, such as palladium in coupling reactions, can remain in trace amounts in the product mixture. Column chromatography can effectively remove these catalysts, which is crucial to prevent contamination of the final drug product.

5. Quality Control and Analytical Purification
Analytical Purification:

- In pharmaceutical quality control, column chromatography is used to purify small amounts of a drug for analytical purposes. This might involve isolating a specific impurity for identification or quantifying the purity of a drug sample before release to the market.
- **Degradation Product Analysis:** During stability testing, drugs can degrade into various products. Column chromatography helps isolate and identify these degradation products, ensuring that the drug remains stable and effective over its shelf life.

6. Large-Scale Purification in Manufacturing
Preparative Chromatography:

- In the manufacturing of pharmaceuticals, column chromatography is scaled up to preparative levels to purify large quantities of APIs. This involves using larger columns and more automated systems to handle the increased volume while maintaining the same principles of separation.
- **High-Purity Products:** The use of preparative column chromatography in drug manufacturing ensures that the final products meet the high purity standards required for pharmaceutical use. This is especially important for drugs administered in small doses, where even trace impurities can have significant effects.

7. Purification of Biopharmaceuticals
Protein and Peptide Purification:

- In the production of biopharmaceuticals, such as therapeutic proteins and peptides, column chromatography is a critical purification step. Techniques like ion-exchange chromatography, affinity chromatography, and size-exclusion chromatography are often used to purify these biologics from cell culture supernatants or fermentation broths.
- **Removal of Host Cell Proteins:** In biopharmaceutical production, it is essential to remove host cell proteins and other impurities that may co-purify with the product. Column chromatography provides a reliable method to achieve the necessary purity levels.

CHAPTER NINE

Thin Layer Chromatography (TLC)

9.1 Principle and Methodology

Stationary Phase, Mobile Phase, and Development Techniques

Thin Layer Chromatography (TLC) is a simple, quick, and effective analytical technique used to separate and identify components in a mixture. The principle of TLC is based on the differential migration of compounds on a stationary phase under the influence of a mobile phase. The separation occurs due to the varying affinities of the compounds for the stationary and mobile phases.

Stationary Phase

The **stationary phase** in TLC is typically a thin layer of an adsorbent material, such as silica gel, alumina, or cellulose, coated onto a flat, rigid support like a glass plate, plastic sheet, or aluminum foil.

- **Silica Gel:** Silica gel is the most commonly used stationary phase in TLC. It is a polar adsorbent, making it suitable for separating polar compounds. Silica gel TLC plates are highly porous, providing a large surface area for interactions between the sample and the stationary phase.
- **Alumina:** Alumina is another polar adsorbent used in TLC, though it is less common than silica gel. It is slightly less polar than silica gel and is often used for separating less polar compounds.
- **Cellulose:** Cellulose-based stationary phases are used for specific applications, such as separating polar compounds, particularly those that are sensitive to the acidic or basic nature of silica gel or alumina.

The stationary phase is typically activated by heating before use to remove any moisture, ensuring consistent results.

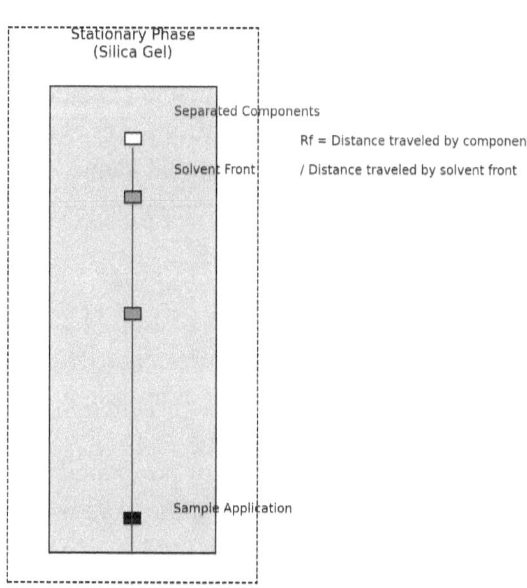

Mobile Phase

The **mobile phase** in TLC is a solvent or a mixture of solvents that moves through the stationary phase by capillary action. The choice of mobile phase is critical for achieving good separation of the components in the mixture.

- **Polarity of the Mobile Phase:** The polarity of the mobile phase relative to the stationary phase determines the separation. A more polar mobile phase will move polar compounds faster along the stationary phase, while a less polar mobile phase will better separate non-polar compounds.
- **Solvent Systems:** Common solvent systems used in TLC include mixtures like hexane/ethyl acetate, chloroform/methanol, and toluene/ acetone. The ratio of solvents can be adjusted to fine-tune the separation, depending on the polarity of the compounds being analyzed.

Development Techniques

After the stationary phase is prepared and the mobile phase is selected, the TLC plate is ready for development. Several techniques can be used to develop the chromatogram:

- **Ascending Development:** In this common method, the TLC plate is placed vertically in a development chamber containing a small amount of the mobile phase. The mobile phase ascends the plate by capillary action, carrying the components of the sample with it. Different compounds travel at different rates depending on their affinity for the stationary and mobile phases.
- **Descending Development:** In descending development, the mobile phase is placed at the top of the TLC plate, and the solvent moves downward by gravity. This technique is less common but can be useful for separating compounds that might streak or migrate poorly in ascending development.
- **Horizontal Development:** In horizontal development, the TLC plate is placed flat, and the mobile phase is allowed to move horizontally across the plate. This technique is used in specific applications, such as two-dimensional TLC, where the plate is developed in one direction, dried, and then developed in a perpendicular direction with a different solvent system.
- **Two-Dimensional TLC:** This advanced technique involves developing the plate in two different solvent systems in perpendicular directions. It is particularly useful for separating complex mixtures where compounds may overlap in a single dimension.

Visualization of Spots

Once the TLC plate has been developed, the separated compounds must be visualized, as many organic compounds are colorless and not visible to the naked eye.

- **UV Light:** Most TLC plates are coated with a fluorescent indicator that makes compounds visible under ultraviolet (UV) light. Under UV light, the spots where compounds have adsorbed will quench the fluorescence, appearing as dark spots on the plate.
- **Chemical Stains:** Various chemical stains can be applied to the plate to visualize different types of compounds. Common stains include iodine

vapor, ninhydrin (for amino acids), and sulfuric acid charring (for organic compounds). The choice of stain depends on the nature of the compounds being analyzed.

Calculation of Rf Values

The **Rf value** (retention factor) is a key parameter in TLC that quantifies the relative distance a compound travels on the TLC plate compared to the solvent front. It is a ratio that helps identify and compare compounds based on their migration behavior.

Calculation of Rf Value:

The Rf value is calculated using the following formula:

$$R_f = \frac{\text{Distance traveled by the compound}}{\text{Distance traveled by the solvent front}}$$

Where:

- **Distance traveled by the compound** is the distance from the baseline (where the sample was originally applied) to the center of the spot representing the compound.
- **Distance traveled by the solvent front** is the distance from the baseline to the solvent front (the furthest point reached by the mobile phase on the plate).

Interpretation of Rf Values:

- **Consistency:** Rf values are characteristic of specific compounds under defined experimental conditions. They provide a reproducible way to compare compounds across different experiments or laboratories, provided the same stationary phase, mobile phase, and development conditions are used.
- **Identification:** By comparing the Rf values of unknown compounds with those of known standards, one can identify the compounds in a mixture.
- **Compound Polarity:** Compounds with higher Rf values are typically less polar and interact less strongly with the polar stationary phase, allowing them to travel further up the plate. Conversely, compounds with lower

Rf values are more polar and remain closer to the baseline.

Factors Affecting Rf Values:

- **Solvent Composition:** Changes in the polarity of the mobile phase will affect the Rf values, with more polar solvents generally increasing Rf values for polar compounds.
- **Stationary Phase:** The nature of the stationary phase (e.g., silica gel, alumina) will also impact the Rf values, as different phases interact differently with the compounds.
- **Temperature:** Variations in temperature can affect the mobility of the compounds on the TLC plate, potentially altering Rf values.
- **Sample Concentration:** Overloading the sample can lead to streaking and inaccurate Rf values, so it's important to apply the correct amount of sample.

9.2 Applications of TLC
Identification of Compounds

Thin Layer Chromatography (TLC) is widely used in the identification of compounds within a mixture due to its simplicity, speed, and ability to provide a visual representation of the components. The identification process in TLC involves comparing the Rf values of the spots obtained from the unknown sample with those of known reference compounds under identical experimental conditions.

Identification of Compounds
1. Comparison with Standards:

- **Reference Standards:** In TLC, known reference standards (pure compounds with established Rf values) are run on the same plate alongside the unknown sample. By comparing the position of the spots of the unknown sample to those of the standards, one can identify the components of the mixture. If a spot from the unknown sample coincides with a spot from a reference standard, it suggests that the unknown compound may be identical to the reference.
- **Rf Value Comparison:** The Rf value is a key metric for identification. Even if the spots do not perfectly align on the plate due to slight experimental variations, comparing the Rf values can confirm the identity of the compound. Matching Rf values between an unknown

sample and a reference standard under identical conditions indicates a likely match.

2. Multi-Component Analysis:

- **Complex Mixtures:** TLC is particularly useful for the identification of components in complex mixtures, such as plant extracts, pharmaceutical formulations, or reaction products. By running a series of reference compounds alongside the unknown sample, it is possible to identify multiple components within a single run.
- **Fingerprinting:** In some applications, such as herbal medicine or quality control, TLC is used to create a "fingerprint" of the sample, which is a pattern of spots that is characteristic of a specific product or raw material. This fingerprint can be compared with reference fingerprints to identify or verify the authenticity of the sample.

3. Detection of Impurities:

- **Impurity Identification:** TLC is effective in identifying impurities within a sample. By comparing the TLC profile of a sample with that of a pure reference standard, any additional spots observed in the sample's chromatogram can be attributed to impurities. This is particularly important in quality control of pharmaceuticals, where the presence of impurities must be minimized.
- **Limitations of Identification:** While TLC is effective for initial identification, it should be noted that Rf values alone may not be sufficient to conclusively identify a compound, especially if multiple compounds have similar Rf values. In such cases, further confirmation using more specific techniques like mass spectrometry (MS) or nuclear magnetic resonance (NMR) spectroscopy may be necessary.

Purity Testing

TLC is also extensively used for assessing the purity of compounds, particularly in the pharmaceutical industry, chemical research, and quality control laboratories. The ability to visually inspect the chromatogram for additional spots makes TLC a straightforward and reliable method for purity testing.

Purity Testing

1. Detection of Contaminants:

- **Visual Inspection:** In purity testing, a pure compound should ideally produce a single, well-defined spot on the TLC plate. The presence of additional spots indicates contamination or impurities in the sample. The number, size, and position of these additional spots provide qualitative information about the level of impurity.
- **Quantitative Analysis:** While TLC is primarily qualitative, densitometry can be used to quantify the intensity of spots, providing semi-quantitative information about the purity of the sample. By comparing the spot intensity of the sample with that of a pure standard, the relative amount of impurities can be estimated.

2. Monitoring Reaction Progress:

- **Reaction Monitoring:** TLC is a valuable tool for monitoring the progress of chemical reactions. By periodically sampling the reaction mixture and running it on a TLC plate, the disappearance of starting materials and the appearance of products can be observed. The purity of the product can be assessed by checking for the presence of unreacted starting materials or by-products.
- **Optimization of Reaction Conditions:** TLC can be used to optimize reaction conditions by identifying the time point at which the desired product is formed with minimal impurities. This helps in achieving the highest possible purity in the final product.

3. Quality Control in Pharmaceuticals:

- **Batch Consistency:** In the pharmaceutical industry, TLC is routinely used for quality control to ensure that each batch of a drug product meets purity standards. Any deviation from the expected TLC profile may indicate issues with the raw materials, synthesis process, or storage conditions, prompting further investigation.
- **Regulatory Compliance:** Regulatory bodies require stringent purity testing for pharmaceuticals, and TLC serves as an initial screening tool. Although more advanced techniques like HPLC or GC are often used for final analysis, TLC remains a quick and cost-effective method for preliminary purity assessment.

4. Stability Testing:

- **Stability Studies:** TLC is employed in stability studies to assess the purity of a compound over time under various environmental conditions, such as temperature, humidity, and light exposure. By comparing the TLC profiles of a compound at different time points, degradation products can be detected, and the stability of the compound can be evaluated.
- **Shelf-Life Determination:** The data obtained from TLC stability testing contribute to determining the shelf-life of pharmaceutical products by identifying the point at which significant degradation occurs, indicating when a product is no longer pure or effective.

CHAPTER TEN

Paper Chromatography

10.1 Introduction to Paper Chromatography

Sample Application and Development Techniques

Paper chromatography is a simple yet effective analytical technique that is widely used for separating and identifying compounds, particularly in mixtures. It is a type of partition chromatography where the stationary phase is a sheet of paper, and the mobile phase is a solvent or mixture of solvents. Paper chromatography is particularly useful in the fields of biochemistry, food science, and forensic analysis.

Sample Application

The process of sample application is crucial in paper chromatography, as it determines the starting point of the analytes on the chromatogram and impacts the clarity and resolution of the separation.

1. Selection of Paper:

- **Chromatography Paper:** The stationary phase in paper chromatography is typically a special type of paper known as chromatography paper. This paper is made from highly purified cellulose and is chosen for its uniformity and consistent absorbency. The paper acts as the stationary phase by retaining water (or another solvent), which facilitates the partitioning of compounds between the mobile phase and the stationary phase.

- **Preparation of the Paper:** The chromatography paper is usually cut into strips or sheets, depending on the experimental setup. The paper may be marked with a pencil line at the baseline, where the sample will be applied.

2. Sample Preparation:

- **Dissolution:** The sample to be analyzed is typically dissolved in a small volume of a suitable solvent. The choice of solvent depends on the nature of the compounds being separated and should ensure that the sample is fully dissolved without affecting the integrity of the compounds.
- **Concentration:** The concentration of the sample should be appropriate for the sensitivity of the technique. Too concentrated a sample can lead to overlapping spots, while too dilute a sample may result in faint or undetectable spots.

3. Application of the Sample:

- **Spotting:** The sample is applied to the paper using a fine capillary tube, micropipette, or syringe. The sample is "spotted" onto the paper at the baseline, which is usually a few centimeters from the bottom edge of the paper. It is important to apply a small, concentrated spot to prevent band broadening and ensure sharp separation.
- **Drying:** After application, the sample spot is allowed to dry completely before the chromatogram is developed. This drying step prevents the sample from diffusing inappropriately during the development process.

Development Techniques

Once the sample has been applied to the paper, the next step in paper chromatography is the development of the chromatogram. This involves allowing the mobile phase to move through the stationary phase, carrying the sample components with it.

1. Selection of the Mobile Phase:

- **Solvent Choice:** The mobile phase in paper chromatography is typically a solvent or a mixture of solvents. The choice of mobile phase depends on the polarity of the compounds being separated. Common solvents include water, ethanol, butanol, acetone, and mixtures of these. The polarity of the solvent system must be carefully chosen to achieve the best separation of the components.
- **Saturation of the Chamber:** Before development, the chromatography chamber is often saturated with the solvent vapor. This helps to maintain a consistent environment during the development process and can improve the resolution of the separation.

2. Ascending Development:

- **Setup:** In ascending development, the paper is suspended vertically in a developing chamber with the lower edge (below the baseline) immersed in the mobile phase. The solvent moves upward by capillary action through the stationary phase (the paper), carrying the components of the sample with it.
- **Migration of Compounds:** As the solvent front moves up the paper, different components of the sample will travel at different rates depending on their solubility in the mobile phase and their interaction with the stationary phase. More soluble compounds in the mobile phase will travel further, while less soluble compounds will stay closer to the baseline.

3. Descending Development:

- **Setup:** In descending development, the paper is suspended from the top of the chamber, and the mobile phase is introduced from the top. The solvent moves downward by gravity, in addition to capillary action.
- **Advantages:** Descending development can sometimes result in better separation, as gravity assists the movement of the solvent, leading to more uniform flow and potentially faster development times.

4. Radial or Circular Development:

- **Setup:** In radial or circular chromatography, the sample is applied at a central point on a circular piece of chromatography paper. The paper is then placed horizontally in a petri dish, with the edge of the paper in contact with the mobile phase.
- **Migration of Compounds:** The solvent moves radially outward from the center, carrying the sample components in a circular pattern. This technique is often used when analyzing a single sample and can provide clear, symmetrical chromatograms.

5. Two-Dimensional Development:

- **Setup:** In two-dimensional chromatography, the sample is first developed in one direction using a mobile phase. After the first development, the paper is rotated 90 degrees, and a second development is performed using a different solvent system.

- **Advantages:** Two-dimensional development is particularly useful for separating complex mixtures where components may overlap in a single dimension. By changing the direction and solvent, compounds that co-migrate in one dimension can be separated in the second.

Visualization and Analysis:

After development, the chromatogram is removed from the chamber and dried. The separated components are then visualized using various techniques:

- **Natural Color:** Some compounds are naturally colored and can be seen directly on the chromatogram.
- **UV Light:** Compounds that are not visible under normal light may fluoresce under UV light. Viewing the chromatogram under a UV lamp can reveal these spots.
- **Chemical Reagents:** Spraying or dipping the chromatogram in chemical reagents can develop colors in otherwise invisible spots. For example, ninhydrin is used to detect amino acids by producing a purple color.

CHAPTER ELEVEN

Electrophoresis

11.1 Introduction to Electrophoresis

Factors Affecting Electrophoretic Mobility

Electrophoresis is a widely used analytical technique that involves the movement of charged particles through a medium under the influence of an electric field. This method is particularly valuable for separating biomolecules such as DNA, RNA, and proteins based on their size, charge, and shape. The speed at which these molecules migrate through the medium, known as electrophoretic mobility, is influenced by several factors. Understanding these factors is essential for optimizing electrophoresis conditions and achieving effective separation.

Factors Affecting Electrophoretic Mobility

1. Charge of the Molecule:

- **Net Charge:** The electrophoretic mobility of a molecule is directly proportional to its net charge. Molecules with a higher net charge will experience a greater force in an electric field and, therefore, migrate faster through the medium. For example, proteins with a higher net positive or negative charge will move more quickly towards the oppositely charged electrode.

- **pH of the Buffer:** The net charge of a molecule, especially proteins and peptides, is influenced by the pH of the electrophoresis buffer. The pH determines the ionization state of the functional groups (such as carboxyl and amino groups) on the molecule. At a pH below the molecule's isoelectric point (pI), it will carry a positive charge, while at a pH above the pI, it will carry a negative charge. Adjusting the pH of the buffer can thus control the charge and, consequently, the mobility of the molecule.

2. Size and Shape of the Molecule:

- **Molecular Size:** Smaller molecules typically move faster through the electrophoresis medium than larger molecules. This is because smaller molecules experience less resistance from the medium. In the case of nucleic acids, such as DNA and RNA, the size is directly correlated with the length of the molecule, with shorter fragments migrating more quickly.
- **Molecular Shape:** The shape of the molecule also affects its mobility. For example, compact, globular proteins migrate differently compared to elongated, fibrous proteins of the same molecular weight. In nucleic acid electrophoresis, supercoiled DNA migrates faster than linear or relaxed circular DNA because of its more compact shape.

3. Strength of the Electric Field:

- **Voltage Applied:** The strength of the electric field, typically expressed as voltage per unit distance (V/cm), is a crucial factor in determining electrophoretic mobility. A higher voltage increases the force acting on the charged molecules, causing them to move faster. However, excessively high voltages can lead to issues such as overheating of the medium, band distortion, or even denaturation of sensitive biomolecules.
- **Field Uniformity:** It is important to maintain a uniform electric field across the gel or medium. Variations in the field strength can lead to uneven migration, resulting in distorted bands and poor resolution.

4. Type of Medium:

- **Gel Matrix:** The medium through which the molecules migrate can significantly impact electrophoretic mobility. Common media include agarose and polyacrylamide gels, each with distinct properties:
  - **Agarose Gel:** Agarose is typically used for the separation of large nucleic acids (e.g., DNA fragments) because it forms a loose gel matrix with large pores. The pore size in agarose gels can be adjusted by varying the concentration of agarose, with lower concentrations creating larger pores and higher concentrations creating smaller

pores.

- ○ **Polyacrylamide Gel:** Polyacrylamide gels have smaller, more uniform pores and are commonly used for separating proteins and small nucleic acids. The pore size in polyacrylamide gels is controlled by adjusting the concentration of acrylamide and the crosslinker (usually bis-acrylamide). Polyacrylamide gels offer higher resolution than agarose gels and are suitable for resolving molecules with small size differences.

- **Gel Concentration:** The concentration of the gel matrix determines the pore size, which in turn affects the migration of molecules. Higher gel concentrations result in smaller pores, which slow down the migration of larger molecules and enhance the resolution of smaller molecules.

5. Temperature:

- **Effect of Heat:** The temperature of the electrophoresis system can influence electrophoretic mobility. Higher temperatures reduce the viscosity of the buffer and increase the mobility of the molecules. However, excessive heating can cause the gel to deform, reduce the resolution, or lead to the denaturation of proteins and nucleic acids. It is common to run electrophoresis at controlled temperatures or to use cooling systems to dissipate heat generated by the electric field.
- **Thermal Effects on Bands:** Uneven heating within the gel can lead to band smearing or distortion, which complicates the interpretation of results. Temperature control is especially important in techniques such as two-dimensional gel electrophoresis, where precise separation is required.

6. Buffer Composition:

- **Buffer Ions:** The composition of the buffer affects both the pH and the ionic strength, which in turn influence the charge and stability of the molecules being separated. Common buffers used in electrophoresis include Tris-acetate-EDTA (TAE) and Tris-borate-EDTA (TBE) for nucleic acids, and Tris-glycine or Tris-tricine for proteins.
- **Ionic Strength:** The ionic strength of the buffer impacts the conductivity of the medium and the sharpness of the bands. High ionic strength

buffers provide better conductivity, leading to faster migration, but can also increase the heat generated. Low ionic strength buffers reduce heat but can lead to broader bands and lower resolution.

- **pH Stability:** Maintaining a stable pH throughout the run is crucial, as fluctuations in pH can alter the charge on the molecules, leading to inconsistent migration. Buffers with good pH buffering capacity are chosen to minimize pH shifts during electrophoresis.

7. Interaction with the Medium:

- **Binding Interactions:** Some molecules may interact with the components of the gel matrix or the buffer, which can affect their mobility. For example, proteins might bind to the gel matrix if it contains charged groups, slowing down their migration. Additives such as SDS (sodium dodecyl sulfate) are used in SDS-PAGE to denature proteins and provide them with a uniform negative charge, minimizing interactions with the gel matrix and allowing separation based primarily on size.
- **Electroendosmosis (EEO):** Electroendosmosis is the movement of buffer ions through the gel matrix under the influence of the electric field. This can lead to the movement of water in the opposite direction of the sample migration, causing sample bands to broaden or distort. Gel materials with low EEO are preferred to minimize these effects.

11.2 Techniques of Electrophoresis

Paper Electrophoresis

Paper electrophoresis is one of the simplest forms of electrophoresis used for the separation and analysis of charged molecules, particularly small biomolecules like amino acids, peptides, nucleotides, and small ions. This technique involves the movement of charged particles across a strip of cellulose paper under the influence of an electric field. Paper electrophoresis is useful for educational purposes, basic research, and preliminary studies where more sophisticated methods may not be necessary.

Principle of Paper Electrophoresis

The principle of paper electrophoresis is based on the differential migration of ions or charged molecules in an electric field. When an electric field is applied across a strip of paper soaked in an electrolyte solution (buffer), charged particles move towards the electrode of opposite charge.

The rate and direction of movement depend on the charge, size, and shape of the molecules, as well as the pH and ionic strength of the buffer.

Procedure of Paper Electrophoresis

1. Preparation of the Paper:

- **Selection of Paper:** The paper used in paper electrophoresis is typically filter paper or chromatography paper made from high-quality cellulose. The paper should be uniform, with consistent pore size and thickness, to ensure reliable results.
- **Buffer Saturation:** The paper is soaked in an appropriate buffer solution that maintains the pH and provides the necessary ionic environment for the separation. Common buffers include phosphate, acetate, or barbiturate buffers, depending on the nature of the analytes and the desired pH.

2. Sample Application:

- **Spotting the Sample:** The sample to be analyzed is applied as a small spot or line at a specific position on the paper. The amount of sample applied should be small and concentrated to ensure clear separation of the components. Care should be taken to apply the sample precisely to avoid smearing or uneven distribution.
- **Drying the Sample:** After application, the sample spots are allowed to dry completely before the electrophoresis run begins. This helps to prevent the sample from diffusing away from the application point when the electric field is applied.

3. Setting Up the Electrophoresis:

- **Electrode Placement:** The paper is placed horizontally in an electrophoresis chamber with its ends dipping into buffer reservoirs connected to the electrodes. The paper should be positioned so that the sample application point is equidistant from both electrodes.
- **Electric Field Application:** The electrodes are connected to a power supply, and a constant voltage is applied across the paper. The duration of the run depends on the desired separation and the nature of the sample. During the run, positively charged particles (cations) migrate towards the cathode (negative electrode), while negatively charged

particles (anions) migrate towards the anode (positive electrode).

4. Visualization and Detection:

- **Detection of Separated Components:** After the electrophoresis run is complete, the paper is removed from the chamber, dried, and the separated components are visualized. Visualization techniques depend on the type of analytes:

  - **Staining:** For proteins, amino acids, or other biomolecules, the paper can be stained using appropriate dyes (e.g., ninhydrin for amino acids) to reveal the separated spots or bands.
  - **UV Light:** If the compounds are UV-active, the paper can be examined under UV light to detect fluorescent or UV-absorbing spots.
  - **Radioactive Labeling:** For radiolabeled compounds, autoradiography can be used to detect the positions of the separated components.

5. Analysis of Results:

- **Rf Value Calculation:** Similar to thin-layer chromatography (TLC), the migration distance of each component can be measured relative to the total distance traveled by the solvent front or buffer front. The Rf value (retention factor) can be calculated to compare and identify the separated components.
- **Qualitative Analysis:** The pattern of spots or bands can provide qualitative information about the components in the mixture, such as their relative mobility and charge properties.
- **Quantitative Analysis:** For quantitative analysis, the intensity of the spots or bands can be measured using densitometry or other techniques, allowing for the estimation of the concentration of each component.

Applications of Paper Electrophoresis
1. Separation of Small Biomolecules:

- Paper electrophoresis is particularly effective for separating small biomolecules such as amino acids, peptides, and nucleotides based on their charge properties. It is often used in basic biochemical research to study these molecules under different pH conditions.

2. Analysis of Inorganic Ions:

- The technique can also be applied to the separation and identification of inorganic ions, particularly metal cations and anions. This application is useful in environmental analysis, geochemistry, and teaching laboratories.

3. Clinical Diagnostics:

- In clinical laboratories, paper electrophoresis has been used historically for the separation and analysis of hemoglobin variants, plasma proteins, and other biologically important molecules. Although more advanced techniques like gel electrophoresis and capillary electrophoresis have largely replaced paper electrophoresis, it remains a valuable tool for specific applications.

4. Educational Demonstrations:

- Due to its simplicity and low cost, paper electrophoresis is commonly used in educational settings to demonstrate the principles of electrophoresis and the behavior of charged particles in an electric field. It provides a clear and visual way to introduce students to basic separation techniques.

Advantages and Disadvantages of Paper Electrophoresis
Advantages:

- **Simplicity:** Paper electrophoresis is easy to set up and requires minimal specialized equipment, making it accessible for a wide range of laboratories.
- **Cost-Effectiveness:** The materials and equipment required for paper electrophoresis are inexpensive, making it an economical choice for many applications.
- **Versatility:** The technique can be adapted to a variety of sample types and can be used with different buffers and pH conditions.

Disadvantages:

- **Limited Resolution:** The separation achieved with paper electrophoresis is generally lower in resolution compared to more advanced methods like gel electrophoresis. This can make it difficult to separate closely related compounds.
- **Slow Separation:** The process of paper electrophoresis is relatively slow, particularly for large molecules or complex mixtures, which may require long run times.
- **Limited Quantitative Precision:** While paper electrophoresis can provide qualitative and semi-quantitative results, it is not as precise as other electrophoretic techniques for quantitative analysis.

Gel Electrophoresis
Introduction to Gel Electrophoresis

Gel electrophoresis is a powerful and widely used technique for separating macromolecules, such as DNA, RNA, and proteins, based on their size and charge. This method involves the migration of these molecules through a gel matrix under the influence of an electric field. Gel electrophoresis is essential in molecular biology, biochemistry, genetics, and forensic science, providing a visual and analytical means to study complex mixtures of biological macromolecules.

Principle of Gel Electrophoresis

The principle of gel electrophoresis is based on the movement of charged molecules through a gel matrix when subjected to an electric field. The speed at which these molecules migrate depends on their size, shape, and charge, as well as the properties of the gel and the strength of the electric field.

- **Charge:** Molecules move towards the electrode of opposite charge. For example, negatively charged DNA and RNA molecules move towards the anode (positive electrode), while positively charged proteins may move towards the cathode (negative electrode).
- **Size:** Smaller molecules migrate faster through the gel pores than larger molecules, allowing for size-based separation.
- **Gel Matrix:** The gel acts as a sieve, slowing down the migration of larger molecules more than smaller ones, thereby facilitating separation based on size.

Types of Gels Used

Two primary types of gels are used in gel electrophoresis, each with its specific applications:

1. Agarose Gel:

- **Composition:** Agarose, a polysaccharide extracted from seaweed, is the most commonly used gel matrix for separating nucleic acids (DNA and RNA). It forms a porous gel when dissolved in a buffer and cooled.
- **Applications:** Agarose gel electrophoresis is primarily used for separating DNA fragments ranging from a few hundred base pairs to several kilobases in length. It is also used for RNA separation, although care must be taken to prevent RNA degradation.
- **Advantages:** Agarose gels are easy to prepare, handle, and cast. The pore size of the gel can be adjusted by varying the concentration of agarose, making it versatile for different fragment sizes.
- **Visualization:** DNA and RNA bands are typically visualized by staining the gel with ethidium bromide (EtBr), which intercalates between the nucleic acid bases and fluoresces under UV light, or with safer alternatives like SYBR Green.

2. Polyacrylamide Gel (PAGE):

- **Composition:** Polyacrylamide gel is a synthetic polymer used primarily for the separation of proteins and smaller nucleic acids. It forms a more rigid and uniform gel compared to agarose, with smaller and more defined pores.
- **Applications:** Polyacrylamide gel electrophoresis (PAGE) is used for separating proteins (SDS-PAGE), small DNA or RNA fragments, and for performing more refined separations where higher resolution is required.
- **Advantages:** PAGE offers high-resolution separation, making it ideal for analyzing proteins based on size, charge, or conformation. The gel concentration can be varied to optimize the separation of molecules with different sizes.
- **Visualization:** Proteins separated by PAGE are often visualized by staining with dyes like Coomassie Brilliant Blue or silver stain. Nucleic acids can be visualized using ethidium bromide or other nucleic acid stains.

Procedure of Gel Electrophoresis
1. Preparation of the Gel:

- **Gel Casting:** The gel is prepared by dissolving agarose or polyacrylamide in an appropriate buffer, heating it to dissolve completely, and then pouring it into a casting tray with a comb to create wells for loading samples. Once the gel has solidified, the comb is removed, leaving wells to hold the sample.
- **Buffer System:** The gel is submerged in an electrophoresis buffer that provides the necessary ions for conducting electricity and maintaining a stable pH. Common buffers include Tris-acetate-EDTA (TAE), Tris-borate-EDTA (TBE) for nucleic acids, and Tris-glycine or Tris-tricine for proteins.

2. Sample Preparation and Loading:

- **Sample Preparation:** The sample is mixed with a loading dye that adds density to the sample (so it sinks into the wells) and provides color for easy visualization during loading. In protein electrophoresis, samples are often treated with SDS (sodium dodecyl sulfate) to denature proteins and give them a uniform negative charge.
- **Loading the Gel:** The prepared samples are carefully pipetted into the wells of the gel. Molecular weight markers or ladders are also loaded into one or more wells to provide a reference for determining the size of the separated molecules.

3. Running the Gel:

- **Electric Field Application:** The electrophoresis apparatus is connected to a power supply, and a constant voltage is applied across the gel. The charged molecules begin to migrate through the gel matrix, with smaller molecules moving faster than larger ones.
- **Monitoring the Run:** The progress of the electrophoresis can be monitored by observing the movement of the loading dye, which typically migrates ahead of the sample molecules.

4. Staining and Visualization:

- **Staining:** After electrophoresis, the gel is stained to visualize the separated molecules. For DNA and RNA, the gel may be stained with ethidium bromide or SYBR Green, while proteins are stained with Coomassie Blue or silver stain.
- **Visualization:** The stained gel is visualized using UV light (for nucleic acids) or visible light (for proteins), and the bands are photographed or scanned for analysis.

5. Analysis of Results:

- **Band Patterns:** The position and intensity of the bands on the gel correspond to the size and quantity of the molecules. By comparing the bands to the molecular weight markers, the size of the separated molecules can be estimated.
- **Quantification:** The intensity of the bands can be quantified using densitometry, allowing for the estimation of the amount of nucleic acid or protein present in the sample.

Applications of Gel Electrophoresis
1. DNA and RNA Analysis:

- **Restriction Fragment Analysis:** Agarose gel electrophoresis is used to separate DNA fragments generated by restriction enzyme digestion, allowing for the analysis of genetic variants, cloning verification, and DNA mapping.
- **PCR Product Analysis:** Gel electrophoresis is essential for checking the success of polymerase chain reaction (PCR) amplifications, verifying the size of PCR products, and confirming the presence or absence of specific DNA sequences.
- **RNA Analysis:** Gel electrophoresis is used to assess the integrity and size distribution of RNA samples, particularly in the context of gene expression studies and RNA sequencing.

2. Protein Analysis:

- **SDS-PAGE:** Sodium dodecyl sulfate-polyacrylamide gel electrophoresis (SDS-PAGE) is the most common technique for separating proteins based on their molecular weight. It is widely used in protein characterization, purity assessment, and molecular weight determination.

- **Native PAGE:** In native PAGE, proteins are separated without denaturation, allowing for the analysis of protein complexes and the study of protein structure and function.
- **Isoelectric Focusing (IEF):** IEF separates proteins based on their isoelectric point (pI), the pH at which the protein has no net charge. It is often used in combination with SDS-PAGE for two-dimensional gel electrophoresis (2D-PAGE), providing high-resolution separation of complex protein mixtures.

3. Forensic Analysis:

- **DNA Fingerprinting:** Gel electrophoresis is a critical technique in forensic science for DNA fingerprinting, where it is used to separate and analyze variable number tandem repeats (VNTRs) and short tandem repeats (STRs) in DNA samples for identification purposes.

4. Genotyping and Mutational Analysis:

- **Allele Discrimination:** Gel electrophoresis is used to detect single-nucleotide polymorphisms (SNPs), insertions, deletions, and other genetic variations in genotyping studies, allowing for the identification of mutations associated with diseases.

5. Quality Control in Biotechnology:

- **Recombinant Protein Production:** Gel electrophoresis is used to monitor the expression and purification of recombinant proteins in biotechnology and pharmaceutical production, ensuring that the final product is of the desired purity and quality.

Advantages and Disadvantages of Gel Electrophoresis
Advantages:

- **High Resolution:** Gel electrophoresis provides excellent resolution for separating molecules of different sizes, allowing for detailed analysis of complex mixtures.

- **Versatility:** The technique can be applied to a wide range of macromolecules, including DNA, RNA, and proteins, with various gel types and configurations available to suit different analytical needs.
- **Visualization:** The separated molecules can be easily visualized and analyzed, with the option to quantify band intensity for more detailed studies.

Disadvantages:

- **Time-Consuming:** Gel electrophoresis can be time-consuming, particularly when running large gels or performing two-dimensional separations.
- **Limited Quantification:** While gel electrophoresis provides qualitative and semi-quantitative results, it is less precise for quantification compared to techniques like qPCR or mass spectrometry.
- **Sample Handling:** The process requires careful sample handling and preparation, with potential for sample loss or contamination during loading and staining.

Capillary Electrophoresis

Introduction to Capillary Electrophoresis

Capillary electrophoresis (CE) is an advanced and highly efficient analytical technique used for the separation of ions and molecules based on their size-to-charge ratio. Unlike traditional gel or paper electrophoresis, CE is performed in narrow capillaries, which allows for high-resolution separations with minimal sample and reagent consumption. This technique is widely applied in fields such as pharmaceuticals, biotechnology, environmental science, and forensic analysis due to its speed, sensitivity, and ability to handle complex mixtures.

Principle of Capillary Electrophoresis

The principle of capillary electrophoresis is based on the migration of charged species through a buffer-filled capillary under the influence of an electric field. The separation occurs due to differences in the electrophoretic mobility of the analytes, which depends on their charge, size, and shape. The capillary's narrow diameter (typically 25-100 micrometers) and the use of high voltage (often 10-30 kV) enable fast and efficient separations.

Key Components of Capillary Electrophoresis

1. Capillary:

- **Material and Size:** The capillary used in CE is typically made of fused silica, which provides good chemical resistance and optical transparency. The internal diameter of the capillary is usually between 25 and 100 micrometers, while the total length can range from 20 to 100 cm, depending on the specific application.
- **Coating:** The inner wall of the capillary may be coated to reduce electroosmotic flow (EOF) or to minimize interactions between the analytes and the capillary surface. Uncoated capillaries are often used for standard applications, while coated capillaries are preferred for specific analyses requiring reduced surface interactions.

2. Buffer System:

- **Composition:** The buffer used in CE is crucial for controlling the pH and ionic strength, which in turn affect the charge and mobility of the analytes. Common buffers include phosphate, borate, and Tris-based buffers. The pH of the buffer is carefully selected to ensure that the analytes are in their ionized form.
- **Electroosmotic Flow (EOF):** In capillary electrophoresis, the movement of the buffer (and thus the bulk of the sample) through the capillary is influenced by EOF, a phenomenon caused by the interaction of the electric field with the charged surface of the capillary. EOF can be controlled or suppressed by adjusting the buffer composition or by using coated capillaries.

3. High Voltage Power Supply:

- **Voltage Application:** A high voltage (typically 10-30 kV) is applied across the capillary to create the electric field that drives the separation. The high voltage allows for rapid separation, with analytes migrating through the capillary based on their electrophoretic mobility. The polarity of the voltage can be adjusted depending on whether the analytes are cations or anions.
- **Heat Management:** The application of high voltage generates heat within the capillary, which can affect the separation. To manage this, the capillary is often placed in a cooling system, such as an air or liquid

coolant, to maintain a consistent temperature during the run.

4. Detection System:

- **UV-Visible Detection:** The most common detection method in CE is UV-visible absorbance, where the analytes are detected as they pass through a detection window near the end of the capillary. The UV detector measures the absorbance of light by the analytes at specific wavelengths.
- **Fluorescence Detection:** For analytes that fluoresce naturally or have been labeled with a fluorescent dye, fluorescence detection provides higher sensitivity than UV detection.
- **Mass Spectrometry (MS) Coupling:** Capillary electrophoresis can be coupled with mass spectrometry (CE-MS) for highly sensitive and selective detection. This combination allows for the identification and quantification of analytes based on their mass-to-charge ratio (m/z).

Modes of Capillary Electrophoresis
1. Capillary Zone Electrophoresis (CZE):

- **Principle:** CZE is the most common mode of capillary electrophoresis, where analytes are separated based on their differences in electrophoretic mobility. The separation occurs in a uniform buffer system, with analytes migrating through the capillary as discrete zones.
- **Applications:** CZE is widely used for the separation of small ions, peptides, nucleotides, and other charged molecules in various analytical applications.

2. Capillary Gel Electrophoresis (CGE):

- **Principle:** In CGE, the capillary is filled with a gel matrix, similar to traditional gel electrophoresis. The gel acts as a molecular sieve, providing an additional size-based separation mechanism alongside charge-based separation.
- **Applications:** CGE is commonly used for DNA sequencing, protein analysis, and the separation of large biomolecules.

3. Micellar Electrokinetic Chromatography (MEKC):

- **Principle:** MEKC is a hybrid technique that combines electrophoresis with chromatography. In MEKC, surfactants are added to the buffer to form micelles, which act as a pseudo-stationary phase. This allows for the separation of neutral molecules, in addition to charged ones, based on their partitioning between the micelles and the buffer.
- **Applications:** MEKC is useful for separating a wide range of analytes, including small organic molecules, drugs, and neutral compounds.

4. Capillary Isoelectric Focusing (CIEF):

- **Principle:** CIEF separates analytes based on their isoelectric points (pI), the pH at which a molecule carries no net charge. The capillary is filled with a pH gradient, and analytes migrate to the point in the gradient where their net charge is zero, effectively focusing into sharp bands.
- **Applications:** CIEF is particularly useful for the separation and analysis of proteins, peptides, and other amphoteric molecules.

5. Capillary Isotachophoresis (CITP):

- **Principle:** In CITP, analytes are separated based on their electrophoretic mobility in a discontinuous buffer system. The analytes form discrete zones with sharp boundaries, which migrate at the same velocity through the capillary.
- **Applications:** CITP is often used as a sample pre-concentration technique before further analysis by CZE or another mode of CE.

Advantages and Disadvantages of Capillary Electrophoresis
Advantages:

- **High Resolution:** CE offers excellent resolution, allowing for the separation of closely related compounds and isomers.
- **Speed:** The high voltage applied in CE enables rapid separations, often completed within minutes.
- **Low Sample and Reagent Consumption:** CE requires very small amounts of sample and buffer, making it cost-effective and reducing waste.
- **Versatility:** CE can be adapted to a wide range of applications, from small ions to large biomolecules, using different modes and detection methods.

- **Automation and Reproducibility:** CE systems are highly automated, providing reproducible results with minimal manual intervention.

Disadvantages:

- **Detection Sensitivity:** The small sample volumes used in CE can limit detection sensitivity, particularly for UV-visible detection. However, this can be mitigated by using more sensitive detectors like fluorescence or mass spectrometry.
- **Complexity of Buffer Optimization:** The need to carefully optimize the buffer composition, pH, and ionic strength for each analysis can be time-consuming.
- **Limited Sample Loading Capacity:** The narrow capillaries used in CE limit the amount of sample that can be loaded, which may be a drawback for applications requiring the analysis of large sample volumes.

Applications of Capillary Electrophoresis
1. Pharmaceutical Analysis:

- **Drug Purity and Stability:** CE is widely used in the pharmaceutical industry for the analysis of drug purity, degradation products, and impurities. Its high resolution makes it ideal for stability testing and quality control.
- **Chiral Separation:** CE is effective for separating enantiomers of chiral drugs, which is important for assessing the pharmacological activity and safety of pharmaceutical compounds.

2. Biotechnology and Proteomics:

- **Protein and Peptide Analysis:** CE is used for analyzing proteins and peptides, including post-translational modifications and isoforms. It is particularly valuable in proteomics for identifying and quantifying proteins in complex mixtures.
- **DNA Sequencing and Genotyping:** CE, particularly in the form of capillary gel electrophoresis, is used for DNA sequencing, fragment analysis, and genotyping in genetic research and forensic applications.

3. Environmental and Food Analysis:

- **Trace Metal Analysis:** CE is employed for the analysis of trace metals and inorganic ions in environmental samples, offering high sensitivity and specificity.
- **Food Quality Control:** In the food industry, CE is used to analyze amino acids, vitamins, preservatives, and other additives to ensure product quality and safety.

4. Clinical Diagnostics:

- **Hemoglobin Variants and Isoenzymes:** CE is used in clinical laboratories to separate and identify hemoglobin variants, isoenzymes, and other biomarkers, aiding in the diagnosis of various diseases.
- **Electrolyte and Metabolite Analysis:** CE can be used to measure electrolytes, metabolites, and small organic acids in biological fluids, providing valuable information for clinical diagnostics.

Pharmaceutical Applications of Capillary Electrophoresis

Capillary electrophoresis (CE) is a highly versatile and efficient analytical technique widely used in the pharmaceutical industry for various applications, including drug development, quality control, and regulatory compliance. The ability of CE to separate and analyze complex mixtures with high resolution and sensitivity makes it an indispensable tool in the pharmaceutical sector.

1. Drug Purity and Impurity Profiling

1.1 Analysis of Drug Purity:

- **Quality Control:** CE is commonly used in the quality control of pharmaceuticals to ensure that the active pharmaceutical ingredient (API) is of high purity. This involves the separation and quantification of the API from any impurities, degradation products, or by-products that may have been introduced during synthesis, formulation, or storage.
- **Regulatory Compliance:** Pharmaceutical products must meet stringent purity standards set by regulatory bodies such as the FDA and EMA. CE provides a reliable method for detecting and quantifying impurities, helping manufacturers comply with these regulations.

1.2 Impurity Profiling:

- **Identification of Impurities:** CE is highly effective for profiling impurities in drug substances and drug products. The technique's high resolution allows for the separation of structurally similar impurities that may be difficult to distinguish using other methods.
- **Degradation Studies:** During stability testing, CE is used to monitor the formation of degradation products over time. This is crucial for understanding the shelf life of a drug and for ensuring that it remains safe and effective throughout its intended shelf life.

2. Chiral Separation and Analysis
2.1 Enantiomeric Purity:

- **Chiral Drugs:** Many pharmaceutical compounds are chiral, meaning they exist as two enantiomers with identical chemical compositions but different three-dimensional structures. These enantiomers can have different pharmacological effects, making it essential to separate and quantify them. CE, particularly using chiral selectors in the buffer or chiral stationary phases, is a powerful tool for separating enantiomers and determining the enantiomeric purity of chiral drugs.
- **Quality Assurance:** Ensuring the correct enantiomeric composition is vital in drug manufacturing, as one enantiomer may be therapeutically active while the other may be inactive or even harmful. CE provides the precision needed for this critical analysis.

2.2 Chiral Method Development:

- **Method Optimization:** The development of chiral separation methods using CE involves optimizing various parameters, such as the choice of chiral selector, buffer composition, and pH. CE's flexibility allows for rapid method development and optimization, which is essential in the early stages of drug development.

3. Drug Formulation and Excipients Analysis
3.1 Formulation Analysis:

- **Complex Mixtures:** CE is used to analyze the composition of pharmaceutical formulations, which often contain multiple components, including the API, excipients, preservatives, and stabilizers. CE can effectively separate and quantify these components, ensuring the consistency and stability of the final product.

- **Drug-Excipient Interactions:** CE can be employed to study interactions between the drug and excipients, which can affect the drug's stability, bioavailability, and overall efficacy. Understanding these interactions is crucial for the development of robust and effective formulations.

3.2 Excipients Purity:

- **Excipients Testing:** Excipients used in drug formulations must meet high purity standards to prevent adverse effects on the drug product. CE is used to analyze the purity of excipients, detecting potential contaminants or degradation products that could impact the quality of the final formulation.

4. Pharmacokinetics and Bioanalysis
4.1 Drug Metabolism and Pharmacokinetics (DMPK):

- **Metabolite Profiling:** CE is used in pharmacokinetic studies to separate and identify drug metabolites in biological fluids such as blood, urine, and plasma. The high resolution and sensitivity of CE allow for the detection of low concentrations of metabolites, providing valuable information on the drug's metabolic pathways and elimination.
- **Quantification of Drugs in Biological Matrices:** CE can be used to quantify the concentration of a drug in biological samples over time, which is essential for determining pharmacokinetic parameters such as absorption, distribution, metabolism, and excretion (ADME).

4.2 Bioanalysis of Biopharmaceuticals:

- **Peptide and Protein Drugs:** Biopharmaceuticals, including therapeutic peptides and proteins, are increasingly important in modern medicine. CE is used to analyze these complex molecules, assessing their purity, stability, and structural integrity.
- **Antibody-Drug Conjugates (ADCs):** CE is employed to characterize antibody-drug conjugates, which are complex biopharmaceuticals consisting of an antibody linked to a cytotoxic drug. CE helps in understanding the drug-to-antibody ratio, conjugation sites, and stability

of the conjugate.

5. Drug-Drug Interaction Studies
5.1 Interaction Mechanisms:

- **Competitive Binding Studies:** CE can be used to study drug-drug interactions by analyzing the binding of multiple drugs to the same target or receptor. Understanding these interactions is critical for predicting potential side effects and optimizing combination therapies.
- **Inhibition and Activation Studies:** CE allows for the investigation of how one drug may inhibit or activate the metabolism of another drug, which can lead to altered drug efficacy or increased toxicity. These studies are important for ensuring the safety and effectiveness of multi-drug regimens.

6. Regulatory Applications and Method Validation
6.1 Method Validation:

- **Regulatory Requirements:** CE methods used in the pharmaceutical industry must be validated according to regulatory guidelines. This includes assessing the method's accuracy, precision, linearity, limit of detection (LOD), limit of quantification (LOQ), specificity, and robustness. CE is well-suited for developing validated methods that meet these stringent criteria.
- **Robustness Testing:** CE methods are tested for robustness by evaluating their performance under slightly varied conditions, such as changes in buffer composition, capillary temperature, or voltage. Robust methods are essential for ensuring consistent and reliable results in routine quality control.

6.2 Stability-Indicating Methods:

- **Stability Testing:** Stability-indicating methods are essential for determining the shelf life and storage conditions of pharmaceutical products. CE is used to develop stability-indicating methods that can detect and quantify degradation products, ensuring the continued safety and efficacy of the drug throughout its shelf life.

11.3 Applications of Electrophoresis

Separation of Nucleic Acids and Proteins

Electrophoresis is a fundamental technique used in the separation and analysis of nucleic acids (DNA and RNA) and proteins. This technique exploits the differences in size, charge, and shape of these biomolecules to achieve effective separation under the influence of an electric field. The separation of nucleic acids and proteins using electrophoresis is essential in various fields, including molecular biology, genetics, biochemistry, and clinical diagnostics.

Separation of Nucleic Acids

1. DNA Separation:

1.1 Agarose Gel Electrophoresis for DNA:

- **Principle:** Agarose gel electrophoresis is the most common method for separating DNA molecules. DNA fragments are negatively charged due to their phosphate backbone, and when an electric field is applied, they migrate towards the positive electrode (anode). The agarose gel acts as a sieve, allowing smaller DNA fragments to move faster than larger ones.

- **Applications:**

  - **Fragment Analysis:** Agarose gel electrophoresis is widely used to separate DNA fragments generated by restriction enzyme digestion, enabling researchers to analyze the size and quantity of DNA fragments. This is crucial in genetic mapping, cloning, and various molecular biology applications.

  - **PCR Product Verification:** After performing polymerase chain reaction (PCR), agarose gel electrophoresis is used to verify the size and presence of amplified DNA products, confirming the success of the PCR process.

  - **Genotyping and DNA Fingerprinting:** Agarose gels are used to separate DNA fragments for genotyping and DNA fingerprinting, which are essential in forensic analysis, paternity testing, and genetic diversity studies.

1.2 Polyacrylamide Gel Electrophoresis for DNA (PAGE):

- **Principle:** For separating smaller DNA fragments or single-stranded DNA, polyacrylamide gel electrophoresis (PAGE) is used.

Polyacrylamide gels have smaller pores than agarose gels, providing higher resolution for small DNA molecules.

- **Applications:**

  - **DNA Sequencing:** PAGE is used in the separation of DNA sequencing products, where single-nucleotide differences can be resolved. This is crucial in determining the precise nucleotide sequence of DNA.
  - **Single-Strand Conformation Polymorphism (SSCP):** PAGE is used in SSCP analysis to detect mutations in DNA by separating single-stranded DNA fragments based on their conformation, which can vary due to sequence differences.

1.3 Pulsed-Field Gel Electrophoresis (PFGE):

- **Principle:** PFGE is a specialized technique used for separating very large DNA molecules (up to several megabases) that cannot be resolved by standard agarose gel electrophoresis. In PFGE, the direction of the electric field is periodically changed, allowing large DNA fragments to reorient and migrate through the gel matrix.
- **Applications:**

  - **Genomic DNA Analysis:** PFGE is used to separate large fragments of genomic DNA, such as those generated by restriction enzyme digestion, for applications in genome mapping, strain typing, and epidemiological studies.

2. RNA Separation:
2.1 Agarose Gel Electrophoresis for RNA:

- **Principle:** Similar to DNA, RNA molecules are separated using agarose gel electrophoresis. However, RNA is more prone to degradation and requires careful handling. Often, RNA samples are treated with denaturing agents (such as formaldehyde) to prevent secondary structures from forming during electrophoresis.
- **Applications:**

  - **mRNA Analysis:** Agarose gel electrophoresis is used to assess the integrity and size distribution of mRNA in gene expression studies,

RNA isolation, and quality control of RNA samples.

- **Ribosomal RNA Analysis:** The separation of ribosomal RNA (rRNA) bands is commonly used as an indicator of RNA integrity in various experimental setups.

2.2 Denaturing Polyacrylamide Gel Electrophoresis for RNA:

- **Principle:** For separating small RNA molecules or detecting subtle differences in RNA sequences, denaturing polyacrylamide gel electrophoresis is used. Denaturing agents like urea are included in the gel to maintain the RNA in a single-stranded form, preventing secondary structure formation.
- **Applications:**

  - **MicroRNA and siRNA Analysis:** PAGE is used to separate and analyze small RNA species such as microRNAs (miRNAs) and small interfering RNAs (siRNAs), which are important in gene regulation and therapeutic research.

Separation of Proteins
1. Sodium Dodecyl Sulfate-Polyacrylamide Gel Electrophoresis (SDS-PAGE):
1.1 Principle:

- **Denaturation and Charge Uniformity:** In SDS-PAGE, proteins are first denatured and coated with sodium dodecyl sulfate (SDS), a detergent that imparts a uniform negative charge to the proteins. This treatment eliminates the effects of the protein's native charge and shape, allowing separation based solely on molecular weight as they migrate through the polyacrylamide gel.

1.2 Applications:

- **Protein Purity and Molecular Weight Determination:** SDS-PAGE is widely used to determine the purity of protein samples and to estimate the molecular weight of proteins by comparing their migration to that of known molecular weight standards.

- **Western Blotting:** After separation by SDS-PAGE, proteins can be transferred to a membrane and detected using specific antibodies in a technique known as Western blotting. This is crucial for identifying specific proteins in complex mixtures.
- **Protein Expression Analysis:** SDS-PAGE is used to analyze protein expression levels in various biological samples, including cell lysates and tissue extracts, making it essential in proteomics and cell biology research.

2. Native Polyacrylamide Gel Electrophoresis (Native PAGE):
2.1 Principle:

- **Non-Denaturing Conditions:** Unlike SDS-PAGE, native PAGE separates proteins based on their native charge, size, and shape without denaturation. This allows proteins to retain their functional and structural integrity during separation.

2.2 Applications:

- **Protein-Protein Interactions:** Native PAGE is used to study protein-protein interactions, as it preserves the quaternary structure of protein complexes, allowing the analysis of intact protein assemblies.
- **Enzyme Activity Assays:** Native PAGE is used to separate enzymes in their active forms, enabling subsequent activity assays to be performed directly on the gel. This is useful in enzyme characterization and functional studies.

3. Isoelectric Focusing (IEF):
3.1 Principle:

- **Separation by Isoelectric Point (pI):** Isoelectric focusing separates proteins based on their isoelectric point (pI), the pH at which a protein carries no net charge. Proteins migrate through a pH gradient in the gel until they reach the point where their net charge is zero and they stop moving.

3.2 Applications:

- **Protein Charge Heterogeneity:** IEF is used to resolve proteins with small differences in pI, making it ideal for detecting charge variants and post-translational modifications, such as phosphorylation or glycosylation.
- **Two-Dimensional Gel Electrophoresis (2D-PAGE):** IEF is often used as the first dimension in 2D-PAGE, where proteins are first separated by pI and then by molecular weight, providing a high-resolution map of complex protein mixtures.

4. Capillary Electrophoresis for Proteins:
4.1 Principle:

- **High-Resolution Separation:** Capillary electrophoresis (CE) offers high-resolution separation of proteins based on their charge-to-mass ratio in a narrow capillary. CE is particularly useful for analyzing small protein samples with high precision.

4.2 Applications:

- **Protein Characterization:** CE is used to characterize proteins, including the analysis of protein isoforms, charge variants, and post-translational modifications. It is widely used in quality control and research applications.
- **Clinical Diagnostics:** CE is employed in clinical laboratories for the analysis of specific proteins in biological fluids, such as serum protein electrophoresis, which is used to diagnose and monitor various diseases.

Pharmaceutical Applications of Electrophoresis

Electrophoresis is a critical tool in the pharmaceutical industry, providing valuable insights into the analysis, development, and quality control of drugs and therapeutic proteins. Its ability to separate molecules based on size, charge, and conformation makes electrophoresis particularly useful for various applications in pharmaceutical research, development, and manufacturing.

1. Quality Control and Purity Testing
1.1 Analysis of Active Pharmaceutical Ingredients (APIs):

- **Purity Assessment:** Electrophoresis, particularly capillary electrophoresis (CE) and SDS-PAGE, is employed to assess the purity of active pharmaceutical ingredients (APIs). Ensuring the purity of APIs is crucial to meet regulatory standards and ensure the safety and efficacy of the final drug product.
- **Impurity Profiling:** Electrophoresis can detect and quantify impurities, including degradation products and residual solvents, that may be present in pharmaceutical formulations. This is essential for maintaining the quality and consistency of pharmaceutical products.

1.2 Protein-Based Therapeutics:

- **Monoclonal Antibodies:** Electrophoresis is widely used to characterize monoclonal antibodies, which are complex protein-based therapeutics. Techniques such as SDS-PAGE and capillary electrophoresis allow for the analysis of protein purity, glycosylation patterns, and the detection of aggregation or fragmentation.
- **Peptides and Hormones:** For peptide-based drugs and hormones, electrophoresis helps in determining the purity, identifying degradation products, and analyzing modifications, such as phosphorylation or deamidation, which can affect the drug's activity.

2. Drug Development and Characterization
2.1 Stability Testing:

- **Stability-Indicating Methods:** Electrophoresis is used in stability testing to monitor the degradation of pharmaceuticals under various conditions, such as temperature, humidity, and light exposure. These stability-indicating methods help in determining the shelf life and appropriate storage conditions for drug products.
- **Degradation Products:** The separation and identification of degradation products by electrophoresis provide insights into the pathways of drug degradation, enabling the formulation of more stable pharmaceutical products.

2.2 Chiral Drug Analysis:

- **Enantiomeric Purity:** Many drugs are chiral, meaning they exist as two enantiomers that may have different pharmacological effects. Capillary electrophoresis, often using chiral selectors, is an effective technique for separating and quantifying the enantiomers in chiral drug formulations, ensuring the desired enantiomeric purity and activity.

3. Biopharmaceutical Analysis
3.1 Protein Characterization:

- **Isoelectric Focusing (IEF):** Isoelectric focusing is used to separate proteins based on their isoelectric points (pI), allowing for the detailed characterization of biopharmaceuticals, including monoclonal antibodies and recombinant proteins. IEF is essential for detecting protein heterogeneity and post-translational modifications.
- **Two-Dimensional Gel Electrophoresis (2D-PAGE):** 2D-PAGE combines isoelectric focusing with SDS-PAGE, providing a high-resolution method for analyzing complex protein mixtures. This technique is used to characterize protein drugs, study their stability, and identify potential impurities or modifications.

3.2 Glycoprotein Analysis:

- **Glycosylation Profiling:** Electrophoresis is used to analyze the glycosylation patterns of glycoproteins, which are critical for the biological activity and stability of many biopharmaceuticals. Understanding glycosylation patterns helps in ensuring the consistency and efficacy of glycoprotein-based drugs.

4. Pharmacokinetics and Drug Metabolism
4.1 Metabolite Analysis:

- **Drug Metabolism Studies:** Electrophoresis, particularly capillary electrophoresis, is used to separate and identify drug metabolites in biological fluids such as blood, urine, and plasma. This information is vital for understanding the pharmacokinetics of a drug, including its absorption, distribution, metabolism, and excretion (ADME).
- **Quantification of Metabolites:** The ability to quantify drug metabolites using electrophoresis aids in assessing the drug's pharmacokinetic

profile and ensuring that metabolites do not pose any safety concerns.

4.2 Bioavailability Studies:

- **Therapeutic Proteins:** Electrophoresis is used to study the bioavailability of therapeutic proteins by analyzing their presence and stability in biological fluids over time. This information is crucial for optimizing dosing regimens and ensuring the therapeutic efficacy of protein-based drugs.

5. Regulatory Compliance and Method Validation
5.1 Method Validation:

- **Regulatory Requirements:** Electrophoresis methods used in the pharmaceutical industry must be validated according to regulatory guidelines to ensure their accuracy, precision, specificity, and robustness. Validated methods are essential for routine quality control and batch release testing.
- **Robustness Testing:** The robustness of electrophoresis methods is tested by assessing their performance under varied conditions, such as changes in buffer composition, voltage, and temperature. Robust methods are critical for ensuring reliable and reproducible results across different batches and laboratories.

5.2 Batch Release Testing:

- **Consistency and Compliance:** Electrophoresis is used in the final testing of pharmaceutical products to ensure that each batch meets the required specifications for purity, potency, and safety. This is particularly important for biopharmaceuticals, where product consistency is essential for regulatory compliance.

6. Forensic and Clinical Applications
6.1 Drug Testing and Monitoring:

- **Clinical Diagnostics:** Electrophoresis is used in clinical laboratories to monitor drug levels in patients, particularly in therapeutic drug monitoring (TDM) for drugs with narrow therapeutic windows. This ensures that patients receive the optimal dose for therapeutic effectiveness while minimizing the risk of toxicity.

- **Forensic Analysis:** Electrophoresis is employed in forensic toxicology to detect and quantify drugs and their metabolites in biological samples, aiding in cases of suspected drug abuse, poisoning, or overdose.

6.2 Biomarker Discovery:

- **Proteomic Profiling:** Electrophoresis, particularly 2D-PAGE, is used in proteomic studies to identify potential biomarkers for diseases, which can lead to the development of new diagnostic tests or targeted therapies. This application is crucial for personalized medicine and drug development.

CHAPTER TWELVE

Gas Chromatography (GC)

12.1 Introduction and Theory of GC

Principles of Gas Chromatography

Gas chromatography (GC) is a powerful analytical technique used to separate and analyze compounds that can be vaporized without decomposition. It is widely employed in various fields, including pharmaceuticals, environmental analysis, food science, and forensic science, to identify and quantify volatile and semi-volatile compounds. The separation of compounds in GC is based on their differential partitioning between a mobile phase (carrier gas) and a stationary phase (a liquid or solid) within a column.

Principles of Gas Chromatography

1. Components of Gas Chromatography:

- **Carrier Gas (Mobile Phase):** The carrier gas is an inert gas, such as helium, nitrogen, or hydrogen, that acts as the mobile phase in GC. It carries the sample vapor through the column and plays a crucial role in determining the efficiency and speed of the separation. The choice of carrier gas depends on factors like the type of detector used, the column, and the nature of the analytes.

- **Injection Port:** The sample is introduced into the GC system through the injection port, where it is rapidly vaporized if it is not already in the gaseous state. The injection port is typically maintained at a high temperature to ensure efficient vaporization of the sample.

- **Column:** The heart of the GC system is the chromatographic column, which is usually a long, narrow tube made of stainless steel, glass, or fused silica. The column contains the stationary phase and is housed within an oven that controls the temperature during the separation process.

- **Detector:** After separation in the column, the analytes are detected as they elute. Various types of detectors can be used in GC, such as flame ionization detectors (FID), thermal conductivity detectors (TCD), electron capture detectors (ECD), and mass spectrometers (MS), depending on the sensitivity and specificity required.

2. Retention Time and Separation:

- **Retention Time (tR):** The retention time is the time it takes for a compound to travel through the column and reach the detector. Each compound has a characteristic retention time under specific conditions, which is used for identification purposes. The retention time depends on the compound's interaction with the stationary phase, its vapor pressure, and the column temperature.
- **Separation Mechanism:** In GC, separation occurs because different compounds interact differently with the stationary phase and the mobile phase. Compounds with a higher affinity for the stationary phase will spend more time in the column, resulting in longer retention times, while compounds with a lower affinity will elute faster. The efficiency of separation is influenced by factors such as column length, stationary phase composition, carrier gas flow rate, and temperature.

Gas-Liquid Partitioning

Gas-liquid partitioning is the fundamental process that drives the separation of compounds in gas chromatography. This process involves the distribution of analytes between the gas phase (mobile phase) and the liquid phase (stationary phase) within the column.

1. Stationary Phase:

- **Liquid Coated on a Solid Support:** In gas-liquid chromatography (GLC), the stationary phase is a liquid that is coated on an inert solid support material, such as diatomaceous earth, or directly bonded to the inner walls of the capillary column. The choice of liquid stationary phase depends on the polarity and chemical nature of the analytes. Common stationary phases include non-polar liquids like polydimethylsiloxane (PDMS) for separating non-polar compounds, and polar liquids like polyethylene glycol (PEG) for separating polar compounds.

- **Polarity Matching:** The principle of "like dissolves like" is applied in gas-liquid partitioning, where non-polar analytes have a higher affinity for non-polar stationary phases and polar analytes have a higher affinity for polar stationary phases. This matching of polarity between the analytes and the stationary phase enhances the separation.

2. Partition Coefficient (K):

- **Definition:** The partition coefficient (K) is a measure of how a compound distributes itself between the stationary phase and the mobile phase. It is defined as the ratio of the concentration of the compound in the stationary phase to its concentration in the mobile phase:

$$K = \frac{\text{Concentration in Stationary Phase}}{\text{Concentration in Mobile Phase}}$$

- **Influence on Retention:** A higher partition coefficient indicates that the compound has a stronger interaction with the stationary phase, leading to longer retention times. Conversely, compounds with lower partition coefficients will spend more time in the mobile phase and elute faster.

3. Temperature Control:

- **Column Oven:** The temperature of the column is controlled by an oven that can be programmed to maintain a constant temperature or to follow a temperature gradient. Temperature is a critical factor in gas-liquid partitioning, as it affects the volatility of the analytes and the viscosity of the stationary phase.
- **Isothermal vs. Temperature-Programmed GC:** In isothermal GC, the column temperature remains constant throughout the separation, which is suitable for analyzing compounds with similar volatilities. In temperature-programmed GC, the column temperature is gradually increased during the run, which helps in separating a mixture of compounds with a wide range of boiling points by reducing the retention time of late-eluting compounds.

4. Factors Affecting Gas-Liquid Partitioning:

- **Nature of the Stationary Phase:** The chemical composition and polarity of the stationary phase directly influence the partitioning behavior of analytes. Choosing an appropriate stationary phase is essential for achieving optimal separation.
- **Carrier Gas Flow Rate:** The flow rate of the carrier gas affects the time analytes spend in the column. A higher flow rate can lead to faster elution but may reduce the resolution between closely eluting compounds. Conversely, a lower flow rate increases the retention time and resolution but may result in broader peaks.
- **Sample Size:** The amount of sample introduced into the GC system can impact the partitioning process. Overloading the column with too much sample can lead to peak broadening and reduced separation efficiency.

12.2 Instrumentation of GC
Carrier Gas, Injector, Column, Detector

The instrumentation of gas chromatography (GC) involves several key components that work together to achieve the separation and analysis of compounds. These components include the carrier gas, injector, chromatographic column, and detector. Each plays a critical role in the overall performance and efficiency of the GC system.

1. Carrier Gas
1.1 Role of the Carrier Gas:

- **Mobile Phase:** The carrier gas serves as the mobile phase in gas chromatography. It transports the vaporized sample through the chromatographic column and is crucial for the separation process. The carrier gas must be inert to prevent reactions with the sample or stationary phase.
- **Common Carrier Gases:** Helium, nitrogen, and hydrogen are the most commonly used carrier gases in GC. Each has specific properties that make it suitable for different applications:

  - **Helium:** Widely used due to its inertness, moderate viscosity, and compatibility with most detectors. Helium provides a good balance between efficiency and analysis time.

- **Nitrogen:** Offers high efficiency at low flow rates but results in longer analysis times. It is often used when cost or availability of helium is a concern.
- **Hydrogen:** Provides the fastest analysis times due to its low viscosity and high diffusivity. However, it requires careful handling because of its flammability.

1.2 Control of Carrier Gas Flow:

- **Flow Rate:** The flow rate of the carrier gas is a critical parameter that affects the retention time, resolution, and overall efficiency of the separation. It is typically controlled by a flow controller or mass flow meter in the GC system.
- **Pressure Regulation:** The carrier gas is supplied from a high-pressure cylinder and regulated to a specific pressure using a pressure regulator. Maintaining a constant pressure ensures consistent flow through the column.

2. Injector
2.1 Purpose of the Injector:

- **Sample Introduction:** The injector is the point at which the sample is introduced into the GC system. The injector must vaporize the sample efficiently and introduce it into the carrier gas stream without causing degradation or loss of sample components.

2.2 Types of Injectors:

- **Split/Splitless Injector:**

  - **Split Mode:** In split mode, only a small portion of the sample is introduced into the column, while the rest is vented out. This mode is used when analyzing high-concentration samples to prevent overloading the column.
  - **Splitless Mode:** In splitless mode, the entire sample is introduced into the column, making it suitable for trace analysis or low-concentration samples. This mode allows for maximum sensitivity and detection.

- **On-Column Injector:**

  - **Direct Injection:** In on-column injection, the sample is introduced directly into the column without vaporization in the injector. This method is used for thermally sensitive samples that may decompose at high injector temperatures.

- **Programmed Temperature Vaporizing (PTV) Injector:**

  - **Temperature Control:** The PTV injector allows the temperature to be programmed, enabling the gradual vaporization of the sample. This method reduces the risk of sample decomposition and is useful for a wide range of sample types.

2.3 Injector Temperature:

- **Temperature Setting:** The injector is typically heated to a temperature above the boiling point of the sample components to ensure complete vaporization. The temperature must be carefully controlled to prevent sample decomposition or the formation of non-volatile residues.

3. Chromatographic Column
3.1 Types of Columns:

- **Packed Columns:**

  - **Construction:** Packed columns are filled with a solid support material coated with a liquid stationary phase. These columns are typically 1-4 meters in length and have an internal diameter of 2-4 mm.
  - **Applications:** Packed columns are used for separating gases and volatile compounds in applications where high sample capacity is required.

- **Capillary Columns:**

  - **Construction:** Capillary columns, also known as open tubular columns, have an internal diameter of 0.1-0.5 mm and are coated with a thin layer of the stationary phase on the inner walls. These columns are much longer, typically 10-100 meters.

- ○ **Applications:** Capillary columns offer higher resolution and faster analysis times compared to packed columns and are widely used for complex mixtures and trace analysis.

3.2 Stationary Phases:

- **Non-Polar Stationary Phases:** Non-polar stationary phases, such as polydimethylsiloxane (PDMS), are used for separating non-polar compounds. They interact weakly with analytes, resulting in shorter retention times for non-polar compounds.
- **Polar Stationary Phases:** Polar stationary phases, such as polyethylene glycol (PEG), are used for separating polar compounds. They interact more strongly with polar analytes, leading to longer retention times.

3.3 Temperature Control:

- **Column Oven:** The chromatographic column is housed in a temperature-controlled oven. The oven temperature can be maintained isothermally or programmed to increase gradually during the run, depending on the complexity of the sample.
- **Isothermal vs. Temperature-Programmed Operation:** Isothermal operation is used for simple mixtures with similar volatilities, while temperature programming is used for complex mixtures with a wide range of boiling points.

4. Detector
4.1 Types of Detectors:

- **Flame Ionization Detector (FID):**

  - ○ **Principle:** FID is the most commonly used detector in GC. It works by ionizing carbon-containing compounds as they elute from the column. The ions are collected to generate a current, which is proportional to the concentration of the compound.
  - ○ **Applications:** FID is highly sensitive and suitable for detecting hydrocarbons, alcohols, aldehydes, and other organic compounds.

- **Thermal Conductivity Detector (TCD):**

  - **Principle:** TCD measures changes in the thermal conductivity of the carrier gas as analytes elute from the column. The change in thermal conductivity is proportional to the concentration of the analyte.
  - **Applications:** TCD is a universal detector, suitable for both organic and inorganic compounds, and is often used when analyzing permanent gases.

- **Electron Capture Detector (ECD):**

  - **Principle:** ECD detects compounds that can capture electrons, such as halogenated compounds. It works by measuring the reduction in current caused by the capture of electrons by the analyte.
  - **Applications:** ECD is highly sensitive to halogens, nitrates, and organometallic compounds, making it ideal for environmental analysis and detecting pesticides.

- **Mass Spectrometry (MS):**

  - **Principle:** MS detects and identifies compounds based on their mass-to-charge ratio (m/z). It provides both qualitative and quantitative information and is often coupled with GC for detailed analysis.
  - **Applications:** GC-MS is used in a wide range of applications, including forensic analysis, environmental monitoring, and drug testing, due to its high sensitivity and specificity.

4.2 Detector Sensitivity and Selectivity:

- **Sensitivity:** The sensitivity of the detector is a measure of its ability to detect small amounts of analyte. FID and MS are highly sensitive detectors, suitable for trace analysis.
- **Selectivity:** Selectivity refers to the detector's ability to distinguish between different compounds. ECD is highly selective for electron-capturing compounds, while FID and TCD are less selective but more universal.

Temperature Programming in Gas Chromatography

Temperature programming is a crucial technique in gas chromatography (GC) that enhances the separation of complex mixtures by varying the column temperature during the analysis. This approach allows for the efficient separation of compounds with a wide range of boiling points, improving both the resolution and the speed of the analysis.

Principles of Temperature Programming

1. Isothermal vs. Temperature-Programmed Operation:

- **Isothermal Operation:** In isothermal GC, the column temperature is held constant throughout the entire analysis. This method is effective for separating compounds with similar volatilities. However, it may not be suitable for mixtures with components that have a wide range of boiling points. In such cases, early-eluting compounds might be well-separated, while late-eluting compounds could have excessively long retention times, leading to broad and poorly resolved peaks.

- **Temperature Programming:** In temperature-programmed GC, the column temperature is gradually increased during the analysis. This method is particularly useful for complex mixtures with components that vary significantly in volatility. Temperature programming allows early-eluting compounds to separate quickly at lower temperatures, while increasing the temperature accelerates the elution of higher boiling point compounds, resulting in sharper and more resolved peaks.

2. Benefits of Temperature Programming:

- **Improved Resolution:** Temperature programming helps to separate compounds that might co-elute under isothermal conditions. By optimizing the temperature ramp, compounds with different volatilities can be separated more effectively, leading to better resolution.

- **Shorter Analysis Time:** By increasing the temperature during the run, temperature programming reduces the retention times of late-eluting compounds, leading to faster analysis times compared to isothermal operation.

- **Peak Shape Improvement:** Temperature programming can improve peak shapes, particularly for high-boiling compounds. As the temperature increases, these compounds are eluted more rapidly, reducing peak broadening and tailing.

Implementing Temperature Programming
1. Temperature Ramp Rate:

- **Ramp Rate Selection:** The rate at which the column temperature is increased during the analysis is known as the temperature ramp rate. It is typically expressed in degrees Celsius per minute (°C/min). The choice of ramp rate is critical and depends on the nature of the sample and the desired separation:

  - **Slow Ramp Rate:** A slow ramp rate (e.g., 1-5°C/min) is used when high resolution is needed, particularly for complex mixtures with closely eluting compounds. This allows ample time for each compound to separate, resulting in well-resolved peaks.
  - **Fast Ramp Rate:** A fast ramp rate (e.g., 10-20°C/min) is used to shorten the analysis time, especially when separating compounds with widely differing boiling points. However, too fast a ramp rate may compromise resolution, leading to co-elution of some compounds.

2. Initial and Final Temperatures:

- **Initial Temperature:** The initial temperature of the column is typically set below the boiling point of the most volatile compound in the sample. This ensures that the early-eluting compounds are separated efficiently before the temperature starts to increase.
- **Final Temperature:** The final temperature is selected based on the boiling points of the highest boiling compounds in the sample. It should be high enough to elute all compounds within a reasonable time frame but not so high as to degrade thermally sensitive analytes or damage the stationary phase.

3. Hold Times:

- **Initial Hold Time:** The initial hold time is the duration for which the column temperature is maintained at the initial temperature before the temperature ramp begins. This allows for the separation of low-boiling compounds before increasing the temperature for higher-boiling components.

- **Final Hold Time:** The final hold time is the period for which the column temperature is maintained at the final temperature after the ramp is complete. This ensures that all high-boiling compounds are fully eluted from the column.

Applications of Temperature Programming
1. Complex Mixtures:

- **Multi-Component Analysis:** Temperature programming is ideal for analyzing complex mixtures containing compounds with a wide range of volatilities. For example, in environmental analysis, GC is used to separate volatile organic compounds (VOCs) along with semi-volatile compounds in a single run, improving the efficiency of the analysis.
- **Petroleum and Hydrocarbon Analysis:** In the analysis of petroleum products and hydrocarbons, temperature programming enables the separation of light alkanes and aromatics along with heavier compounds such as polycyclic aromatic hydrocarbons (PAHs) in a single chromatographic run.

2. High Boiling Point Compounds:

- **Pesticide Analysis:** Temperature programming is frequently used in the analysis of pesticides, which often include both volatile and semi-volatile compounds. By starting at a lower temperature and gradually increasing it, both classes of compounds can be effectively separated and detected.
- **Flavor and Fragrance Analysis:** The separation of complex mixtures of volatile and semi-volatile flavor and fragrance compounds is enhanced by temperature programming, allowing for the detailed analysis of these intricate mixtures.

3. Optimization of Analysis Conditions:

- **Method Development:** During method development, temperature programming provides flexibility in optimizing separation conditions. By adjusting the ramp rate, initial, and final temperatures, analysts can tailor the GC method to achieve the desired balance between resolution and analysis time.

- **Thermally Labile Compounds:** For thermally sensitive compounds that may degrade at high temperatures, temperature programming allows for controlled heating, reducing the risk of thermal decomposition and ensuring accurate quantification.

12.3 Applications of GC
Analysis of Volatile Compounds

Gas chromatography (GC) is particularly well-suited for the analysis of volatile compounds, making it a widely used technique in various industries, including pharmaceuticals, environmental science, food and beverage, and petrochemicals. The ability of GC to separate, identify, and quantify volatile substances with high precision and sensitivity makes it an indispensable tool for the analysis of a wide range of compounds.

Analysis of Volatile Compounds
1. Environmental Analysis:
1.1 Volatile Organic Compounds (VOCs):

- **Air Quality Monitoring:** GC is extensively used in environmental analysis to monitor volatile organic compounds (VOCs) in the atmosphere. VOCs are a significant group of pollutants that can arise from industrial processes, vehicle emissions, and natural sources. GC enables the separation and quantification of VOCs such as benzene, toluene, ethylbenzene, and xylene (collectively known as BTEX) in ambient air, providing crucial data for air quality assessment and regulatory compliance.
- **Soil and Water Analysis:** GC is also employed to detect and quantify VOCs in soil and water samples. This is important for assessing contamination at industrial sites, landfills, and groundwater sources. By analyzing soil and water samples, GC helps in identifying sources of pollution and determining the extent of contamination.

1.2 Persistent Organic Pollutants (POPs):

- **Pesticides and Herbicides:** Many pesticides and herbicides are volatile or semi-volatile compounds that can persist in the environment, leading to contamination of soil, water, and air. GC is used to analyze these compounds in environmental samples, helping to monitor and regulate their presence in ecosystems.

- **Polychlorinated Biphenyls (PCBs):** PCBs are a group of persistent organic pollutants that are harmful to the environment and human health. GC, often coupled with electron capture detection (ECD), is used to detect and quantify PCBs in environmental samples, aiding in pollution control and remediation efforts.

2. Food and Beverage Industry:
2.1 Flavor and Fragrance Analysis:

- **Essential Oils and Aroma Compounds:** GC is a primary tool for analyzing the volatile components of essential oils, flavors, and fragrances. The technique allows for the separation and identification of individual compounds that contribute to the overall aroma and flavor profile of food and beverages. This is essential for quality control, product development, and ensuring consistency in the production of flavors and fragrances.
- **Alcoholic Beverages:** In the analysis of alcoholic beverages, GC is used to quantify volatile compounds such as ethanol, methanol, esters, and higher alcohols. These compounds influence the taste, aroma, and quality of the beverage. GC helps in the quality control of products like wine, beer, and spirits by ensuring that the volatile composition meets industry standards.

2.2 Residual Solvents:

- **Food Packaging Materials:** GC is used to detect residual solvents in food packaging materials to ensure that they do not migrate into the food product. This is important for maintaining food safety and complying with regulatory standards.
- **Food Contaminants:** Volatile contaminants such as pesticides, fumigants, and plasticizers in food products can be analyzed using GC. This analysis is crucial for ensuring that food products are free from harmful levels of these substances, thereby protecting consumer health.

3. Pharmaceutical Industry:
3.1 Residual Solvent Analysis:

- **Pharmaceutical Production:** During the manufacturing of pharmaceuticals, organic solvents are often used in the synthesis and purification processes. Residual solvents left in the final product can pose safety risks to consumers. GC, particularly with headspace sampling, is the preferred method for detecting and quantifying residual solvents in pharmaceutical products. This analysis is essential for ensuring that residual solvent levels comply with guidelines set by regulatory authorities such as the International Council for Harmonisation of Technical Requirements for Pharmaceuticals for Human Use (ICH).
- **Quality Control:** In addition to residual solvent analysis, GC is used in the pharmaceutical industry for the quality control of volatile impurities and degradation products in drug formulations. This ensures the safety, efficacy, and stability of pharmaceutical products.

3.2 Analysis of Volatile Active Pharmaceutical Ingredients (APIs):

- **Volatile APIs:** Some active pharmaceutical ingredients (APIs) are volatile in nature, and GC is an effective technique for analyzing their purity and concentration in formulations. This is particularly important for drugs administered by inhalation, where the volatility of the API is a key factor in its delivery and efficacy.

4. Petrochemical Industry:
4.1 Hydrocarbon Analysis:

- **Crude Oil and Natural Gas:** GC is extensively used in the petrochemical industry to analyze hydrocarbons in crude oil, natural gas, and refined petroleum products. The technique helps in characterizing the composition of hydrocarbons, including alkanes, alkenes, and aromatic compounds, which is crucial for refining processes, quality control, and product specification.
- **Gasoline and Diesel Fuels:** GC is used to analyze the volatile components of gasoline and diesel fuels, including additives and impurities. This analysis ensures that the fuel meets regulatory standards for composition, performance, and emissions.

4.2 Volatile Components in Petrochemical Products:

- **Plasticizers and Additives:** GC is used to detect and quantify volatile plasticizers, solvents, and other additives in petrochemical products. This analysis is important for product safety, regulatory compliance, and ensuring that the final products meet quality standards.

5. Forensic Science:
5.1 Analysis of Volatile Compounds in Forensic Samples:

- **Arson Investigation:** GC is used in forensic science to analyze volatile accelerants (e.g., gasoline, kerosene) in fire debris samples from suspected arson cases. The ability to detect trace levels of these accelerants is crucial for determining the cause of a fire and identifying potential suspects.
- **Toxicology:** In forensic toxicology, GC is used to analyze volatile substances such as alcohols, solvents, and other volatile poisons in biological samples (e.g., blood, urine). This analysis is essential for determining the presence of toxic substances in cases of suspected poisoning or substance abuse.

5.2 Drug Analysis:

- **Controlled Substances:** GC is employed to analyze volatile and semi-volatile controlled substances, including certain drugs of abuse and their precursors. This application is vital for law enforcement and regulatory agencies in the identification and quantification of illicit drugs.

Pharmaceutical and Environmental Applications of Gas Chromatography (GC)

Gas chromatography (GC) is a highly versatile and widely used analytical technique in both the pharmaceutical and environmental fields. Its ability to separate, identify, and quantify volatile and semi-volatile compounds makes it an essential tool for ensuring product quality, safety, and compliance with regulatory standards, as well as for monitoring and protecting environmental health.

Pharmaceutical Applications
1. Quality Control and Assurance
1.1 Residual Solvent Analysis:

- **Importance in Pharmaceuticals:** Residual solvents are organic volatile chemicals used during the manufacturing of active pharmaceutical ingredients (APIs), excipients, or drug products. These solvents must be controlled and minimized due to their potential toxicity. GC, especially with headspace sampling, is the method of choice for detecting and quantifying residual solvents in pharmaceuticals.
- **Regulatory Compliance:** The International Council for Harmonisation of Technical Requirements for Pharmaceuticals for Human Use (ICH) has established guidelines (ICH Q3C) that specify acceptable limits for residual solvents. GC ensures that pharmaceutical products meet these limits, safeguarding patient safety and meeting regulatory requirements.

1.2 Purity and Impurity Profiling:

- **API Analysis:** GC is used to assess the purity of APIs and to identify and quantify any volatile impurities that may be present. This is crucial for ensuring the safety, efficacy, and stability of the drug product.
- **Degradation Products:** During the stability testing of pharmaceuticals, GC is employed to monitor the formation of volatile degradation products over time. Identifying these products helps in understanding the degradation pathways and ensuring that the drug remains within its specifications throughout its shelf life.

1.3 Analysis of Volatile Active Pharmaceutical Ingredients (APIs):

- **Volatile APIs:** Certain APIs are volatile in nature, and GC is particularly effective in analyzing their purity, concentration, and stability within pharmaceutical formulations. This is especially relevant for inhalation drugs, where the volatility of the API is a key factor in drug delivery and therapeutic effectiveness.

2. Drug Formulation and Development
2.1 Optimization of Formulations:

- **Excipient Interaction:** GC is used to study the interactions between volatile components, such as flavoring agents or preservatives, and other excipients in drug formulations. Understanding these interactions is essential for optimizing the formulation for stability, efficacy, and patient acceptability.

- **Inhalation Products:** For inhalation therapies, such as asthma medications, GC is used to analyze the propellants and other volatile components to ensure proper delivery and dosing.

2.2 Process Development and Validation:

- **Process Control:** During the development and validation of pharmaceutical manufacturing processes, GC is used to monitor volatile intermediates and by-products. This ensures that the process is efficient, reproducible, and yields a product of consistent quality.
- **Validation Studies:** GC methods must be validated to ensure accuracy, precision, specificity, and sensitivity. Validation studies are critical for regulatory approval and for ensuring that the analytical methods are robust and reliable.

3. Pharmacokinetics and Metabolism Studies
3.1 Analysis of Drug Metabolites:

- **Pharmacokinetic Studies:** GC is used in pharmacokinetic studies to analyze volatile metabolites in biological fluids such as blood, urine, and plasma. Understanding the metabolic profile of a drug helps in determining its absorption, distribution, metabolism, and excretion (ADME) characteristics.
- **Bioavailability Studies:** GC aids in quantifying the bioavailability of volatile drugs by analyzing their concentration in biological samples over time, providing essential data for dosage optimization and therapeutic effectiveness.

Environmental Applications
1. Air Quality Monitoring
1.1 Volatile Organic Compounds (VOCs):

- **Air Pollution Monitoring:** GC is extensively used to monitor volatile organic compounds (VOCs) in the atmosphere. VOCs, which can originate from industrial emissions, vehicle exhaust, and natural sources, are significant contributors to air pollution and can have harmful effects on human health and the environment.

- **Indoor Air Quality:** GC is also employed to assess indoor air quality by detecting VOCs emitted from building materials, furnishings, and household products. This is important for identifying and mitigating sources of indoor air pollution, ensuring a healthy living environment.

1.2 Greenhouse Gases:

- **Climate Change Research:** GC is used to measure the concentration of greenhouse gases, such as methane (CH_4) and carbon dioxide (CO_2), in the atmosphere. Monitoring these gases is essential for understanding their impact on global warming and for developing strategies to mitigate climate change.

2. Water and Soil Analysis
2.1 Water Contamination:

- **Detection of Organic Pollutants:** GC is a key tool in analyzing organic pollutants, such as pesticides, herbicides, and industrial chemicals, in water samples. This is crucial for ensuring that water sources, including drinking water, meet safety standards and are free from harmful contaminants.
- **Monitoring of Volatile Contaminants:** GC is used to detect and quantify volatile organic compounds (VOCs) in groundwater and surface water. VOCs can contaminate water sources through industrial discharges, landfill leachates, and agricultural runoff, posing risks to both human health and aquatic ecosystems.

2.2 Soil Contamination:

- **Environmental Remediation:** GC is employed in the analysis of soil samples to detect the presence of volatile organic contaminants, such as hydrocarbons, solvents, and pesticides. This information is critical for assessing the extent of contamination, developing remediation strategies, and monitoring the effectiveness of cleanup efforts.
- **Agricultural Applications:** In agriculture, GC is used to monitor the levels of pesticides and herbicides in soil, ensuring that they are within safe limits to prevent environmental damage and protect crop health.

3. Environmental Forensics
3.1 Source Identification:

- **Pollution Source Tracking:** GC is used in environmental forensics to identify the sources of pollution, such as oil spills, chemical leaks, or illegal discharges. By analyzing the chemical composition of pollutants, GC helps in tracing them back to their origin, supporting legal and regulatory actions.
- **Fingerprinting of Contaminants:** GC allows for the "fingerprinting" of complex mixtures, such as petroleum hydrocarbons, enabling the identification of specific sources or types of contamination. This is important for environmental liability assessments and remediation planning.

3.2 Ecotoxicology:

- **Impact Assessment:** GC is used to analyze the presence and concentration of toxic organic compounds in environmental samples. This data is essential for assessing the impact of these contaminants on wildlife and ecosystems, and for developing strategies to mitigate their effects.
- **Long-Term Monitoring:** GC plays a role in the long-term monitoring of environmental contaminants, helping to track changes in pollutant levels over time and assess the effectiveness of environmental policies and regulations.

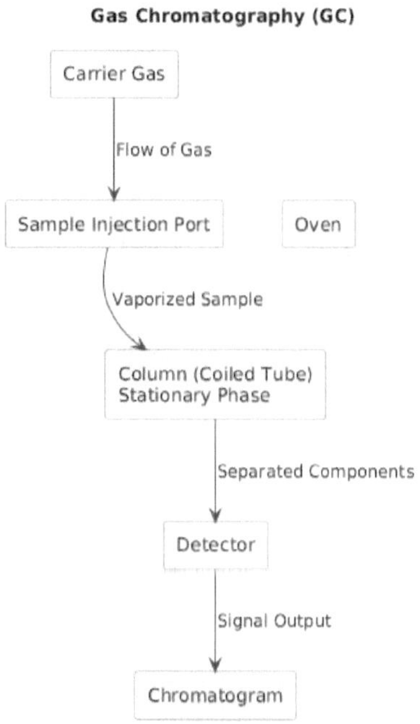

Gas Chromatography: Process Flow and Key Components

CHAPTER THIRTEEN

High-Performance Liquid Chromatography (HPLC)

13.1 Introduction and Theory of HPLC

Principles of HPLC

High-Performance Liquid Chromatography (HPLC) is an advanced analytical technique widely used for the separation, identification, and quantification of components in complex mixtures. It is a highly efficient form of column chromatography that utilizes high pressure to push solvents through a column filled with a solid stationary phase. The technique is particularly valuable in pharmaceuticals, biotechnology, environmental analysis, and food science due to its ability to handle a wide range of sample types, including those that are non-volatile, thermally labile, or complex in nature.

Principles of HPLC

1. Basic Components of HPLC:

1.1 Mobile Phase:

- **Liquid Solvent System:** The mobile phase in HPLC is a liquid solvent or a mixture of solvents that transports the sample through the chromatographic column. The choice of mobile phase is critical as it influences the separation process and the interaction between the sample components and the stationary phase. Common solvents used include water, methanol, acetonitrile, and buffers.
- **Gradient vs. Isocratic Elution:** The mobile phase can be delivered in two modes:

  ○ **Isocratic Elution:** In isocratic elution, the composition of the mobile phase remains constant throughout the run. This is suitable for separating compounds with similar polarities.

- ◦ **Gradient Elution:** In gradient elution, the composition of the mobile phase changes gradually over time, usually from a lower to a higher percentage of organic solvent. This allows for the efficient separation of compounds with a wide range of polarities and retention times.

1.2 Stationary Phase:

- **Column Packing Material:** The stationary phase in HPLC is typically made of small, porous particles, usually silica-based, that are packed tightly into a column. These particles are coated or chemically bonded with different functional groups (such as C18, C8, phenyl, or cyano) to provide varying degrees of interaction with the analytes.
- **Types of Stationary Phases:** The choice of stationary phase depends on the nature of the analytes and the type of separation required:

  - ◦ **Reversed-Phase (RP-HPLC):** The most common type, where the stationary phase is non-polar (e.g., C18 or C8), and the mobile phase is polar. Reversed-phase HPLC is ideal for separating polar and moderately polar compounds.
  - ◦ **Normal-Phase (NP-HPLC):** The stationary phase is polar (e.g., silica), and the mobile phase is non-polar. Normal-phase HPLC is used for separating non-polar compounds.
  - ◦ **Ion-Exchange HPLC:** The stationary phase contains charged groups, which interact with oppositely charged analytes. This method is used for separating ionic compounds, such as proteins, peptides, and nucleotides.
  - ◦ **Size-Exclusion HPLC:** The stationary phase consists of porous particles that separate molecules based on their size. Larger molecules elute first, followed by smaller ones. This method is used for analyzing polymers, proteins, and other macromolecules.

2. Separation Mechanism in HPLC:
2.1 Interaction of Analytes with Stationary and Mobile Phases:

- **Partitioning:** The separation of compounds in HPLC is based on their differential partitioning between the mobile phase and the stationary phase. Compounds with a higher affinity for the stationary phase will spend more time in the column, resulting in longer retention times, while those with a higher affinity for the mobile phase will elute faster.

- **Adsorption:** In normal-phase HPLC, the separation is based on the adsorption of analytes onto the polar stationary phase. Compounds that strongly adsorb to the stationary phase will elute more slowly.
- **Ion Exchange:** In ion-exchange HPLC, analytes are separated based on their charge and their interaction with the charged groups on the stationary phase. Stronger ionic interactions result in longer retention times.
- **Size Exclusion:** In size-exclusion HPLC, also known as gel filtration or gel permeation chromatography, molecules are separated based on their size. Larger molecules pass through the column more quickly because they cannot enter the pores of the stationary phase, while smaller molecules are retained longer as they diffuse into the pores.

2.2 Retention Time (tR):

- **Definition:** Retention time (tR) is the time it takes for an analyte to pass through the column and reach the detector. Each compound has a characteristic retention time under specific conditions, which is used for identification purposes.
- **Factors Affecting Retention Time:** Retention time is influenced by several factors, including the composition of the mobile phase, the type of stationary phase, the flow rate of the mobile phase, the temperature of the column, and the nature of the analytes.

3. High Pressure and Efficiency:
3.1 Role of High Pressure:

- **Increased Efficiency:** In HPLC, high pressure is applied to the mobile phase to push it through the densely packed column at a high flow rate. This pressure, typically in the range of 400-6000 psi (pounds per square inch), increases the efficiency of the separation by reducing the time the analytes spend in the column and by minimizing band broadening.
- **Narrower Peaks:** The use of high pressure results in narrower peaks and better resolution, allowing for the separation of closely related compounds with high precision.

3.2 Van Deemter Equation:

- **Theoretical Plates:** The efficiency of an HPLC column is often described in terms of the number of theoretical plates (N), a concept borrowed from distillation theory. The higher the number of theoretical plates, the more efficient the column.
- **Van Deemter Equation:** The Van Deemter equation describes the relationship between flow rate and column efficiency, accounting for factors such as eddy diffusion, longitudinal diffusion, and mass transfer. It helps in optimizing the flow rate to achieve the best resolution.

4. Detection Methods:
4.1 Common Detectors:

- **UV-Visible Detector:** The most commonly used detector in HPLC, which measures the absorbance of analytes at specific wavelengths. It is suitable for compounds that absorb UV or visible light, such as aromatic compounds and conjugated systems.
- **Fluorescence Detector:** More sensitive than UV detectors, the fluorescence detector measures the emission of light by analytes after excitation. It is ideal for detecting trace amounts of fluorescent compounds or for analyzing compounds that can be derivatized to become fluorescent.
- **Refractive Index Detector (RID):** Measures changes in the refractive index of the mobile phase as analytes elute. It is a universal detector suitable for compounds that do not absorb UV light, such as sugars and polymers.
- **Mass Spectrometry (MS):** Provides both qualitative and quantitative information by detecting analytes based on their mass-to-charge ratio (m/z). HPLC-MS is highly sensitive and specific, making it suitable for complex mixtures, including biomolecules and environmental samples.

4.2 Sensitivity and Selectivity:

- **Sensitivity:** The sensitivity of the detector determines its ability to detect low concentrations of analytes. Fluorescence and MS detectors are generally more sensitive than UV-Visible and RID detectors.

- **Selectivity:** Selectivity refers to the detector's ability to distinguish between different analytes. MS offers the highest selectivity due to its ability to differentiate compounds based on their molecular weight and fragmentation patterns.

Modes of Separation: Normal and Reverse Phase

In High-Performance Liquid Chromatography (HPLC), the mode of separation is determined by the polarity of the stationary phase and the mobile phase used in the process. The two primary modes of separation in HPLC are Normal Phase (NP-HPLC) and Reverse Phase (RP-HPLC). Each mode has distinct characteristics and is suited for different types of analytes, depending on their polarity and the nature of the separation required.

1. Normal Phase HPLC (NP-HPLC)

1.1 Principles of Normal Phase HPLC:

- **Stationary Phase:** In Normal Phase HPLC, the stationary phase is polar, typically consisting of unmodified silica particles or silica particles modified with polar groups such as amino, cyano, or diol groups. These polar stationary phases interact strongly with polar analytes through mechanisms such as hydrogen bonding, dipole-dipole interactions, and adsorption.
- **Mobile Phase:** The mobile phase in NP-HPLC is non-polar or moderately polar, usually consisting of organic solvents such as hexane, chloroform, ethyl acetate, or a mixture of these solvents. The non-polar mobile phase interacts weakly with polar analytes, allowing them to spend more time interacting with the polar stationary phase.

1.2 Mechanism of Separation:

- **Polarity-Based Separation:** In NP-HPLC, the separation of analytes is based on their polarity. Polar compounds interact more strongly with the polar stationary phase, leading to longer retention times, while non-polar compounds have weaker interactions and elute more quickly. As a result, compounds are separated based on their differential affinity for the stationary and mobile phases.
- **Elution Order:** Typically, non-polar compounds elute first, followed by increasingly polar compounds. The elution order reflects the relative

strength of the interactions between the analytes and the stationary phase.

1.3 Applications of Normal Phase HPLC:

- **Separation of Polar Compounds:** NP-HPLC is particularly well-suited for the separation of polar compounds that may not interact well with non-polar stationary phases. It is commonly used for the separation of vitamins, amino acids, nucleotides, and other polar small molecules.
- **Chiral Separation:** NP-HPLC is also used in chiral separations, where the stationary phase contains chiral selectors that differentiate between enantiomers based on their interactions with the polar stationary phase.
- **Natural Product Analysis:** NP-HPLC is employed in the analysis of natural products, such as plant extracts, where the compounds of interest often have polar functional groups.

2. Reverse Phase HPLC (RP-HPLC)
2.1 Principles of Reverse Phase HPLC:

- **Stationary Phase:** In Reverse Phase HPLC, the stationary phase is non-polar or weakly polar. The most common stationary phases are silica particles modified with non-polar alkyl chains, such as C18 (octadecylsilane), C8 (octylsilane), or phenyl groups. These non-polar stationary phases interact strongly with non-polar analytes.
- **Mobile Phase:** The mobile phase in RP-HPLC is polar or moderately polar, typically consisting of water or aqueous buffers mixed with organic solvents like methanol, acetonitrile, or tetrahydrofuran (THF). The polar mobile phase interacts more strongly with polar analytes, reducing their interaction with the stationary phase.

2.2 Mechanism of Separation:

- **Hydrophobic Interaction:** In RP-HPLC, separation is primarily based on hydrophobic interactions between the analytes and the non-polar stationary phase. Non-polar compounds have stronger interactions with the stationary phase, resulting in longer retention times, while polar compounds interact more with the polar mobile phase and elute faster.

- **Elution Order:** In RP-HPLC, polar compounds elute first, followed by non-polar compounds. The strength of the interaction between the analytes and the stationary phase determines their elution order, with more hydrophobic compounds being retained longer.

2.3 Applications of Reverse Phase HPLC:

- **Separation of Non-Polar and Moderately Polar Compounds:** RP-HPLC is the most widely used mode of separation in HPLC, suitable for a broad range of analytes, including non-polar and moderately polar compounds. It is commonly used in pharmaceutical analysis, including the separation and quantification of drugs, metabolites, and impurities.
- **Biomolecule Analysis:** RP-HPLC is frequently used for the analysis of biomolecules such as peptides, proteins, and nucleic acids, as these molecules often have hydrophobic regions that interact well with non-polar stationary phases.
- **Food and Beverage Analysis:** RP-HPLC is used to analyze compounds in food and beverages, such as caffeine, flavor compounds, and preservatives. The method is also employed in the analysis of lipids, fatty acids, and vitamins.

2.4 Advantages of RP-HPLC:

- **Versatility:** RP-HPLC is highly versatile and can separate a wide range of compounds, making it the most commonly used mode of HPLC.
- **Reproducibility:** The use of aqueous-organic mobile phases allows for better control and reproducibility of separations, which is critical in method development and routine analysis.
- **Compatibility with Detectors:** RP-HPLC is compatible with various detectors, including UV-Visible, fluorescence, and mass spectrometry, enhancing its applicability in diverse analytical fields.

13.2 Instrumentation of HPLC
Pumps, Injectors, Columns, Detectors

The instrumentation of High-Performance Liquid Chromatography (HPLC) is designed to achieve precise, efficient, and reproducible separations of complex mixtures. Each component plays a critical role in ensuring the accuracy and reliability of the chromatographic process. The key components of an HPLC system include the pumps, injectors, columns, and detectors. Understanding the function and optimization of each component is essential for successful HPLC operation.

1. Pumps

1.1 Role of Pumps in HPLC:

- **Mobile Phase Delivery:** Pumps are responsible for delivering the mobile phase at a consistent flow rate and pressure through the HPLC system. This is essential for maintaining the separation efficiency and reproducibility of the chromatographic process.
- **High Pressure:** HPLC pumps operate at high pressures, typically ranging from 400 to 6000 psi (pounds per square inch), to push the mobile phase through the tightly packed chromatographic column. This high pressure is necessary to achieve fast and efficient separations, particularly when using small particle size columns.

1.2 Types of HPLC Pumps:

- **Constant Flow Pumps (Isocratic Pumps):** These pumps deliver the mobile phase at a constant flow rate, making them ideal for isocratic separations where the mobile phase composition remains unchanged throughout the analysis.
- **Gradient Pumps:** Gradient pumps can vary the composition of the mobile phase over time, enabling gradient elution. This type of pump is essential for complex separations where the polarity of the mobile phase needs to change to separate analytes with different retention times.

1.3 Features of HPLC Pumps:

- **Flow Rate Accuracy:** The accuracy of the flow rate is crucial for maintaining consistent retention times and peak areas. High-quality HPLC pumps are designed to deliver highly accurate and stable flow rates.
- **Pressure Stability:** Pumps must maintain stable pressure to ensure reproducible separations, especially when using long or narrow columns. Pressure fluctuations can lead to variations in retention time and peak shape.

2. Injectors
2.1 Purpose of the Injector:

- **Sample Introduction:** The injector is used to introduce the sample into the HPLC system. It must deliver the sample accurately and reproducibly to ensure consistent results. The sample is typically introduced into the mobile phase stream before it enters the column.

2.2 Types of Injectors:

- **Manual Injectors:** Manual injectors are operated by the user, who manually introduces the sample into the system using a syringe. While they offer simplicity and are less expensive, they require skill and consistency from the operator to ensure reproducibility.
- **Auto-Samplers:** Auto-samplers automate the injection process, allowing for high-throughput analysis and reducing variability associated with manual injections. They can handle multiple samples in sequence, improving laboratory efficiency and reproducibility.

2.3 Injection Volume:

- **Variable Injection Volumes:** Injectors can be adjusted to deliver different volumes of sample, typically ranging from a few microliters to several milliliters, depending on the sample concentration and the sensitivity required for the analysis.
- **Minimizing Sample Loss:** Injectors are designed to minimize sample loss during the injection process. Precision and accuracy in injection volume are critical for quantitation, especially when dealing with small sample amounts or low concentrations.

3. Columns
3.1 Role of the Column:

- **Separation of Analytes:** The column is the heart of the HPLC system, where the separation of analytes occurs. It contains the stationary phase, which interacts with the analytes as they pass through, leading to their differential retention and separation.

- **Column Composition:** Columns are typically made of stainless steel or PEEK (polyether ether ketone) and are packed with stationary phase particles. The choice of column material and stationary phase depends on the nature of the analytes and the type of separation required.

3.2 Types of HPLC Columns:

- **Reversed-Phase Columns:** The most commonly used columns in HPLC, typically packed with non-polar stationary phases such as C18 (octadecylsilane) or C8 (octylsilane). They are ideal for separating polar and moderately polar compounds using polar mobile phases.
- **Normal-Phase Columns:** Packed with polar stationary phases like bare silica or amino-modified silica, these columns are used for separating non-polar compounds with non-polar mobile phases.
- **Ion-Exchange Columns:** Contain charged groups that interact with oppositely charged analytes, making them suitable for separating ionic compounds, such as proteins, peptides, and nucleotides.
- **Size-Exclusion Columns:** Used for separating molecules based on size, with larger molecules eluting first. These columns are commonly used in the analysis of polymers and biomolecules.

3.3 Column Dimensions:

- **Length and Diameter:** HPLC columns vary in length (typically 5 to 30 cm) and internal diameter (typically 2.1 to 4.6 mm). Longer columns provide better resolution but require higher pressure, while shorter columns offer faster analysis times.
- **Particle Size:** The stationary phase particles in HPLC columns range from 3 to 10 micrometers in diameter. Smaller particle sizes offer higher efficiency and better resolution but also require higher pressure to maintain flow.

3.4 Temperature Control:

- **Column Oven:** The column is often housed in a temperature-controlled oven, which maintains a consistent temperature during the separation. Temperature control is important for reproducibility and can be used to optimize separation by influencing analyte interaction with the stationary phase.

4. Detectors
4.1 Purpose of the Detector:

- **Detection of Analytes:** The detector is responsible for identifying and quantifying the analytes as they elute from the column. The choice of detector depends on the nature of the analytes and the required sensitivity and selectivity.

4.2 Types of HPLC Detectors:

- **UV-Visible Detector:** The most common detector in HPLC, which measures the absorbance of analytes at specific wavelengths. It is widely used for detecting compounds that absorb UV or visible light, such as organic molecules with conjugated double bonds.
- **Fluorescence Detector:** A highly sensitive detector that measures the fluorescence emitted by analytes after excitation with a specific wavelength of light. It is ideal for detecting compounds that are naturally fluorescent or can be derivatized to fluoresce.
- **Refractive Index Detector (RID):** Measures changes in the refractive index of the mobile phase as analytes elute. It is a universal detector, suitable for compounds that do not absorb UV light, such as sugars, alcohols, and lipids.
- **Mass Spectrometry (MS) Detector:** Provides detailed information on the molecular weight and structure of analytes based on their mass-to-charge ratio (m/z). HPLC-MS is highly sensitive and specific, making it ideal for complex mixtures and trace analysis.

4.3 Detector Sensitivity and Selectivity:

- **Sensitivity:** Sensitivity refers to the detector's ability to detect small amounts of analytes. Fluorescence and MS detectors are among the most sensitive, suitable for trace analysis.
- **Selectivity:** Selectivity is the detector's ability to distinguish between different analytes. MS detectors offer the highest selectivity, allowing for the identification of specific compounds within complex mixtures.

13.3 Applications of HPLC

Drug Analysis and Purity Testing

High-Performance Liquid Chromatography (HPLC) is an essential analytical technique widely used in the pharmaceutical industry for drug analysis and purity testing. The precision, accuracy, and versatility of HPLC make it an indispensable tool for ensuring the quality, safety, and efficacy of pharmaceutical products. Below are the key applications of HPLC in drug analysis and purity testing.

1. Drug Analysis

1.1 Identification and Quantification of Active Pharmaceutical Ingredients (APIs):

- **Role in Quality Control:** HPLC is used to identify and quantify the active pharmaceutical ingredients (APIs) in drug formulations. This ensures that the correct dosage of the API is present in each batch of the product, which is critical for the drug's therapeutic effectiveness.
- **Method Development:** Pharmaceutical companies develop and validate HPLC methods for the routine analysis of APIs. These methods are tailored to the specific chemical properties of the API, such as polarity, solubility, and stability, ensuring accurate quantification.
- **Stability Testing:** HPLC is employed to monitor the stability of APIs over time under various environmental conditions (e.g., temperature, humidity, light). Stability testing ensures that the drug remains effective and safe throughout its shelf life.

1.2 Analysis of Drug Metabolites:

- **Pharmacokinetics and Bioavailability Studies:** HPLC is used to analyze drug metabolites in biological samples, such as blood, urine, and plasma. These studies are crucial for understanding the pharmacokinetics (absorption, distribution, metabolism, and excretion) and bioavailability of drugs, helping to optimize dosing regimens and improve therapeutic outcomes.
- **Metabolite Profiling:** HPLC allows for the separation and identification of drug metabolites, which can provide insights into the metabolic pathways of drugs and help predict potential drug interactions and side effects.

1.3 Analysis of Complex Drug Formulations:

- **Combination Drugs:** Many pharmaceutical products contain multiple APIs. HPLC is used to analyze these complex formulations, ensuring that each API is present at the correct concentration and that there is no interaction between them that could affect efficacy or safety.
- **Drug Delivery Systems:** HPLC is also used to analyze advanced drug delivery systems, such as sustained-release tablets, transdermal patches, and liposomal formulations. This analysis ensures that the drug is released at the desired rate and maintains its therapeutic activity.

2. Purity Testing
2.1 Impurity Profiling:

- **Detection of Impurities:** HPLC is highly sensitive and can detect and quantify impurities at very low levels, often down to parts per million (ppm) or even parts per billion (ppb). Impurity profiling is essential for ensuring that the levels of impurities in drug products are within acceptable limits set by regulatory authorities.
- **Identification of Degradation Products:** During manufacturing, storage, or use, drugs can degrade to form impurities. HPLC is used to identify and quantify these degradation products, which is critical for assessing the drug's stability and ensuring it remains safe and effective over time.
- **Regulatory Compliance:** Regulatory agencies, such as the U.S. Food and Drug Administration (FDA) and the European Medicines Agency (EMA), require that pharmaceutical companies submit detailed impurity profiles for new drug products. HPLC plays a central role in generating the data needed to meet these regulatory requirements.

2.2 Purity Assessment of APIs:

- **Batch-to-Batch Consistency:** HPLC is used to ensure that the purity of APIs remains consistent from batch to batch during production. This is vital for maintaining the quality and therapeutic efficacy of the final drug product.
- **Process Control:** During the synthesis of APIs, HPLC is employed to monitor the purity at various stages of the manufacturing process. This helps in optimizing the process and ensuring that the final product meets

the required purity specifications.

- **Isolation of Impurities:** In cases where impurities are detected, HPLC can be used in conjunction with preparative chromatography to isolate and identify the impurities. This information is then used to refine the manufacturing process and improve the purity of the API.

2.3 Analysis of Excipients:

- **Excipients Quality Control:** Excipients are inactive substances used in drug formulations to provide bulk, stability, or other functional properties. HPLC is used to analyze the purity of excipients to ensure they do not contain contaminants that could affect the safety or efficacy of the drug product.
- **Interaction Studies:** HPLC can also be used to study the interactions between APIs and excipients, ensuring that the excipients do not interfere with the stability or release profile of the drug.

3. Validation and Method Development
3.1 Method Validation:

- **Accuracy and Precision:** HPLC methods used for drug analysis and purity testing must be validated to ensure they provide accurate and precise results. Validation includes assessing parameters such as linearity, sensitivity, specificity, repeatability, and robustness.
- **Regulatory Standards:** Method validation is carried out according to guidelines provided by regulatory agencies, such as the International Council for Harmonisation of Technical Requirements for Pharmaceuticals for Human Use (ICH). Compliance with these guidelines is mandatory for the approval of pharmaceutical products.

3.2 Robustness Testing:

- **Consistency Across Conditions:** Robustness testing evaluates the performance of an HPLC method under varying conditions, such as changes in pH, temperature, flow rate, or mobile phase composition. This ensures that the method produces reliable results even when minor variations occur during routine analysis.

- **Transferability:** Robust HPLC methods can be transferred between laboratories or scaled up from analytical to preparative chromatography, ensuring consistency and reliability across different settings.

Bioavailability Studies

High-Performance Liquid Chromatography (HPLC) plays a pivotal role in bioavailability studies, which are crucial for understanding the pharmacokinetics of a drug and ensuring its therapeutic efficacy. Bioavailability refers to the proportion of a drug that enters the systemic circulation in an active form after administration, thereby becoming available to exert its intended biological effect. HPLC is employed to accurately quantify the drug and its metabolites in biological matrices, such as blood, plasma, urine, and tissues, throughout the study.

1. Importance of Bioavailability Studies

1.1 Determining Drug Absorption:

- **Oral vs. Intravenous Administration:** Bioavailability studies are essential to compare the absorption of a drug when administered orally (where absorption can be incomplete due to factors like first-pass metabolism) versus intravenous administration, which provides 100% bioavailability. HPLC quantifies the concentration of the drug in plasma over time, allowing for the calculation of key pharmacokinetic parameters such as the area under the curve (AUC), maximum concentration (Cmax), and time to reach maximum concentration (Tmax).
- **Formulation Development:** The data obtained from bioavailability studies help in optimizing the formulation of the drug to enhance its absorption and ensure consistent therapeutic effects. For example, if a drug shows low bioavailability, formulation scientists might develop strategies such as using prodrugs, nanoparticles, or lipid-based delivery systems to improve absorption.

1.2 Assessing Drug Efficacy and Safety:

- **Therapeutic Monitoring:** By analyzing the drug concentration in the bloodstream, HPLC helps determine whether a drug reaches its therapeutic concentration without exceeding toxic levels. This ensures that the drug is effective while minimizing the risk of adverse effects.

- **Dose Adjustment:** The results from bioavailability studies can lead to adjustments in the dosing regimen to achieve the desired therapeutic effect. For example, a drug with low bioavailability might require a higher dose or more frequent administration to maintain effective blood levels.

1.3 Regulatory Approval:

- **Generic Drug Approval:** For generic drugs, bioavailability studies are conducted to demonstrate bioequivalence with the brand-name reference product. HPLC is used to compare the pharmacokinetic profiles of the generic and reference drugs, ensuring that the generic version provides the same therapeutic effect as the original.
- **New Drug Applications:** For new drug applications, bioavailability data is required by regulatory authorities such as the FDA or EMA to support the approval of the drug. These studies provide essential information on how the drug behaves in the human body.

2. Role of HPLC in Bioavailability Studies
2.1 Quantification of Drug and Metabolites:

- **Accurate Measurement:** HPLC is renowned for its ability to accurately and precisely quantify drugs and their metabolites in complex biological matrices. This is critical in bioavailability studies, where the concentration of the drug must be monitored over time to assess its absorption, distribution, metabolism, and excretion (ADME) profiles.
- **Sample Preparation:** Biological samples are often complex and require careful preparation before analysis by HPLC. Techniques such as protein precipitation, liquid-liquid extraction, or solid-phase extraction are used to isolate the drug and its metabolites from plasma, urine, or other matrices.

2.2 Pharmacokinetic Analysis:

- **Data Collection:** HPLC is used to collect concentration data at various time points after drug administration. This data is then used to construct a pharmacokinetic profile, showing how the drug concentration changes over time.

- **Parameter Calculation:** From the HPLC data, key pharmacokinetic parameters are calculated, including:

  - **Area Under the Curve (AUC):** Represents the total drug exposure over time.
  - **Maximum Concentration (Cmax):** The highest concentration of the drug observed in plasma.
  - **Time to Maximum Concentration (Tmax):** The time it takes to reach Cmax.
  - **Half-Life (t1/2):** The time it takes for the plasma concentration of the drug to reduce by half.
  - **Clearance (CL):** The rate at which the drug is removed from the body.
  - **Volume of Distribution (Vd):** Indicates how extensively the drug is distributed in body tissues.

2.3 Bioequivalence Testing:

- **Comparative Studies:** In bioequivalence studies, HPLC is used to compare the pharmacokinetic profiles of two drug formulations (typically a generic and a brand-name drug). The goal is to demonstrate that the generic drug's bioavailability falls within an acceptable range (usually 80-125% of the reference drug) to be considered equivalent.
- **Statistical Analysis:** The concentration data obtained from HPLC is subjected to statistical analysis to determine if there are significant differences between the test and reference formulations. Bioequivalence ensures that the generic product is therapeutically interchangeable with the original.

2.4 Monitoring Metabolites:

- **Metabolic Profiling:** HPLC is used to monitor not only the parent drug but also its metabolites, which can be pharmacologically active or toxic. This is important for understanding the full pharmacokinetic profile of the drug and for ensuring that metabolites do not accumulate to harmful levels.
- **Metabolite Identification:** By using HPLC in combination with detectors like mass spectrometry (HPLC-MS), researchers can identify and

quantify specific metabolites, providing insights into the drug's metabolism and potential drug-drug interactions.

3. Challenges and Considerations in HPLC for Bioavailability Studies
3.1 Sensitivity and Selectivity:

- **Detection Limits:** The sensitivity of the HPLC method must be sufficient to detect low concentrations of the drug, especially during the later stages of the pharmacokinetic profile. Selective detectors like mass spectrometry can enhance the detection of specific analytes in complex matrices.
- **Matrix Effects:** Biological samples can contain endogenous compounds that interfere with the analysis. Careful method development and validation are required to minimize matrix effects and ensure accurate quantification.

3.2 Method Validation:

- **Regulatory Standards:** HPLC methods used in bioavailability studies must be validated according to regulatory guidelines (e.g., ICH guidelines) to ensure they are accurate, precise, and reproducible. Validation parameters include linearity, sensitivity, specificity, accuracy, precision, and robustness.
- **Stability Testing:** The stability of the drug and metabolites in biological matrices must be confirmed to ensure that the concentrations measured by HPLC accurately reflect the in vivo situation.

3.3 Sample Throughput:

- **High-Throughput Analysis:** Bioavailability studies often involve large numbers of samples collected over multiple time points. HPLC methods must be optimized for high-throughput analysis, allowing for the rapid and efficient processing of samples.

CHAPTER FOURTEEN

Ion Exchange Chromatography

14.1 Introduction to Ion Exchange Chromatography

Classification and Types of Ion Exchange Resins

Ion exchange chromatography (IEC) is a powerful and widely used analytical technique that separates ions and polar molecules based on their affinity to ion exchange resins. These resins contain charged functional groups that can exchange ions with the sample ions in a solution, facilitating the separation of different components. Ion exchange chromatography is commonly used in the purification of proteins, peptides, nucleic acids, and other biomolecules, as well as in water treatment and other industrial processes.

Classification of Ion Exchange Resins

Ion exchange resins are classified based on the nature of the charged functional groups attached to the polymer matrix. The two main types of ion exchange resins are cation exchange resins and anion exchange resins. These resins can be further categorized based on the strength of the ion exchange groups as either strong or weak exchangers.

1. Cation Exchange Resins

1.1 Definition:

- **Cation Exchange Resins:** Cation exchange resins contain negatively charged functional groups that can exchange their associated cations (positive ions) with cations in the sample solution. These resins are used to separate and purify positively charged molecules, such as metal ions, proteins, and peptides.

1.2 Types of Cation Exchange Resins:

- **Strong Cation Exchange Resins (SCX):**

  - **Functional Groups:** Strong cation exchange resins contain strong acidic functional groups, typically sulfonic acid groups ($-SO_3 H$). These groups are fully ionized across a wide pH range, making SCX resins effective for separating cations at varying pH levels.
  - **Applications:** SCX resins are commonly used in the separation of metal ions, basic proteins, and peptides. Due to their strong ion-exchange capacity, they are also used in industrial applications such as water softening and metal recovery.

- **Weak Cation Exchange Resins (WCX):**

  - **Functional Groups:** Weak cation exchange resins contain weak acidic functional groups, such as carboxylic acid groups ($-COOH$). These groups are only partially ionized depending on the pH of the solution, making WCX resins more sensitive to changes in pH.
  - **Applications:** WCX resins are used for the separation of weakly basic proteins and peptides. They are particularly useful when a controlled and gradual elution of bound cations is required, allowing for fine-tuned separations.

2. Anion Exchange Resins
2.1 Definition:

- **Anion Exchange Resins:** Anion exchange resins contain positively charged functional groups that can exchange their associated anions (negative ions) with anions in the sample solution. These resins are used to separate and purify negatively charged molecules, such as nucleic acids, proteins, and anions.

2.2 Types of Anion Exchange Resins:

- **Strong Anion Exchange Resins (SAX):**

  - **Functional Groups:** Strong anion exchange resins contain strong basic functional groups, typically quaternary ammonium groups ($-N^+ (CH_3)_3$). These groups are fully ionized across a wide pH range, making SAX resins effective for separating anions at different pH levels.

- ○ **Applications:** SAX resins are widely used in the separation of nucleic acids, acidic proteins, and inorganic anions. They are also employed in water treatment processes to remove anions such as chloride, sulfate, and nitrate.

- **Weak Anion Exchange Resins (WAX):**

  - ○ **Functional Groups:** Weak anion exchange resins contain weak basic functional groups, such as primary, secondary, or tertiary amines ($-NH_2$, -NHR, $-NR_2$). These groups are only partially ionized depending on the pH, allowing WAX resins to be more selective based on pH conditions.
  - ○ **Applications:** WAX resins are used for the separation of weakly acidic proteins, peptides, and other biomolecules. They are particularly useful for applications where a gentle elution of bound anions is desired, enabling precise control over the separation process.

Properties of Ion Exchange Resins
1. Polymer Matrix:

- **Structure:** The polymer matrix of ion exchange resins is typically made of cross-linked polystyrene or polymethacrylate, providing a stable and inert support for the functional groups. The degree of cross-linking affects the porosity, mechanical strength, and ion exchange capacity of the resin.
- **Porosity:** The porosity of the resin beads determines the accessibility of the functional groups to the ions in solution. Highly porous resins allow for faster ion exchange and are preferred for large biomolecules, while less porous resins offer greater selectivity for small ions.

2. Ion Exchange Capacity:

- **Measurement:** The ion exchange capacity of a resin is measured in milliequivalents per gram (meq/g) and represents the number of charged sites available for ion exchange. This capacity influences the resin's ability to bind and separate ions from a solution.

- **Optimization:** In practical applications, the ion exchange capacity must be optimized based on the sample type, target ions, and desired separation efficiency. Higher capacities allow for the separation of larger quantities of ions, while lower capacities may offer better selectivity.

3. Particle Size:

- **Influence on Separation:** The particle size of ion exchange resins affects the resolution and speed of the separation process. Smaller particles provide higher resolution due to increased surface area and more efficient ion exchange but may require higher pressure for flow through the column.
- **Choice of Particle Size:** In analytical applications, smaller particle sizes (5-10 micrometers) are preferred for high-resolution separations, while larger particles (20-100 micrometers) are often used in preparative and industrial applications for faster flow rates and higher sample throughput.

Applications of Ion Exchange Chromatography
1. Protein Purification:

- **Separation of Charged Proteins:** Ion exchange chromatography is widely used to separate proteins based on their net charge at a given pH. By adjusting the pH and ionic strength of the mobile phase, specific proteins can be selectively bound to or eluted from the ion exchange resin.
- **Process Optimization:** The choice between strong and weak ion exchange resins allows for tailored purification strategies, optimizing yield, purity, and recovery of target proteins.

2. Nucleic Acid Purification:

- **DNA and RNA Purification:** Anion exchange chromatography is commonly used for the purification of nucleic acids, including plasmid DNA, RNA, and oligonucleotides. SAX resins are particularly effective in binding negatively charged nucleic acids, enabling their separation from other cellular components.

- **High Purity:** This technique is essential for applications requiring high-purity nucleic acids, such as gene therapy, molecular cloning, and sequencing.

3. Water Treatment:

- **Removal of Contaminants:** Ion exchange resins are extensively used in water treatment to remove unwanted cations and anions, such as hardness ions (calcium and magnesium), heavy metals, and dissolved salts. The process improves water quality for industrial, municipal, and residential use.
- **Regeneration of Resins:** In water treatment, the resins can be regenerated by washing them with a concentrated solution of the counter-ion, restoring their ion exchange capacity for continued use.

4. Industrial Applications:

- **Chemical Production:** Ion exchange chromatography is used in the purification of chemicals, including the removal of ionic impurities from organic compounds and the recovery of valuable ions from industrial effluents.
- **Bioprocessing:** In bioprocessing, ion exchange chromatography is employed for the large-scale purification of biopharmaceuticals, enzymes, and other biologically active molecules, ensuring the final product meets stringent purity and quality standards.

Properties and Mechanism of Ion Exchange

Ion exchange chromatography (IEC) is a method that separates ions and polar molecules based on their charge properties and interactions with ion exchange resins. The properties and mechanism of ion exchange are fundamental to understanding how this technique can efficiently separate and purify various charged species, including proteins, peptides, nucleic acids, and inorganic ions.

1. Properties of Ion Exchange Resins

Ion exchange resins are the core components of ion exchange chromatography, and their properties determine the efficiency and specificity of the separation process. These properties include the type of ion exchange groups, ion exchange capacity, particle size, and the physical structure of the resin.

1.1 Type of Ion Exchange Groups:

- **Cation Exchange Resins:** These resins possess negatively charged functional groups (e.g., sulfonic acid or carboxylic acid) that attract and bind positively charged ions (cations) from the sample solution. The strength of the ion exchange interaction can vary depending on the pH and ionic strength of the mobile phase.
- **Anion Exchange Resins:** These resins contain positively charged functional groups (e.g., quaternary ammonium or amino groups) that bind negatively charged ions (anions). The binding affinity of anions to the resin is influenced by the pH and composition of the mobile phase.

1.2 Ion Exchange Capacity:

- **Definition:** Ion exchange capacity refers to the number of exchangeable ions that a resin can bind and is typically measured in milliequivalents per gram (meq/g) of dry resin. This capacity reflects the density of functional groups available for ion exchange and determines the resin's ability to separate and purify ions.
- **Factors Affecting Capacity:** The capacity of an ion exchange resin is influenced by factors such as the degree of cross-linking in the resin, the nature of the functional groups, and the ionic strength of the solution. Higher capacity resins are more effective for separating larger quantities of ions, while lower capacity resins may offer greater selectivity.

1.3 Particle Size and Porosity:

- **Particle Size:** The size of the resin particles affects the resolution and speed of the ion exchange process. Smaller particles provide a larger surface area for ion exchange, leading to higher resolution but requiring higher pressure for the mobile phase to flow through the column. Larger particles allow for faster flow rates but may result in lower resolution.
- **Porosity:** The porosity of the resin beads determines the accessibility of the functional groups to the ions in solution. Highly porous resins allow for faster ion exchange and are particularly useful for the separation of large biomolecules, such as proteins.

1.4 Physical Structure:

- **Matrix Composition:** The matrix of ion exchange resins is usually made of cross-linked polymers such as polystyrene or polymethacrylate. The degree of cross-linking affects the rigidity, swelling behavior, and mechanical strength of the resin, which are important for maintaining column stability and performance during repeated use.
- **Swelling Properties:** Ion exchange resins swell in the presence of water, which increases the accessibility of the functional groups to the ions in solution. The extent of swelling depends on the degree of cross-linking and the nature of the functional groups.

2. Mechanism of Ion Exchange

The mechanism of ion exchange involves the reversible exchange of ions between the ion exchange resin and the sample solution. This process is governed by the principles of electrostatic attraction, ion affinity, and equilibrium dynamics.

2.1 Electrostatic Attraction:

- **Binding of Ions:** The primary driving force for ion exchange is the electrostatic attraction between the charged functional groups on the resin and the oppositely charged ions in the sample solution. Cations are attracted to cation exchange resins, while anions are attracted to anion exchange resins.
- **Reversible Process:** Ion exchange is a reversible process, meaning that bound ions can be displaced by other ions with a higher affinity for the resin. This reversibility is key to the selective separation and elution of target ions during chromatography.

2.2 Selectivity and Ion Affinity:

- **Selectivity Coefficient:** The selectivity of the resin for different ions is quantified by the selectivity coefficient, which describes the relative affinity of the resin for one ion over another. Ions with higher charge density or smaller hydrated radius typically have higher affinity for the resin.
- **Influence of pH and Ionic Strength:** The affinity of ions for the resin can be modulated by adjusting the pH and ionic strength of the mobile phase.

For example, increasing the ionic strength can reduce the binding of weakly bound ions, facilitating their elution from the column. Similarly, pH changes can alter the ionization state of the functional groups on the resin and the sample ions, affecting the binding strength.

2.3 Equilibrium Dynamics:

- **Ion Exchange Equilibrium:** The ion exchange process reaches an equilibrium state, where the rate of ions binding to the resin equals the rate of ions being displaced and eluted. The position of this equilibrium is influenced by the concentration of ions in the mobile phase, the ion exchange capacity of the resin, and the selectivity of the resin for different ions.
- **Isotherms:** The relationship between the concentration of ions in the solution and the amount of ions bound to the resin is described by ion exchange isotherms. These isotherms provide insights into the binding capacity and efficiency of the resin under different conditions.

2.4 Elution of Bound Ions:

- **Gradient Elution:** In ion exchange chromatography, bound ions are typically eluted by gradually increasing the concentration of a competing ion in the mobile phase or by changing the pH. This technique, known as gradient elution, allows for the selective elution of ions based on their affinity for the resin.
- **Stepwise Elution:** Alternatively, stepwise elution can be used, where the mobile phase composition is changed in discrete steps to sequentially elute ions with different binding strengths. This approach is useful for separating ions with distinct affinities for the resin.

3. Applications of Ion Exchange Mechanism
3.1 Protein Purification:

- **Charge-Based Separation:** Ion exchange chromatography is extensively used to purify proteins based on their net charge at a given pH. By selecting the appropriate ion exchange resin and optimizing the pH and ionic strength, specific proteins can be selectively bound and eluted, achieving high-purity preparations.

- **Isoelectric Focusing:** The isoelectric point (pI) of a protein determines its charge at a specific pH, making ion exchange chromatography a powerful tool for separating proteins with different pIs.

3.2 Nucleic Acid Purification:

- **Separation of DNA and RNA:** Anion exchange chromatography is widely used for purifying nucleic acids, including DNA and RNA, based on their negative charge. Strong anion exchange resins are particularly effective in binding nucleic acids, which can then be eluted by increasing the salt concentration or altering the pH.
- **High-Purity Applications:** The ability to achieve high-purity nucleic acid preparations makes ion exchange chromatography indispensable in applications such as gene therapy, molecular cloning, and diagnostic testing.

3.3 Industrial Applications:

- **Water Softening and Purification:** Ion exchange resins are commonly used in water treatment to remove hardness ions (calcium and magnesium) and other contaminants, improving water quality for industrial and residential use.
- **Chemical Production:** Ion exchange chromatography is used in the chemical industry for the purification of organic compounds, removal of ionic impurities, and recovery of valuable ions from process streams.

14.2 Methodology of Ion Exchange Chromatography
Sample Preparation

Sample preparation is a critical step in ion exchange chromatography (IEC) to ensure accurate, efficient, and reproducible separation of target molecules. Proper sample preparation helps to maintain the integrity of the sample, optimize the interaction with the ion exchange resin, and prevent issues such as column clogging or poor resolution. Below are the key aspects of sample preparation for ion exchange chromatography.

1. Buffer Selection and Preparation
1.1 Importance of Buffering the Sample:

- **Maintaining pH:** The pH of the sample is crucial because it influences the charge of the target molecules and the ion exchange resin. Proper buffering ensures that the pH is consistent, allowing for optimal interaction between the sample and the resin. The buffer should be chosen based on the pH range in which the target analytes are most stable and maintain their desired charge.
- **Buffer Capacity:** The buffer used should have a high capacity to resist pH changes during the chromatographic process, particularly when dealing with samples that might affect the pH of the solution.

1.2 Common Buffers:

- **Phosphate Buffers:** Widely used in ion exchange chromatography due to their effective buffering capacity in the pH range of 6-8, which is suitable for many biological molecules such as proteins and nucleic acids.
- **Tris Buffers:** Commonly used for protein separation, particularly when the pH needs to be in the range of 7-9. Tris buffers are often used in combination with other reagents to optimize protein stability.
- **Acetate Buffers:** Typically used in the pH range of 4-6, making them suitable for the separation of acidic proteins or peptides.
- **Preparation:** Buffers should be prepared with high-purity water and filtered to remove particulates. The ionic strength of the buffer should be adjusted according to the requirements of the ion exchange process, as higher ionic strengths can reduce the binding of weakly interacting ions.

2. Sample Clarification
2.1 Filtration:

- **Removing Particulates:** Before loading the sample onto the ion exchange column, it is important to remove any particulates that might clog the column or interfere with the separation process. Filtration through a 0.22 or 0.45 micrometer filter is commonly used to achieve this.
- **Sterilization:** For biological samples, especially those containing proteins or nucleic acids, sterile filtration can prevent microbial contamination and degradation of the sample during the separation process.

2.2 Centrifugation:

- **Pelleting Debris:** Centrifugation is another method to clarify the sample by pelleting cellular debris, precipitates, or other particulates. This is particularly important when working with crude biological extracts or cell lysates.
- **Supernatant Collection:** After centrifugation, the clear supernatant containing the target analytes is carefully collected and may be further processed, such as through filtration, to ensure that it is free of particulates.

3. Adjustment of Ionic Strength and pH
3.1 pH Adjustment:

- **Maintaining Desired Charge:** The pH of the sample may need to be adjusted to ensure that the target molecules have the appropriate charge for interaction with the ion exchange resin. For example, proteins should be in a pH environment that is above or below their isoelectric point (pI) to ensure they carry a net charge.
- **pH Titration:** pH can be adjusted using small volumes of acid or base, with careful monitoring using a pH meter. The chosen pH should align with the buffer system used in the chromatographic process.

3.2 Ionic Strength Adjustment:

- **Enhancing Binding:** The ionic strength of the sample should be optimized to facilitate the binding of the target analytes to the resin. In some cases, reducing the ionic strength of the sample can enhance binding to the resin, while in other cases, increasing the ionic strength may be necessary to weaken non-specific interactions.
- **Dialysis or Desalting:** If the sample contains salts or other components that interfere with the binding process, dialysis or desalting may be performed to reduce the ionic strength. This can be done using dialysis membranes or desalting columns, which help remove small ions while retaining the larger target molecules.

4. Sample Concentration
4.1 Concentration Techniques:

- **Lyophilization (Freeze-Drying):** This technique is used to concentrate samples by removing water under vacuum, resulting in a dry powder that can be reconstituted in a smaller volume. It is particularly useful for concentrating large volumes of dilute samples.
- **Ultrafiltration:** Ultrafiltration uses membranes with specific molecular weight cut-offs to concentrate the sample by removing solvents and small molecules while retaining the larger target molecules. It is commonly used for concentrating proteins and nucleic acids.

4.2 Avoiding Sample Overloading:

- **Optimal Concentration:** The sample should be concentrated to an optimal level that ensures efficient binding to the resin without overloading the column. Overloading can lead to poor resolution, broad peaks, and incomplete separation.
- **Volume Considerations:** The volume of the sample should be appropriate for the size of the ion exchange column. Loading a large volume of dilute sample can result in dilution of the analytes as they pass through the column, reducing the efficiency of the separation.

5. Pre-Equilibration of the Column
5.1 Equilibration with Buffer:

- **Buffer Matching:** Before loading the sample onto the ion exchange column, the column should be equilibrated with the buffer that matches the pH and ionic strength conditions of the sample. This ensures that the column environment is conducive to the binding of target analytes.
- **Column Conditioning:** Equilibration is typically done by passing several column volumes of buffer through the column until the effluent matches the desired pH and ionic strength of the buffer. This step is crucial to avoid sudden changes in conditions that could affect the binding of the analytes.

5.2 Sample Loading:

- **Gentle Loading:** The sample should be loaded onto the column gently to avoid disturbing the resin bed. This can be achieved using a peristaltic pump or gravity flow, depending on the scale and requirements of the separation.

- **Uniform Distribution:** Ensuring uniform distribution of the sample across the column is important for achieving consistent interaction with the resin and maximizing binding efficiency.

Elution Techniques in Ion Exchange Chromatography

Elution is a critical step in ion exchange chromatography (IEC) where bound ions or molecules are selectively removed from the ion exchange resin and collected for further analysis or use. The choice of elution technique depends on the nature of the target molecules, the type of ion exchange resin, and the specific goals of the separation. Below are the common elution techniques used in ion exchange chromatography.

1. Gradient Elution

1.1 Principle of Gradient Elution:

- **Continuous Change:** Gradient elution involves a continuous change in the composition of the mobile phase, typically by increasing the concentration of a counter-ion (such as salt) or altering the pH. This gradually decreases the affinity of the bound ions or molecules for the resin, leading to their sequential elution from the column.
- **Resolution Improvement:** Gradient elution is particularly useful for separating mixtures of compounds with varying affinities for the resin. By gradually changing the elution conditions, closely related species can be resolved more effectively.

1.2 Salt Gradient:

- **Increasing Ionic Strength:** In a salt gradient, the concentration of a salt (e.g., NaCl or KCl) in the mobile phase is gradually increased. As the ionic strength increases, it competes with the bound ions for the exchange sites on the resin, leading to the elution of ions with weaker binding affinities first, followed by those with stronger affinities.
- **Common Applications:** This technique is widely used in the purification of proteins, peptides, and nucleic acids, where the target molecules are eluted in order of increasing affinity to the resin.

1.3 pH Gradient:

- **Changing pH:** A pH gradient involves gradually altering the pH of the mobile phase. This changes the charge on the target molecules and/or the functional groups on the resin, affecting their binding affinity. As the pH shifts, molecules with different isoelectric points (pI) or ionization properties are eluted at different times.
- **Application in Protein Purification:** pH gradient elution is particularly useful for the separation of proteins, where slight changes in pH can lead to significant changes in protein charge, facilitating their elution from the column.

2. Stepwise Elution
2.1 Principle of Stepwise Elution:

- **Discrete Steps:** In stepwise elution, the composition of the mobile phase is changed in discrete steps rather than continuously. Each step involves a sudden increase in salt concentration or a shift in pH, leading to the elution of bound ions or molecules with specific affinities.
- **Simplicity and Control:** Stepwise elution is simpler to implement than gradient elution and allows for precise control over the separation process. It is particularly useful when a clear separation between different fractions is desired.

2.2 Salt Step Elution:

- **Sequential Salt Addition:** In this method, the mobile phase composition is changed by sequentially adding higher concentrations of salt. Each step is designed to elute a specific group of molecules with similar binding affinities, resulting in the collection of distinct fractions.
- **Application in Industrial Processes:** Stepwise salt elution is often used in large-scale industrial processes where simplicity and cost-effectiveness are important. It allows for the efficient separation of target molecules in a controlled manner.

2.3 pH Step Elution:

- **pH Shifts:** Similar to salt step elution, pH step elution involves discrete changes in the pH of the mobile phase. This technique is particularly effective for eluting molecules with specific pH-dependent binding properties, such as proteins with well-defined pI values.

- **Purification of Biomolecules:** pH step elution is commonly used in the purification of proteins and other biomolecules, allowing for the collection of fractions that are enriched in specific target molecules.

3. Isocratic Elution
3.1 Principle of Isocratic Elution:

- **Constant Conditions:** Isocratic elution involves using a mobile phase with a constant composition throughout the chromatographic run. There are no changes in ionic strength or pH, and the molecules are eluted based on their inherent affinities for the ion exchange resin under the given conditions.
- **Simplicity:** Isocratic elution is straightforward to implement and is often used when the sample contains a narrow range of components with similar binding properties.

3.2 Applications:

- **Simple Mixtures:** Isocratic elution is most effective for separating simple mixtures where the components have similar affinities for the resin. It is also used when the target molecule is known to have a specific, predictable elution profile under the constant conditions.
- **Routine Analysis:** This technique is often employed in routine analytical processes where the focus is on reproducibility and ease of use rather than high resolution.

4. Displacement Elution
4.1 Principle of Displacement Elution:

- **Displacing Agents:** In displacement elution, a high-affinity displacing agent is introduced into the mobile phase. This agent has a stronger affinity for the ion exchange sites on the resin than the target molecules, effectively displacing them and causing their elution.
- **High Resolution:** Displacement elution can achieve high resolution because the displacing agent pushes the bound ions off the resin in a well-defined order, leading to the sharp separation of different components.

4.2 Applications:

- **Purification of Rare or Valuable Compounds:** Displacement elution is particularly useful when purifying rare or valuable compounds that require a high degree of separation purity. It is often used in the pharmaceutical industry for the purification of high-value biomolecules.
- **Complex Mixtures:** This technique is effective for separating complex mixtures where the target molecules have varying affinities for the resin, and high-resolution separation is needed.

5. Affinity Elution
5.1 Principle of Affinity Elution:

- **Specific Ligands:** Affinity elution involves using a ligand or a specific agent that has a strong affinity for the target molecule. The ligand binds to the target molecule, reducing its affinity for the ion exchange resin and facilitating its elution.
- **High Specificity:** Affinity elution is highly specific, as the elution is driven by the interaction between the ligand and the target molecule. This method is often used in conjunction with ion exchange chromatography for the purification of proteins, enzymes, and antibodies.

5.2 Applications:

- **Protein Purification:** Affinity elution is commonly used in the purification of proteins, where ligands such as antibodies, enzyme inhibitors, or metal ions are used to specifically elute the target protein from the ion exchange resin.
- **Biochemical Studies:** This technique is also used in biochemical studies where the interaction between a ligand and its target molecule is of interest, allowing for the selective isolation of the molecule for further analysis.

14.3 Applications of Ion Exchange Chromatography
Water Softening

Water softening is one of the most common and practical applications of ion exchange chromatography. This process is used to remove hardness-causing ions, primarily calcium (Ca^{2+}) and magnesium (Mg^{2+}), from water. Hard water can cause scale buildup in pipes, boilers, and household appliances, reducing their efficiency and lifespan. The ion exchange method provides an effective solution to this problem by exchanging hardness ions with sodium ions, thereby softening the water.

1. Principle of Water Softening Using Ion Exchange

1.1 Hardness of Water:

- **Calcium and Magnesium Ions:** Hard water contains high concentrations of calcium and magnesium ions, which react with soap to form insoluble precipitates, reducing the soap's effectiveness. These ions also precipitate out as scale in heating systems, leading to blockages and reduced efficiency.

- **Temporary and Permanent Hardness:** Water hardness can be temporary (due to bicarbonates of calcium and magnesium) or permanent (due to sulfates, chlorides, and nitrates of calcium and magnesium). Ion exchange chromatography is effective in removing both types of hardness.

1.2 Ion Exchange Process:

- **Cation Exchange Resins:** The ion exchange resin used in water softening is typically a cation exchange resin with sulfonic acid groups ($-SO_3\ H^+$) that are strongly acidic and fully ionized. These resins are initially in the sodium (Na^+) form, meaning they are saturated with sodium ions.

- **Exchange Mechanism:** As hard water passes through the ion exchange resin, calcium (Ca^{2+}) and magnesium (Mg^{2+}) ions in the water are exchanged for sodium ions (Na^+) from the resin. The hardness ions are retained on the resin, and the water exiting the system is softened, containing increased levels of sodium ions instead of calcium and magnesium ions.

$$2R\text{-}Na^+ + Ca^{2+} \rightarrow R_2 - Ca^{2+} + 2Na^+$$

$$2R\text{-}Na^+ + Mg^{2+} \rightarrow R_2 - Mg^{2+} + 2Na^+$$

1.3 Regeneration of the Resin:

- **Regeneration Process:** Over time, the resin becomes saturated with calcium and magnesium ions, reducing its effectiveness. To restore its softening capacity, the resin is regenerated by washing it with a concentrated solution of sodium chloride (NaCl), commonly known as brine. The high concentration of sodium ions in the brine displaces the calcium and magnesium ions from the resin, which are then flushed away with the excess brine.
- **Reusability:** After regeneration, the resin is restored to its original sodium form and can be reused for further water softening cycles. This regeneration process is a key advantage of ion exchange resins, making them cost-effective for long-term use.

2. Advantages of Ion Exchange Water Softening
2.1 Effective Removal of Hardness Ions:

- **High Efficiency:** Ion exchange is highly efficient in removing calcium and magnesium ions from water, reducing the hardness to very low levels and preventing scale formation in plumbing and appliances.
- **Consistent Water Quality:** The process provides consistent water quality, ensuring that the softened water remains within the desired hardness range throughout its use.

2.2 Long-Term Cost Savings:

- **Extended Appliance Lifespan:** By preventing scale buildup, water softening extends the lifespan of water heaters, boilers, dishwashers, and other appliances, reducing maintenance and replacement costs.
- **Reduced Energy Consumption:** Softened water improves the efficiency of heating systems, leading to lower energy consumption and cost savings over time.

2.3 Environmental and User Benefits:

- **Reduced Soap and Detergent Use:** Softened water improves the effectiveness of soaps and detergents, reducing the amount needed for cleaning tasks. This not only saves money but also reduces the environmental impact of detergent use.

- **Improved Comfort:** Softened water is more pleasant for bathing and washing, leaving skin and hair feeling softer and less prone to irritation caused by hard water minerals.

3. Industrial and Domestic Applications
3.1 Residential Water Softeners:

- **Home Water Softening Systems:** Ion exchange-based water softeners are commonly installed in homes to provide softened water for daily use. These systems are compact, easy to maintain, and designed for continuous operation, with automatic regeneration cycles.
- **Point-of-Entry Systems:** Residential water softeners are typically installed at the point of entry, where the water supply enters the home, ensuring that all the water used in the house is softened.

3.2 Commercial and Industrial Applications:

- **Boiler Feedwater Treatment:** In industrial settings, ion exchange water softeners are used to treat boiler feedwater, preventing scale formation in boilers and heat exchangers, which can lead to inefficiencies and costly repairs.
- **Food and Beverage Industry:** Softened water is essential in the food and beverage industry, where consistent water quality is required for product consistency and equipment maintenance.
- **Cooling Towers:** In cooling towers, softened water helps prevent scale buildup on heat exchange surfaces, improving the efficiency of the cooling process and reducing energy consumption.

4. Limitations and Considerations
4.1 Sodium Content in Softened Water:

- **Increased Sodium Levels:** The ion exchange process replaces calcium and magnesium ions with sodium ions, increasing the sodium content in the softened water. While this is generally not a concern for most uses, it may be an issue for individuals on sodium-restricted diets.
- **Alternative Solutions:** For applications where low sodium levels are required, such as in certain industrial processes or for drinking water,

alternative methods or additional treatment steps (e.g., reverse osmosis) may be necessary.

4.2 Environmental Impact of Regeneration:

- **Brine Discharge:** The regeneration process generates brine waste, which must be managed to prevent environmental contamination. Proper disposal or recycling of brine is essential to minimize the environmental impact of water softening operations.
- **Sustainability Considerations:** Advances in ion exchange technology are focused on improving the efficiency of the regeneration process and reducing the environmental impact of brine disposal.

Drug Purification Using Ion Exchange Chromatography

Ion exchange chromatography (IEC) is a powerful and versatile technique used extensively in the pharmaceutical industry for the purification of drugs and biologically active molecules. The ability to separate compounds based on their charge properties makes ion exchange chromatography particularly effective in removing impurities, isolating active pharmaceutical ingredients (APIs), and purifying complex mixtures such as proteins, peptides, and nucleic acids.

1. Importance of Drug Purification

1.1 Ensuring Drug Safety and Efficacy:

- **Removal of Impurities:** The presence of impurities in pharmaceutical products can compromise their safety and efficacy. Ion exchange chromatography helps in selectively removing these impurities, ensuring that the final product meets stringent regulatory standards.
- **Purity of Active Ingredients:** High purity of the active pharmaceutical ingredient (API) is essential for the consistent therapeutic performance of the drug. IEC plays a crucial role in achieving the desired purity levels, especially for complex biologics.

1.2 Regulatory Compliance:

- **Meeting Regulatory Standards:** Regulatory agencies such as the FDA and EMA require pharmaceutical products to meet specific purity criteria. Ion exchange chromatography is often employed in the purification process to ensure compliance with these standards, thereby facilitating drug approval.

2. Mechanism of Drug Purification by Ion Exchange Chromatography
2.1 Charge-Based Separation:

- **Interaction with Ion Exchange Resins:** Ion exchange chromatography separates molecules based on their net charge at a given pH. Drug molecules or impurities with different charge properties are differentially retained on the ion exchange resin, allowing for selective purification.
- **Cation and Anion Exchange:** Depending on the nature of the target molecule, either cation exchange resins (for positively charged molecules) or anion exchange resins (for negatively charged molecules) are used. The choice of resin and elution conditions are optimized to maximize the purity of the target compound.

2.2 Optimization of Purification Conditions:

- **pH Control:** The pH of the mobile phase is carefully controlled to ensure that the target drug or impurity carries the appropriate charge for effective binding to the resin. Adjusting the pH can also influence the elution profile, aiding in the separation of closely related species.
- **Ionic Strength:** The ionic strength of the buffer can be manipulated to weaken or strengthen the interaction between the target molecule and the resin. This allows for fine-tuning of the purification process, ensuring that the desired compound is eluted with high purity.

3. Applications in Drug Purification
3.1 Purification of Small Molecule Drugs:

- **API Isolation:** For small molecule drugs, ion exchange chromatography is used to isolate the API from reaction by-products, unreacted starting materials, and other impurities. This is particularly important in multi-step synthesis processes where each step can introduce different impurities.
- **Salt Form Conversion:** Ion exchange chromatography can be used to convert a drug into its desired salt form, which may have better stability,

solubility, or bioavailability. For example, an acidic drug might be converted to its sodium salt using a cation exchange resin.

3.2 Purification of Biologics:

- **Protein Purification:** Ion exchange chromatography is a key method for purifying therapeutic proteins, including monoclonal antibodies, enzymes, and hormones. Proteins with different isoelectric points (pI) can be separated by adjusting the pH and ionic strength, allowing for the removal of impurities such as host cell proteins, DNA, and other contaminants.
- **Peptide Purification:** Synthetic peptides often contain impurities such as truncated sequences or side products from the synthesis process. Ion exchange chromatography can effectively separate these impurities based on charge differences, ensuring the purity of the therapeutic peptide.
- **Nucleic Acid Purification:** In the production of gene therapies and vaccines, ion exchange chromatography is used to purify nucleic acids such as plasmid DNA, mRNA, and oligonucleotides. Anion exchange resins are particularly effective for binding and eluting these negatively charged molecules.

3.3 Industrial-Scale Purification:

- **Large-Scale Production:** Ion exchange chromatography is scalable, making it suitable for both laboratory-scale and industrial-scale drug purification. In large-scale biopharmaceutical manufacturing, IEC is integrated into purification trains that include other chromatographic and filtration methods to achieve the desired purity and yield.
- **Continuous Purification:** Advances in ion exchange technology have led to the development of continuous chromatography systems, where the purification process is carried out without interruption. This is particularly advantageous in the production of biologics, where maintaining consistency and reducing batch-to-batch variability is critical.

4. Advantages of Ion Exchange Chromatography in Drug Purification
4.1 High Selectivity and Resolution:

- **Targeted Purification:** Ion exchange chromatography offers high selectivity, allowing for the targeted purification of the desired molecule while efficiently removing impurities. This results in high-resolution separations that are essential for pharmaceutical applications.
- **Flexibility:** The technique can be tailored to different types of molecules, from small organic compounds to large biomolecules, by adjusting parameters such as pH, ionic strength, and resin type.

4.2 Scalability:

- **Laboratory to Industrial Scale:** Ion exchange chromatography is easily scalable, enabling its use in both research and development settings as well as in large-scale pharmaceutical manufacturing. This scalability ensures that the same purification principles can be applied across different stages of drug development and production.
- **Automation and Process Control:** The technique can be automated, allowing for precise control over the purification process and ensuring consistent results. This is particularly important in industrial settings where large volumes of product are purified.

4.3 Cost-Effectiveness:

- **Regeneration of Resins:** Ion exchange resins can be regenerated and reused multiple times, reducing the overall cost of the purification process. This is particularly beneficial in large-scale manufacturing, where cost efficiency is a critical factor.
- **Minimal Use of Organic Solvents:** Ion exchange chromatography typically requires aqueous buffers rather than organic solvents, reducing costs and environmental impact. This also makes the process safer and easier to handle.

5. Challenges and Considerations
5.1 Protein Stability:

- **Denaturation Risk:** During ion exchange chromatography, changes in pH or ionic strength can potentially denature proteins or alter their biological activity. Careful optimization of the conditions is necessary to maintain protein stability and functionality.

- **Buffer Compatibility:** The choice of buffer must be compatible with the target molecule and the downstream processing steps. In some cases, buffer exchange or dialysis may be required after purification.

5.2 Resin Fouling and Degradation:

- **Fouling:** Over time, ion exchange resins can become fouled by proteins, lipids, or other contaminants, reducing their effectiveness. Regular cleaning and maintenance of the resin are necessary to prevent fouling and extend the life of the resin.
- **Degradation:** Repeated regeneration cycles can lead to the gradual degradation of the resin's functional groups, reducing its ion exchange capacity. Monitoring resin performance and replacing it when necessary are important for maintaining consistent purification results.

CHAPTER FIFTEEN

Gel Chromatography

15.1 Introduction and Theory of Gel Chromatography
Size Exclusion Principles

Gel chromatography, also known as size exclusion chromatography (SEC) or gel filtration chromatography, is a chromatographic technique that separates molecules based on their size as they pass through a porous gel matrix. This technique is widely used in the purification and analysis of proteins, nucleic acids, polymers, and other macromolecules. The primary principle behind gel chromatography is size exclusion, where molecules are separated according to their hydrodynamic volume or molecular weight.

1. Basics of Size Exclusion Chromatography
1.1 Definition and Mechanism:

- **Size Exclusion:** In size exclusion chromatography, the separation of molecules is based on their size as they traverse through a column filled with porous gel beads. The gel beads have a defined pore size that allows smaller molecules to enter and diffuse through the pores, while larger molecules are excluded from entering the pores and, therefore, move through the column more quickly.
- **Molecular Sieving:** The process is often described as molecular sieving, where molecules are sorted by size. Smaller molecules experience a longer path due to their ability to enter and exit the pores of the gel beads, leading to longer retention times, while larger molecules, which are excluded from the pores, elute earlier.

1.2 Gel Matrix and Pore Size:

- **Gel Beads:** The stationary phase in gel chromatography consists of gel beads made from materials such as cross-linked dextran (Sephadex), agarose (Sepharose), polyacrylamide, or silica. These materials are chosen based on their chemical stability, inertness, and ability to form uniform pore sizes.

- **Pore Size Distribution:** The gel beads are characterized by a range of pore sizes, which determines the molecular weight range that can be effectively separated. The pore size distribution is crucial for optimizing the separation of molecules of different sizes. For instance, gels with larger pores are used for separating large biomolecules like proteins or DNA, while smaller pores are suitable for smaller molecules or peptides.

2. Principles of Size Exclusion
2.1 Separation Based on Molecular Size:

- **Exclusion Limit:** The exclusion limit refers to the maximum molecular size that can enter the pores of the gel beads. Molecules larger than this limit are completely excluded from the pores and elute in the void volume, which is the volume outside the beads.
- **Fractionation Range:** The fractionation range is the molecular weight range over which the gel can separate molecules. Within this range, molecules of different sizes elute at different times based on their ability to penetrate the pores. Molecules smaller than the lower limit of the fractionation range will be retained longer as they penetrate deeper into the pores.

2.2 Elution Order:

- **Larger Molecules Elute First:** In size exclusion chromatography, the elution order is the reverse of other chromatographic techniques like ion exchange or reverse phase chromatography. Larger molecules that are excluded from the pores elute first, followed by smaller molecules that can enter the pores and take longer to traverse the column.
- **Elution Profile:** The elution profile typically consists of sharp, well-resolved peaks corresponding to molecules of different sizes. The position of these peaks can be used to estimate the molecular weight of the separated molecules when compared to a standard calibration curve.

2.3 Void Volume and Total Volume:

- **Void Volume (V^0):** The void volume is the volume of the mobile phase outside the gel beads. It corresponds to the elution volume of molecules that are too large to enter any of the pores and, therefore, travel through the column unimpeded. The void volume is typically determined using a high molecular weight standard.
- **Total Volume (Vt):** The total volume of the column is the sum of the void volume and the volume of the pores within the gel beads. It represents the total elution volume of very small molecules that can fully penetrate all the pores in the gel.

2.4 Calibration Curve:

- **Molecular Weight Estimation:** The relationship between the elution volume and the logarithm of the molecular weight is typically linear within the fractionation range of the gel. A calibration curve is generated using standards of known molecular weight, which allows the estimation of the molecular weight of unknown samples based on their elution volume.
- **Use of Standards:** Calibration standards are chosen based on the expected molecular weight range of the sample. The accuracy of molecular weight estimation depends on the precision of the calibration curve and the similarity of the sample's behavior to the standards.

3. Applications of Size Exclusion Chromatography
3.1 Protein Purification and Analysis:

- **Desalting and Buffer Exchange:** Size exclusion chromatography is commonly used for desalting and buffer exchange in protein purification. By separating proteins from small salts and buffer components, it allows for the preparation of samples suitable for further analysis or applications.
- **Protein Aggregation Studies:** SEC is used to analyze protein aggregation by separating monomers from oligomers and aggregates. This is important in assessing protein stability, particularly for therapeutic proteins and biologics.
- **Molecular Weight Determination:** SEC can be used to determine the molecular weight and oligomeric state of proteins. This information is critical for understanding protein function, structure, and interactions.

3.2 Nucleic Acid Purification:

- **Purification of DNA and RNA:** Size exclusion chromatography is used to purify nucleic acids, such as DNA and RNA, from smaller contaminants like nucleotides, salts, and small molecules. It is particularly useful in the preparation of high-purity nucleic acids for sequencing, cloning, or other molecular biology applications.
- **Analysis of Nucleic Acid Conformation:** SEC can also be used to analyze the conformation and molecular weight of nucleic acids, providing insights into their structural properties.

3.3 Polymer Characterization:

- **Molecular Weight Distribution:** In polymer science, size exclusion chromatography, often referred to as gel permeation chromatography (GPC), is used to determine the molecular weight distribution of synthetic and natural polymers. This is crucial for understanding the physical properties and behavior of polymers in various applications.
- **Polydispersity Index:** SEC provides information on the polydispersity index (PDI), which indicates the distribution of molecular weights in a polymer sample. A low PDI suggests a uniform polymer, while a high PDI indicates a broad distribution of molecular weights.

3.4 Pharmaceutical and Biopharmaceutical Applications:

- **Quality Control:** Size exclusion chromatography is used in the pharmaceutical industry for the quality control of biopharmaceuticals, ensuring that products like monoclonal antibodies and vaccines are free from aggregates and contaminants.
- **Drug Delivery Systems:** SEC is also employed to analyze and optimize drug delivery systems, such as liposomes and nanoparticles, by assessing their size distribution and stability.

Gel Filtration vs. Gel Permeation

Gel filtration chromatography (GFC) and gel permeation chromatography (GPC) are two closely related techniques under the broader umbrella of size exclusion chromatography (SEC). Both methods separate molecules based on their size as they pass through a column filled with a porous gel matrix. Despite their similarities, GFC and GPC are typically applied in different contexts and involve slight differences in their principles and applications. Understanding these differences is crucial for selecting the appropriate method for specific analytical or preparative tasks.

1. Gel Filtration Chromatography (GFC)

1.1 Principle of Gel Filtration:

- **Aqueous-Based Separation:** Gel filtration chromatography is primarily performed in an aqueous environment, making it ideal for the separation of water-soluble molecules, particularly biological macromolecules such as proteins, nucleic acids, and polysaccharides. The gel matrix used in GFC is typically hydrophilic and interacts minimally with the sample, allowing for size-based separation without significant adsorption.

- **Size Exclusion:** In GFC, molecules are separated based on their hydrodynamic volume or size. Larger molecules are excluded from entering the pores of the gel beads and elute first, while smaller molecules enter the pores and elute later. The process is non-destructive, preserving the native structure and activity of sensitive biomolecules.

1.2 Applications of Gel Filtration:

- **Protein Purification:** GFC is widely used for protein purification, particularly in the final polishing steps. It is effective in removing aggregates, buffer salts, and other small impurities, resulting in high-purity protein preparations.

- **Desalting and Buffer Exchange:** GFC is commonly used for desalting and buffer exchange, allowing for the removal of small molecules like salts and buffer components from protein or nucleic acid solutions.

- **Molecular Weight Determination:** GFC is also used to estimate the molecular weight of proteins and other macromolecules by comparing their elution volume to that of known molecular weight standards.

2. Gel Permeation Chromatography (GPC)

2.1 Principle of Gel Permeation:

- **Organic Solvent-Based Separation:** Gel permeation chromatography is typically performed in organic solvents, making it suitable for the separation of hydrophobic and non-polar molecules, such as synthetic polymers, plastics, and rubbers. The gel matrix used in GPC is usually hydrophobic or chemically inert, compatible with the organic solvents required for polymer analysis.

- **Size Exclusion in Polymers:** Like GFC, GPC separates molecules based on size, but the focus is primarily on synthetic polymers and other materials that are soluble in organic solvents. The separation mechanism is based on the ability of polymer molecules to penetrate the pores of the gel beads, with larger polymers eluting first and smaller ones eluting later.

2.2 Applications of Gel Permeation:

- **Polymer Characterization:** GPC is the standard method for determining the molecular weight distribution of synthetic polymers. It provides critical information about the polymer's average molecular weight, molecular weight distribution, and polydispersity index (PDI), which are important for understanding the physical properties and performance of the material.
- **Quality Control in Polymer Production:** GPC is used extensively in the polymer industry for quality control, ensuring that polymer products meet the required specifications for molecular weight and distribution, which directly influence their mechanical, thermal, and chemical properties.
- **Analysis of Biodegradable Polymers:** GPC is also used in the analysis of biodegradable polymers and other advanced materials where molecular weight and distribution are crucial for predicting degradation behavior and performance in biological environments.

3. Key Differences Between GFC and GPC
3.1 Sample Type:

- **GFC:** Primarily used for the separation of biological macromolecules such as proteins, nucleic acids, and polysaccharides in aqueous environments.
- **GPC:** Primarily used for the analysis of synthetic polymers and hydrophobic materials in organic solvents.

3.2 Mobile Phase:

- **GFC:** Uses aqueous buffers or water as the mobile phase, which is compatible with biological molecules and helps maintain their native structure.
- **GPC:** Uses organic solvents like tetrahydrofuran (THF), chloroform, or toluene, which are suitable for dissolving non-polar polymers but may denature biological molecules.

3.3 Gel Matrix:

- **GFC:** The gel matrix is hydrophilic and inert, minimizing interactions with water-soluble molecules. Common materials include agarose, dextran, and polyacrylamide.
- **GPC:** The gel matrix is hydrophobic or chemically inert, compatible with organic solvents. Common materials include polystyrene-divinylbenzene (PS-DVB) copolymers and silica-based gels.

3.4 Applications:

- **GFC:** Used in biochemistry, molecular biology, and biotechnology for protein purification, desalting, and molecular weight estimation of biomolecules.
- **GPC:** Used in polymer chemistry, materials science, and industrial applications for determining the molecular weight distribution of synthetic polymers and quality control.

3.5 Calibration and Standards:

- **GFC:** Calibration typically involves water-soluble standards such as proteins or polysaccharides with known molecular weights.
- **GPC:** Calibration involves synthetic polymer standards with known molecular weights, such as polystyrene standards, to create a calibration curve for molecular weight determination.

15.2 Instrumentation of Gel Chromatography

Column Packing

Column packing is a critical aspect of gel chromatography, influencing the efficiency, resolution, and reproducibility of the separation process. Proper packing ensures that the gel matrix is evenly distributed within the column, providing a uniform flow of the mobile phase and consistent interaction between the sample molecules and the stationary phase. Below are the key considerations and techniques involved in column packing for gel chromatography.

1. Selection of Gel Matrix
1.1 Material Selection:

- **Agarose and Dextran:** For gel filtration chromatography (GFC), which operates in aqueous environments, hydrophilic gels such as agarose (e.g., Sepharose) and dextran (e.g., Sephadex) are commonly used. These materials are biocompatible and ideal for separating biological macromolecules like proteins, nucleic acids, and polysaccharides.
- **Polyacrylamide:** Another commonly used material in GFC, polyacrylamide gels offer a range of pore sizes and are suitable for high-resolution separations of proteins and peptides.
- **Polystyrene-Divinylbenzene (PS-DVB):** For gel permeation chromatography (GPC), which typically uses organic solvents, hydrophobic gels such as polystyrene-divinylbenzene copolymers are preferred. These materials are chemically inert and stable in organic solvents, making them ideal for polymer analysis.

1.2 Pore Size Consideration:

- **Fractionation Range:** The pore size of the gel matrix determines the fractionation range, which is the range of molecular weights that can be effectively separated. Selecting a gel with the appropriate pore size is essential for optimizing the separation of the target molecules.
- **Uniformity:** The uniformity of pore sizes in the gel beads is crucial for achieving high resolution. Gels with a narrow pore size distribution provide sharper peaks and better separation of molecules within the desired size range.

2. Preparation of the Gel Slurry
2.1 Hydration of Gel Beads:

- **Hydration Process:** The gel matrix is typically supplied as dry beads and must be fully hydrated before packing the column. Hydration involves soaking the dry beads in a suitable buffer (for GFC) or organic solvent (for GPC) until they swell to their full size. This process can take several hours to overnight, depending on the type of gel and the bead size.

- **Degassing:** To prevent air bubbles from forming during column packing, the hydrated gel slurry should be degassed. This can be done using a vacuum or by gentle sonication. Air bubbles can disrupt the uniformity of the packing and lead to uneven flow through the column.

2.2 Slurry Concentration:

- **Optimal Slurry Concentration:** The concentration of the gel slurry must be optimized for the column size and the desired packing density. A slurry that is too concentrated may result in excessive packing pressure, while a slurry that is too dilute may lead to uneven packing and poor resolution.
- **Viscosity Considerations:** The viscosity of the slurry is also important, particularly for high-viscosity gels like agarose. The slurry should be fluid enough to allow even distribution during packing but not so dilute that it leads to loose packing.

3. Packing the Column
3.1 Column Preparation:

- **Column Selection:** The column must be selected based on the intended application, with consideration for factors such as column length, diameter, and material. Columns made of glass, stainless steel, or plastic are common, depending on the chemical compatibility with the mobile phase.
- **Column Conditioning:** Before packing, the column should be conditioned by flushing it with the buffer or solvent that will be used in the separation process. This step ensures that the column is free of contaminants and equilibrated with the desired mobile phase.

3.2 Gravity Packing:

- **Slow and Controlled Packing:** Gravity packing is a method where the gel slurry is poured into the column, and gravity allows it to settle naturally. The column is packed slowly to avoid trapping air bubbles and to ensure that the gel matrix is evenly distributed.

- **Monitoring Packing:** The packing process should be monitored carefully to ensure that the gel beads settle uniformly and that the bed height remains consistent. If necessary, the column can be tapped gently to help the gel settle more evenly.

3.3 Pressure Packing:

- **Using Pressure to Pack the Column:** Pressure packing involves applying moderate pressure to the slurry as it enters the column, which speeds up the packing process and can result in a more compact and uniform gel bed. Pressure can be applied using a peristaltic pump or a pressure reservoir.
- **Avoiding Overpacking:** Care must be taken to avoid overpacking the column, as excessive pressure can compress the gel beads, reduce the pore size, and negatively impact the separation efficiency. The pressure should be gradually increased and carefully controlled throughout the packing process.

3.4 Ensuring Uniformity:

- **Checking for Uniform Bed Height:** Once the column is packed, the bed height should be uniform across the entire column. Uneven bed height can lead to uneven flow rates and inconsistent separation.
- **Avoiding Channeling:** Channeling occurs when there are gaps or channels within the gel bed, leading to non-uniform flow and poor separation. Proper packing techniques help minimize the risk of channeling, ensuring that the sample flows evenly through the column.

4. Post-Packing Column Conditioning
4.1 Column Equilibration:

- **Equilibrating with Mobile Phase:** After packing, the column should be equilibrated with several column volumes of the mobile phase to ensure that the gel matrix is fully conditioned and that any loosely packed beads are flushed out. This step also stabilizes the bed height and ensures consistent flow rates during the separation.
- **Monitoring Flow Rate:** The flow rate should be monitored and adjusted during equilibration to ensure that it remains stable and within the

desired range. Stable flow rates are essential for achieving reproducible results.

4.2 Performance Testing:

- **Testing with Standards:** Before using the column for actual separations, it is recommended to test its performance using standards of known molecular weight or size. This allows for the assessment of the column's resolution, efficiency, and reproducibility.
- **Adjusting Packing if Necessary:** If the test results indicate poor resolution or uneven flow, the column may need to be repacked or adjusted to optimize performance.

15.2 Instrumentation of Gel Chromatography
Detectors

In gel chromatography, detectors play a crucial role in identifying and quantifying the separated components as they elute from the column. The choice of detector depends on the nature of the analytes, the sensitivity required, and the specific application of the chromatographic method. Detectors convert the physical or chemical properties of the eluting compounds into measurable signals, which are then recorded and analyzed to produce a chromatogram. Below are the common types of detectors used in gel chromatography, along with their principles and applications.

1. Ultraviolet-Visible (UV-Vis) Absorbance Detectors
1.1 Principle of UV-Vis Detection:

- **Absorbance Measurement:** UV-Vis detectors measure the absorbance of light by the analytes as they pass through the detector cell. Many biological molecules, such as proteins and nucleic acids, absorb light in the ultraviolet (UV) range (typically 190-400 nm) due to the presence of aromatic amino acids, nucleotides, or other chromophores. The absorbance at specific wavelengths is directly proportional to the concentration of the analyte, according to the Beer-Lambert law.
- **Wavelength Selection:** Most UV-Vis detectors allow for the selection of specific wavelengths to monitor, enabling the detection of specific compounds within a mixture. Dual-wavelength and diode-array detectors (DAD) can monitor multiple wavelengths simultaneously, providing more comprehensive data.

1.2 Applications of UV-Vis Detection:

- **Protein and Nucleic Acid Analysis:** UV-Vis detectors are widely used in gel filtration chromatography for detecting proteins (typically at 280 nm) and nucleic acids (at 260 nm). These detectors are ideal for applications where these biomolecules are the primary analytes of interest.
- **Peptide and Small Molecule Detection:** UV-Vis detectors are also used for detecting peptides and small molecules that absorb UV light. In gel permeation chromatography (GPC), UV-Vis detection can be employed for monitoring small molecules or additives that contain chromophores.

1.3 Advantages and Limitations:

- **High Sensitivity:** UV-Vis detectors offer high sensitivity, particularly for analytes with strong absorbance in the UV range. They are suitable for detecting low concentrations of analytes in complex mixtures.
- **Specificity:** The ability to select specific wavelengths allows for selective detection of target analytes. However, compounds that do not absorb UV light cannot be detected using this method.

2. Refractive Index (RI) Detectors
2.1 Principle of Refractive Index Detection:

- **Refractive Index Measurement:** RI detectors measure the change in refractive index of the mobile phase as analytes elute from the column. The refractive index is a measure of how much light is bent, or refracted, when it passes through a substance. As the concentration of analytes in the mobile phase changes, so does the refractive index, allowing for detection.
- **Universal Detection:** Unlike UV-Vis detectors, which require analytes to absorb light, RI detectors are universal and can detect any compound that causes a change in the refractive index of the mobile phase, making them suitable for a broad range of analytes.

2.2 Applications of Refractive Index Detection:

- **Polymer Analysis:** RI detectors are commonly used in gel permeation chromatography (GPC) for analyzing synthetic polymers, where the analytes may not have strong UV absorbance. RI detection is particularly useful for determining the molecular weight distribution of polymers.
- **Carbohydrate and Lipid Analysis:** RI detectors are also used for the analysis of carbohydrates, lipids, and other compounds that lack chromophores and do not absorb UV light.

2.3 Advantages and Limitations:

- **Broad Applicability:** RI detectors can detect virtually any compound, making them versatile and broadly applicable across different types of gel chromatography.
- **Lower Sensitivity:** RI detectors are generally less sensitive than UV-Vis detectors, and their performance can be affected by temperature fluctuations and changes in mobile phase composition.

3. Light Scattering Detectors
3.1 Principle of Light Scattering Detection:

- **Molecular Weight Determination:** Light scattering detectors measure the scattering of light by molecules as they elute from the column. The intensity of scattered light is related to the molecular weight and size of the analytes. Multi-angle light scattering (MALS) detectors can provide detailed information about the molecular weight distribution and the size of macromolecules without requiring calibration standards.
- **Static and Dynamic Scattering:** Light scattering detectors can measure both static light scattering (SLS) for absolute molecular weight determination and dynamic light scattering (DLS) for size distribution analysis.

3.2 Applications of Light Scattering Detection:

- **Protein and Polymer Characterization:** Light scattering detectors are widely used in gel filtration chromatography (GFC) and gel permeation chromatography (GPC) for characterizing the molecular weight and size of proteins, polysaccharides, and synthetic polymers. They provide valuable information about the aggregation state and conformation of these macromolecules.

- **Quality Control in Biopharmaceuticals:** In the biopharmaceutical industry, light scattering detectors are used to monitor the purity and stability of protein therapeutics, ensuring that products meet stringent quality standards.

3.3 Advantages and Limitations:

- **Absolute Molecular Weight:** Light scattering detectors can determine the absolute molecular weight of analytes without the need for calibration standards, providing more accurate and reliable data.
- **Complexity and Cost:** Light scattering detectors are more complex and expensive than other types of detectors, and their operation requires specialized expertise.

4. Fluorescence Detectors
4.1 Principle of Fluorescence Detection:

- **Emission of Light:** Fluorescence detectors measure the emission of light by analytes that have been excited by a specific wavelength of light. The emitted light is typically of a longer wavelength and lower energy than the excitation light. Fluorescence detection is highly sensitive, often allowing for the detection of analytes at very low concentrations.
- **Selective Detection:** Fluorescence detectors are particularly useful for detecting specific compounds that exhibit natural fluorescence, such as certain amino acids, or compounds that have been derivatized to become fluorescent.

4.2 Applications of Fluorescence Detection:

- **Trace Analysis:** Fluorescence detectors are used in applications requiring high sensitivity, such as the detection of trace amounts of proteins, peptides, or nucleic acids in gel filtration chromatography.
- **Environmental and Clinical Testing:** Fluorescence detection is also used in environmental and clinical testing for detecting pollutants, toxins, or biomarkers that fluoresce naturally or after derivatization.

4.3 Advantages and Limitations:

- **High Sensitivity:** Fluorescence detectors offer the highest sensitivity among chromatographic detectors, capable of detecting picogram levels of analytes.
- **Selective:** While highly sensitive, fluorescence detection is limited to analytes that either fluoresce naturally or can be chemically modified to fluoresce.

5. Mass Spectrometry (MS) Detectors
5.1 Principle of Mass Spectrometry Detection:

- **Mass-to-Charge Ratio (m/z):** MS detectors measure the mass-to-charge ratio (m/z) of ionized analytes as they elute from the column. The analytes are first ionized, and then separated based on their mass-to-charge ratio in a mass analyzer, producing a mass spectrum that provides detailed information about the molecular weight and structure of the analytes.
- **Structural Information:** MS detection not only provides molecular weight information but also can be used to determine the structural features and composition of the analytes through fragmentation patterns.

5.2 Applications of Mass Spectrometry Detection:

- **Proteomics and Metabolomics:** MS detectors are widely used in proteomics and metabolomics to analyze complex mixtures of proteins, peptides, and small molecules. They are often coupled with gel filtration chromatography to identify and quantify biomolecules with high specificity.
- **Polymer Analysis:** In GPC, MS detectors can be used to analyze synthetic polymers, providing detailed information about the molecular weight distribution and the chemical composition of the polymers.

5.3 Advantages and Limitations:

- **High Specificity and Sensitivity:** MS detectors offer unparalleled specificity and sensitivity, making them ideal for identifying and quantifying complex mixtures.

- **Complexity and Cost:** MS detectors are highly complex and expensive, requiring specialized training and maintenance. They are generally used in research and advanced analytical applications.

15.3 Applications of Gel Chromatography
Protein Separation

Gel chromatography, particularly gel filtration chromatography (GFC), is widely used for the separation and purification of proteins. This technique exploits the size exclusion principle, where proteins are separated based on their size as they pass through a porous gel matrix. The ability to separate proteins without denaturing them and the high resolution offered by this technique make it a preferred method in various biological and biochemical applications.

1. Principle of Protein Separation Using Gel Filtration Chromatography

1.1 Size Exclusion Mechanism:

- **Separation by Size:** In gel filtration chromatography, proteins are separated based on their hydrodynamic volume (size) rather than their molecular weight, charge, or binding affinity. The gel matrix consists of porous beads that allow smaller proteins to enter and traverse through the pores, leading to a longer elution time. Larger proteins, which cannot enter the pores, are excluded and elute more quickly.
- **Non-Denaturing Conditions:** One of the significant advantages of using GFC for protein separation is that it operates under non-denaturing conditions. This ensures that the proteins maintain their native structure and biological activity throughout the separation process.

1.2 Fractionation Range:

- **Optimal Pore Size:** The fractionation range of the gel, determined by the pore size, is crucial for effective protein separation. Selecting a gel with the appropriate pore size is important to achieve good separation of the target proteins. For example, larger pore sizes are used for separating large proteins or protein complexes, while smaller pore sizes are suitable for smaller proteins or peptides.
- **Calibration with Standards:** The calibration of the column using protein standards of known molecular weight allows for the estimation of the

molecular weight of unknown proteins based on their elution volume.

2. Applications of Gel Filtration Chromatography in Protein Separation

2.1 Purification of Native Proteins:

- **High Purity Separation:** Gel filtration chromatography is often used as a final polishing step in protein purification workflows. It is particularly effective in removing aggregates, contaminants, and other unwanted components from the protein sample, resulting in highly pure protein preparations.
- **Buffer Exchange and Desalting:** GFC is also used for buffer exchange and desalting, where proteins are separated from small molecules, salts, and buffer components. This is especially important when preparing proteins for downstream applications such as crystallization, enzymatic assays, or structural studies.

2.2 Isolation of Protein Complexes:

- **Maintaining Quaternary Structure:** GFC is ideal for separating protein complexes without disrupting their quaternary structure. This is crucial for studying the interactions and functions of multi-subunit proteins or protein-protein interactions.
- **Separation of Oligomers and Aggregates:** GFC can effectively separate monomers from oligomers, dimers, or higher-order aggregates. This is particularly important in studying the oligomerization state of proteins and in ensuring that therapeutic proteins are free from aggregates that could lead to immunogenic responses.

2.3 Analysis of Protein Conformation:

- **Conformational Studies:** The elution profile of proteins in GFC can provide insights into their conformation and folding state. Changes in the elution volume can indicate alterations in the protein's hydrodynamic volume, which may result from conformational changes, denaturation, or aggregation.
- **Quality Control in Biopharmaceuticals:** GFC is used in the biopharmaceutical industry for quality control of therapeutic proteins,

such as monoclonal antibodies. It ensures that the final product has the correct size distribution and is free from aggregates or degradation products.

2.4 Molecular Weight Determination:

- **Estimation of Molecular Weight:** By comparing the elution volume of a protein to a set of standards with known molecular weights, GFC allows for the estimation of the molecular weight of the protein. This is valuable in characterizing new proteins or confirming the identity of known proteins.
- **Analysis of Post-Translational Modifications:** GFC can be used to analyze proteins with post-translational modifications, such as glycosylation, which may alter the protein's size and affect its elution profile. This information is critical in understanding the role of these modifications in protein function.

3. Advantages of Gel Filtration Chromatography in Protein Separation
3.1 Non-Destructive Method:

- **Preservation of Protein Integrity:** Since GFC operates under mild, non-denaturing conditions, it preserves the native structure and biological activity of proteins. This is essential for applications where the functional properties of the protein must be maintained.

3.2 High Resolution and Purity:

- **Efficient Separation:** GFC offers high resolution and the ability to separate proteins with minimal cross-contamination. The technique is particularly effective in purifying proteins to a high degree of homogeneity, which is necessary for detailed structural and functional studies.
- **Scalability:** GFC can be easily scaled from analytical to preparative or industrial scales, making it a versatile tool for both research and production purposes.

4. Limitations and Considerations
4.1 Limited Capacity:

- **Sample Load:** The capacity of GFC columns is generally lower than other chromatographic methods, meaning only relatively small volumes of sample can be processed at a time. This limitation must be considered when working with large sample volumes or in industrial applications.

4.2 Long Run Times:

- **Slower Separation:** Gel filtration chromatography typically has longer run times compared to other chromatographic techniques due to the size-based separation mechanism. This can be a drawback when rapid analysis is required.

4.3 Potential for Sample Dilution:

- **Dilution of Eluted Proteins:** During the separation process, proteins may become diluted as they elute from the column, particularly when using large column volumes. Concentration steps may be required after GFC to achieve the desired protein concentration.

15.3 Applications of Gel Chromatography
Molecular Weight Determination

Molecular weight determination is one of the key applications of gel chromatography, particularly gel filtration chromatography (GFC) or size exclusion chromatography (SEC). This technique allows for the estimation of the molecular weight of proteins, nucleic acids, polymers, and other macromolecules based on their elution profile from a gel matrix. Understanding the molecular weight of these molecules is crucial for characterizing their structure, function, and interactions.

1. Principle of Molecular Weight Determination in Gel Filtration Chromatography

1.1 Size Exclusion Mechanism:

- **Separation by Size:** Gel filtration chromatography separates molecules based on their size, with larger molecules eluting first because they are excluded from entering the pores of the gel beads, while smaller molecules penetrate the pores and elute later. The elution volume of a molecule is inversely related to its size.

- **Hydrodynamic Volume:** The technique separates molecules based on their hydrodynamic volume, which is influenced by both the molecular weight and the shape of the molecule. For spherical molecules, the elution volume can be directly correlated with molecular weight.

1.2 Calibration Curve:

- **Use of Standards:** To determine the molecular weight of an unknown sample, a calibration curve is generated using a set of standards with known molecular weights. These standards are typically well-characterized proteins or polymers that cover the range of molecular weights expected in the sample.
- **Logarithmic Relationship:** The calibration curve plots the logarithm of the molecular weight of the standards against their elution volume or elution time. This relationship is usually linear within the fractionation range of the gel. By comparing the elution volume of the unknown sample to the calibration curve, its molecular weight can be estimated.

1.3 Fractionation Range:

- **Pore Size Selection:** The fractionation range of the gel, determined by its pore size, is critical for accurate molecular weight determination. Gels with a broad fractionation range can separate a wide range of molecular weights, while gels with a narrower range provide higher resolution for specific size ranges.
- **Accuracy of Determination:** The accuracy of molecular weight determination depends on the quality of the calibration curve and the appropriateness of the gel's fractionation range for the sample being analyzed.

2. Applications of Molecular Weight Determination
2.1 Protein Characterization:

- **Estimating Protein Size:** Molecular weight determination by GFC is a fundamental technique in protein chemistry, used to estimate the size of native proteins. This information is essential for understanding the protein's structure, function, and interactions.

- **Determining Oligomeric State:** GFC can be used to assess whether a protein exists as a monomer, dimer, trimer, or higher-order oligomer in solution. This is particularly important in studying protein-protein interactions and the functional assembly of protein complexes.
- **Post-Translational Modifications:** The technique can also detect changes in the molecular weight of proteins due to post-translational modifications, such as glycosylation or phosphorylation, which can alter the protein's elution profile.

2.2 Nucleic Acid Analysis:

- **DNA and RNA Sizing:** Gel filtration chromatography can be used to estimate the molecular weight of nucleic acids, such as DNA and RNA, by comparing their elution volume to that of known standards. This is useful in determining the size of plasmids, RNA transcripts, or fragmented nucleic acids.
- **Conformational Studies:** The elution profile of nucleic acids can provide insights into their conformation, such as whether DNA exists in a linear, circular, or supercoiled form.

2.3 Polymer Science:

- **Polymer Molecular Weight Distribution:** In gel permeation chromatography (GPC), the molecular weight distribution of synthetic polymers is determined by analyzing their elution profile. This information is crucial for understanding the physical properties of polymers, such as strength, elasticity, and viscosity.
- **Polydispersity Index:** The polydispersity index (PDI) is a measure of the distribution of molecular weights within a polymer sample. GPC allows for the calculation of PDI, which is important in assessing the uniformity and quality of polymer products.

2.4 Biopharmaceuticals:

- **Quality Control of Therapeutic Proteins:** Molecular weight determination is a critical quality control measure in the production of biopharmaceuticals, such as monoclonal antibodies and recombinant proteins. Ensuring that the therapeutic protein has the correct molecular weight and is free from aggregates is essential for efficacy and safety.

- **Stability Testing:** GFC is used to monitor the stability of biopharmaceuticals by detecting changes in molecular weight that may occur due to degradation, aggregation, or other forms of instability during storage or handling.

3. Advantages of Molecular Weight Determination by Gel Filtration
3.1 Non-Denaturing Conditions:

- **Preservation of Native Structure:** Gel filtration chromatography operates under mild, non-denaturing conditions, making it ideal for determining the molecular weight of proteins and other biomolecules in their native state. This is essential for understanding their biological function and interactions.

3.2 High Resolution:

- **Accurate Separation:** The technique provides high-resolution separation of molecules with different sizes, allowing for precise molecular weight estimation. The use of well-calibrated standards enhances the accuracy of the measurements.

3.3 Versatility:

- **Wide Range of Applications:** Gel filtration chromatography can be used to determine the molecular weight of a wide variety of molecules, from small peptides and nucleic acids to large proteins and polymers. This versatility makes it a valuable tool in many fields of research and industry.

4. Limitations and Considerations
4.1 Dependence on Shape and Conformation:

- **Hydrodynamic Volume vs. Molecular Weight:** The separation in GFC is based on hydrodynamic volume rather than absolute molecular weight. Molecules with unusual shapes or extended conformations may elute at volumes that do not correspond directly to their molecular weight, leading to potential inaccuracies.

- **Calibration with Similar Standards:** To improve accuracy, it is important to use calibration standards that closely resemble the shape and conformation of the sample molecules.

4.2 Limited by Fractionation Range:

- **Pore Size Limitations:** The accuracy of molecular weight determination is limited by the fractionation range of the gel. Molecules that are too large or too small relative to the pore size of the gel may elute in the void volume or the total volume, respectively, leading to less accurate molecular weight estimations.

4.3 Sample Dilution:

- **Dilution Effect:** As molecules elute from the column, they may become diluted, especially if the column volume is large relative to the sample size. This dilution can affect the accuracy of concentration-dependent measurements and may require post-column concentration steps.

CHAPTER SIXTEEN

Affinity Chromatography

16.1 Introduction and Theory of Affinity Chromatography
Principle of Affinity Binding

Affinity chromatography is a highly selective and powerful chromatographic technique used to purify proteins, nucleic acids, enzymes, antibodies, and other biomolecules. The method relies on the specific and reversible interaction between a target molecule (ligand) and a binding partner (analyte) immobilized on a solid support matrix. This selective interaction allows for the efficient separation of the target molecule from a complex mixture, making affinity chromatography one of the most precise methods for purification and isolation.

1. Basic Principle of Affinity Binding
1.1 Specificity of Binding:

- **Biological Interactions:** The fundamental principle of affinity chromatography is the highly specific interaction between a ligand and its binding partner, often mimicking natural biological interactions. These interactions can include antigen-antibody binding, enzyme-substrate interactions, receptor-ligand binding, and other similar specific molecular recognition events.

- **Reversible Binding:** The interaction between the ligand and the target molecule is reversible. This reversibility is crucial for the elution of the target molecule after it has been captured by the ligand on the chromatography matrix. The strength and specificity of the binding can be modulated by altering the conditions, such as pH, ionic strength, or the presence of competing substances.

1.2 Immobilization of the Ligand:

- **Matrix Support:** The ligand is covalently attached or adsorbed onto an inert and stable solid support, often made of agarose, sepharose, or other polymeric materials. The choice of support depends on its chemical compatibility with the ligand and its ability to withstand the conditions used during the chromatographic process.

- **Orientation and Accessibility:** It is essential that the ligand is immobilized in such a way that its binding site is accessible to the target molecule in the sample. Proper orientation and density of the ligand on the matrix are critical for achieving high binding efficiency and capacity.

1.3 Binding Process:

- **Sample Application:** The sample containing the target molecule is applied to the affinity column, where it passes through the matrix. As the sample flows through the column, the target molecule specifically binds to the immobilized ligand, while other components of the sample are washed away.

- **Selective Retention:** The target molecule is selectively retained on the column due to its specific interaction with the ligand. Non-specific interactions are minimized by carefully optimizing the buffer conditions, such as pH, ionic strength, and the presence of detergents or other additives.

2. Types of Affinity Binding
2.1 Antigen-Antibody Interactions:

- **Immunoaffinity Chromatography:** One of the most common forms of affinity chromatography involves the use of antibodies as ligands to capture specific antigens or proteins. This technique, known as immunoaffinity chromatography, is highly selective and is widely used for purifying specific proteins from complex biological samples.

- **Specificity and Sensitivity:** The high specificity of antigen-antibody interactions allows for the purification of trace amounts of target proteins with minimal contamination from other proteins.

2.2 Enzyme-Substrate Interactions:

- **Enzyme Affinity Chromatography:** Enzymes can be used as ligands to capture their specific substrates or inhibitors. This type of affinity chromatography is valuable for isolating enzymes or identifying enzyme inhibitors in drug discovery processes.
- **Activity Retention:** It is important that the enzyme retains its catalytic activity after immobilization, as this ensures effective binding of the substrate or inhibitor.

2.3 Receptor-Ligand Interactions:

- **Receptor Affinity Chromatography:** Receptors immobilized on a matrix can be used to capture specific ligands, such as hormones, neurotransmitters, or drugs. This technique is useful for studying receptor-ligand interactions and for purifying ligands from complex mixtures.
- **Mimicking Biological Conditions:** The binding conditions should mimic physiological conditions to maintain the native conformation and activity of the receptor-ligand complex.

2.4 Nucleic Acid Interactions:

- **DNA/RNA Affinity Chromatography:** Nucleic acids, such as DNA or RNA sequences, can be used as ligands to capture complementary strands, transcription factors, or other nucleic acid-binding proteins. This is particularly useful in studying gene regulation and nucleic acid-protein interactions.
- **Sequence-Specific Binding:** The high specificity of nucleic acid interactions allows for the isolation of sequence-specific binding proteins or nucleic acids with high fidelity.

3. Elution of Bound Molecules
3.1 Competitive Elution:

- **Using Free Ligand:** One common method to elute the bound target molecule is to introduce a solution containing a free ligand that competes with the immobilized ligand for binding to the target molecule. The target molecule is released from the matrix as it binds to the free ligand in the mobile phase.

- **Elution Conditions:** The concentration of the free ligand and the conditions such as pH or ionic strength must be carefully controlled to ensure efficient elution without denaturing the target molecule.

3.2 pH-Dependent Elution:

- **Altering pH:** Changing the pH of the mobile phase can disrupt the interaction between the ligand and the target molecule, leading to elution. For example, lowering the pH can protonate amino acid residues involved in binding, weakening the interaction and allowing the target molecule to be released.
- **Gentle Elution:** pH-dependent elution is often used for sensitive biomolecules that require mild conditions to maintain their activity and structure.

3.3 Ionic Strength Elution:

- **High Salt Concentrations:** Increasing the ionic strength of the mobile phase, typically by adding salt, can weaken electrostatic interactions between the ligand and the target molecule, leading to elution. This method is effective for molecules that bind through ionic interactions.
- **Control of Ionic Strength:** The concentration and type of salt used must be optimized to achieve efficient elution while preserving the integrity of the target molecule.

3.4 Denaturing Elution:

- **Use of Denaturants:** In some cases, particularly when very strong interactions are involved, denaturing agents such as urea, guanidine hydrochloride, or organic solvents are used to disrupt the ligand-target binding. This method is generally employed when the target molecule can withstand denaturing conditions or when refolding is possible after elution.
- **Trade-offs:** While effective, denaturing elution may alter the structure and function of the target molecule, so it is typically used as a last resort when other elution methods fail.

4. Applications of Affinity Chromatography

4.1 Protein Purification:

- **Highly Selective Purification:** Affinity chromatography is widely used for the purification of proteins, including enzymes, antibodies, and recombinant proteins. The high selectivity and efficiency of the technique make it ideal for obtaining pure proteins from complex mixtures, such as cell lysates or serum.
- **Tag-Based Purification:** Recombinant proteins can be engineered with affinity tags (e.g., His-tag, GST-tag) that allow for specific binding to affinity matrices, simplifying the purification process.

4.2 Enzyme and Receptor Studies:

- **Isolation of Active Enzymes:** Affinity chromatography is used to isolate and purify active enzymes, which can then be studied for their kinetic properties, substrate specificity, and inhibitor interactions.
- **Receptor-Ligand Interaction Analysis:** The technique is also used to study receptor-ligand interactions, which are critical for understanding signaling pathways and drug-receptor interactions.

4.3 Nucleic Acid Purification:

- **Purification of Nucleic Acids:** Affinity chromatography is employed to purify DNA, RNA, and their binding proteins. This is especially useful in molecular biology research for studying gene regulation and nucleic acid-protein interactions.

4.4 Drug Discovery:

- **Target Identification:** In drug discovery, affinity chromatography is used to identify and isolate target proteins that interact with potential drug candidates. This technique is critical for the identification of drug targets and the study of drug mechanisms.

16.1 Introduction and Theory of Affinity Chromatography
Ligand Selection

Ligand selection is a critical step in affinity chromatography, as the ligand directly determines the specificity, efficiency, and success of the separation process. The ligand is the molecule that is immobilized on the solid support matrix and is responsible for binding the target molecule with high specificity. The choice of ligand depends on the nature of the target molecule, the desired application, and the type of interaction required for selective binding.

1. Importance of Ligand Selection
1.1 Specificity of Binding:

- **Target Interaction:** The ligand must have a high affinity and specificity for the target molecule to ensure effective binding. This specificity is often based on biological interactions, such as antigen-antibody, enzyme-substrate, or receptor-ligand interactions. The better the specificity, the more efficient the separation will be.
- **Minimizing Non-Specific Binding:** A well-chosen ligand will minimize non-specific interactions, reducing the binding of unwanted molecules and improving the purity of the target molecule.

1.2 Stability and Reusability:

- **Chemical Stability:** The ligand must be chemically stable under the conditions used in the chromatographic process, including the binding and elution steps. It should resist denaturation or degradation to maintain its binding capacity over multiple cycles.
- **Regeneration:** A stable ligand allows the affinity column to be regenerated and reused multiple times, which is economically beneficial and ensures consistent performance.

2. Types of Ligands
2.1 Biological Ligands:

- **Antibodies:**

  - **Immunoaffinity Chromatography:** Antibodies are among the most specific ligands used in affinity chromatography. They bind to their corresponding antigens with high affinity, making them ideal for purifying specific proteins from complex mixtures.
  - **Monoclonal vs. Polyclonal:** Monoclonal antibodies offer higher specificity as they recognize a single epitope, while polyclonal

antibodies can bind to multiple epitopes, potentially capturing a broader range of target molecules.

- **Enzymes:**

  - **Enzyme-Substrate Interaction:** Enzymes can act as ligands to bind their specific substrates or inhibitors. This interaction is highly specific and is used to isolate enzymes or to identify and purify substrates and inhibitors.
  - **Activity Considerations:** The enzyme ligand must retain its catalytic activity after immobilization to ensure effective binding of the target molecule.

- **Receptors:**

  - **Receptor-Ligand Binding:** Receptors can be immobilized to capture specific ligands, such as hormones, drugs, or neurotransmitters. This type of ligand is useful in studying receptor-ligand interactions and purifying ligands from complex biological samples.
  - **Mimicking Physiological Conditions:** The receptor-ligand interaction should ideally occur under conditions that mimic physiological environments to maintain the native conformation and function of the receptor.

2.2 Synthetic Ligands:

- **Aptamers:**

  - **Nucleic Acid-Based Ligands:** Aptamers are synthetic oligonucleotides or peptides that can fold into specific three-dimensional structures to bind target molecules with high affinity and specificity. They can be designed to bind a wide range of targets, including proteins, small molecules, and ions.
  - **Advantages:** Aptamers are highly versatile and can be synthesized in vitro, allowing for the design of ligands tailored to specific targets. They are also stable and can be regenerated easily.

- **Metal Chelates:**

- ○ **Metal-Affinity Chromatography:** Metal ions, such as nickel (Ni^{2+}), cobalt (Co^{2+}), or zinc (Zn^{2+}), can be immobilized on a matrix to create metal chelate ligands. These ligands are used in immobilized metal affinity chromatography (IMAC) to bind histidine-tagged proteins or other metal-binding proteins.
- ○ **Versatility:** Metal chelate ligands are highly effective for purifying recombinant proteins that have been engineered with a polyhistidine tag, allowing for straightforward and efficient purification.

- **Small Molecules:**

  - ○ **Drug-Affinity Chromatography:** Small molecule ligands, such as drugs or inhibitors, can be used to capture specific proteins, enzymes, or receptors. These ligands are particularly useful in drug discovery for identifying and isolating drug targets.
  - ○ **Custom Design:** Small molecule ligands can be designed to target specific binding sites on proteins, allowing for the selective purification of the target molecule.

3. Considerations in Ligand Selection
3.1 Affinity and Binding Strength:

- **Kd (Dissociation Constant):** The affinity between the ligand and the target molecule is often quantified by the dissociation constant (Kd). A lower Kd indicates stronger binding and is desirable for efficient capture of the target molecule. However, extremely strong binding may complicate the elution process.
- **Binding Kinetics:** The kinetics of the interaction, including association (on-rate) and dissociation (off-rate), should be considered to ensure that the target molecule binds and elutes efficiently under the chosen conditions.

3.2 Ligand Density:

- **Optimal Coverage:** The density of the ligand on the matrix surface should be optimized to maximize binding capacity without causing steric hindrance or non-specific interactions. Too high a density may lead to overcrowding, reducing the accessibility of the ligand's binding sites.

- **Adjusting Conditions:** Ligand density can be controlled during the immobilization process, and its impact on binding efficiency should be evaluated experimentally.

3.3 Ligand Stability:

- **Chemical and Thermal Stability:** The ligand must be stable under the conditions of the chromatography process, including pH, temperature, and the presence of detergents or organic solvents. Ligands that degrade or lose their binding capacity under these conditions will reduce the efficiency and reproducibility of the purification process.
- **Reusability:** Ligands that remain stable over multiple cycles allow the column to be regenerated and reused, providing cost-effectiveness and consistent results.

3.4 Non-Specific Binding:

- **Minimizing Non-Specific Interactions:** The ligand should be chosen to minimize non-specific binding of other molecules in the sample. This can be achieved by optimizing the ligand's structure, the buffer composition, and the washing conditions during chromatography.
- **Blocking Agents:** In some cases, blocking agents can be used to prevent non-specific binding to the matrix or the ligand itself, thereby improving the purity of the target molecule.

4. Applications of Ligand-Target Interactions
4.1 Protein Purification:

- **Antibody Purification:** Affinity chromatography using Protein A or G as ligands is a common method for purifying antibodies from serum or cell culture supernatants. The specificity of the ligand-antibody interaction allows for high purity and yield.
- **Enzyme Isolation:** Enzymes can be purified based on their affinity for specific substrates or inhibitors immobilized on the column. This method is used in research and industrial applications where high-purity enzymes are required.

4.2 Drug Discovery:

- **Target Identification:** Small molecule ligands are used in affinity chromatography to identify and isolate drug targets, such as enzymes or receptors, from complex biological samples. This application is critical in the early stages of drug discovery.
- **Ligand Fishing:** In this technique, a known ligand is used to "fish" for its binding partner (e.g., a receptor or enzyme) from a mixture, facilitating the identification of potential drug targets or biomarkers.

4.3 Biomolecular Interaction Studies:

- **Receptor-Ligand Binding:** Affinity chromatography is used to study the interactions between receptors and their ligands, providing insights into signaling pathways, drug-receptor interactions, and the mechanisms of action of therapeutic agents.
- **Nucleic Acid-Protein Interactions:** DNA or RNA ligands can be used to capture and study proteins that interact with specific nucleotide sequences, aiding in the investigation of gene regulation and transcriptional control.

16.2 Instrumentation of Affinity Chromatography
Column Preparation

The preparation of the affinity chromatography column is a crucial step in ensuring the successful separation and purification of target molecules. Proper column preparation involves selecting the appropriate matrix, immobilizing the ligand, packing the column, and conditioning it for the chromatographic process. Each of these steps must be carefully controlled to maintain the integrity of the ligand, ensure efficient binding, and achieve high-resolution separation.

1. Selection of the Matrix
1.1 Matrix Materials:

- **Agarose and Sepharose:** These are the most commonly used matrices in affinity chromatography due to their hydrophilicity, chemical inertness, and ability to support a wide range of ligands. Agarose-based matrices, such as Sepharose, are preferred for their low non-specific binding and good flow properties.
- **Polyacrylamide:** Another popular matrix, polyacrylamide offers a high degree of chemical stability and can be used for a variety of ligands. It is

particularly useful in applications requiring a more rigid support.

- **Magnetic Beads:** Magnetic bead-based matrices allow for easy separation of bound complexes by applying a magnetic field. These are commonly used in small-scale purifications and diagnostic applications.
- **Silica and Glass Beads:** These are used in high-performance affinity chromatography (HPAC) where high-pressure systems are employed. Silica-based matrices provide excellent mechanical strength and are often used in analytical and preparative applications.

1.2 Matrix Properties:

- **Pore Size and Bead Size:** The pore size and bead size of the matrix influence the flow rate and binding capacity of the column. Larger pores are suitable for large biomolecules such as proteins and nucleic acids, while smaller pores may be better for small peptides or small molecule ligands. The bead size affects the surface area available for ligand attachment and the resolution of the separation.
- **Chemical Stability:** The matrix must be chemically stable under the conditions of the chromatography process, including the binding, washing, and elution steps. It should resist degradation or deformation to maintain consistent performance over multiple uses.

2. Ligand Immobilization
2.1 Methods of Immobilization:

- **Covalent Coupling:** Ligands are often covalently attached to the matrix through reactive groups such as amines, carboxyls, or hydroxyls. This method provides a stable and permanent attachment, minimizing the risk of ligand leaching during chromatography.
- **Affinity Tags:** Ligands can be tagged with specific sequences (e.g., His-tag, biotin) that facilitate immobilization on matrices with complementary binding sites (e.g., nickel for His-tag, streptavidin for biotin). This allows for reversible binding and easy removal or exchange of the ligand.
- **Physical Adsorption:** In some cases, ligands can be physically adsorbed onto the matrix surface without covalent bonding. This method is less stable but may be suitable for applications where gentle binding is required.

2.2 Considerations for Immobilization:

- **Ligand Orientation:** The ligand should be immobilized in a way that preserves its active binding site and ensures accessibility to the target molecule. Incorrect orientation can reduce binding efficiency and the overall performance of the column.
- **Ligand Density:** The density of the ligand on the matrix surface must be optimized to maximize binding capacity without causing steric hindrance or non-specific interactions. High ligand density can increase binding capacity, but too much can lead to overcrowding and reduced efficiency.

2.3 Spacer Arms:

- **Use of Spacer Arms:** Spacer arms are often used to extend the ligand away from the matrix surface, reducing steric hindrance and improving the accessibility of the binding site. Spacer arms are particularly useful when the ligand is small or when the target molecule is large and bulky.
- **Length and Flexibility:** The length and flexibility of the spacer arm must be optimized for the specific interaction. A flexible spacer can enhance binding by allowing the ligand to move freely, while a rigid spacer may be necessary for certain applications.

3. Column Packing
3.1 Preparing the Slurry:

- **Hydration of the Matrix:** If the matrix is supplied in a dry form, it must be fully hydrated in a suitable buffer before packing. Hydration should be complete to ensure uniform packing and avoid air bubbles in the column.
- **Degassing:** To prevent the formation of air bubbles during packing, the slurry should be degassed by applying a vacuum or gentle sonication. Air bubbles can disrupt the uniformity of the packed bed and reduce column performance.

3.2 Packing the Column:

- **Gravity Packing:** In gravity packing, the hydrated matrix slurry is slowly poured into the column, allowing it to settle by gravity. This method is suitable for low-pressure systems and ensures gentle packing, which is important for maintaining the activity of sensitive ligands.
- **Pressure Packing:** Pressure packing involves applying moderate pressure to pack the matrix more tightly. This method is often used for high-performance affinity chromatography (HPAC) to achieve a more uniform and compact bed, which is necessary for high-resolution separations.
- **Ensuring Uniformity:** The packed bed should be uniform and free from channels or voids, which can lead to uneven flow and poor separation. Careful monitoring during packing can help achieve a consistent and uniform bed height.

4. Column Conditioning
4.1 Equilibration:

- **Buffer Equilibration:** After packing, the column should be equilibrated with several column volumes of the binding buffer to ensure that the matrix is fully conditioned and that any loosely packed beads are flushed out. This step also stabilizes the bed height and ensures consistent flow rates during the separation process.
- **Monitoring Flow Rate:** The flow rate should be stable and within the desired range. Any fluctuations can indicate issues with the packing or the matrix, which may need to be addressed before proceeding with the chromatography.

4.2 Testing Binding Capacity:

- **Test Run:** Before using the column for actual separations, a test run with a known standard or target molecule should be performed to assess the binding capacity and efficiency of the column. This step helps ensure that the ligand is properly immobilized and that the column is functioning as expected.
- **Adjustments if Necessary:** If the test run indicates suboptimal performance, adjustments to the packing, ligand density, or buffer conditions may be necessary. This could involve re-packing the column, optimizing the ligand immobilization process, or modifying the buffer

composition.

4.3 Regeneration:

- **Regeneration Protocols:** After each use, the column should be regenerated to remove any bound target molecules and restore the ligand's binding capacity. This typically involves washing the column with a regeneration buffer that disrupts the ligand-target interaction, followed by re-equilibration with the binding buffer.
- **Stability and Reusability:** The stability of the ligand and matrix during regeneration is critical for the column's reusability. Columns with stable ligands can be reused multiple times with consistent performance, reducing costs and improving efficiency.

16.3 Applications of Affinity Chromatography
Purification of Antibodies

Affinity chromatography is a widely used technique for the purification of antibodies, leveraging the specific and high-affinity interactions between antibodies and their respective ligands. This method allows for the isolation of antibodies from complex mixtures, such as serum, cell culture supernatants, or ascites fluid, with high purity and yield. The purification process is critical in both research and therapeutic applications, where antibodies must be obtained in a form that is free from contaminants and retains full biological activity.

1. Principle of Antibody Purification Using Affinity Chromatography
1.1 Specific Binding:

- **Protein A and Protein G Ligands:** The most common ligands used in antibody purification are Protein A and Protein G. These bacterial proteins have a strong affinity for the Fc region of IgG antibodies, allowing for the selective capture of antibodies from a mixture. Protein A and Protein G differ slightly in their binding specificities; Protein A has a higher affinity for certain subclasses of IgG, while Protein G binds a broader range of IgG subclasses and some IgA and IgM.
- **Antigen-Antibody Interaction:** Alternatively, antibodies can be purified using their specific antigens as ligands. This method is particularly useful when a high degree of specificity is required, such as in the isolation of monoclonal antibodies against a particular antigen.

1.2 Binding and Elution:

- **Sample Application:** The sample containing the antibodies is passed through the affinity column, where the antibodies bind specifically to the immobilized ligand. Non-antibody proteins and other contaminants are washed away using a buffer that maintains the binding interaction.
- **Elution:** Bound antibodies are eluted by disrupting the interaction between the antibody and the ligand. This is typically achieved by lowering the pH, which weakens the binding, or by using a competitive agent. The elution buffer is chosen to ensure that the antibodies are released from the column while retaining their biological activity.

2. Advantages of Affinity Chromatography for Antibody Purification
2.1 High Specificity and Purity:

- **Selective Capture:** Affinity chromatography provides a highly specific method for isolating antibodies, leading to high purity of the final product. The use of ligands like Protein A or G ensures that only the antibodies of interest are captured, while other proteins and contaminants are effectively removed.
- **High Yield:** The strong interaction between the ligand and the antibody ensures that a high percentage of the antibodies in the sample are captured and eluted, resulting in a high yield of purified antibody.

2.2 Preservation of Antibody Activity:

- **Mild Elution Conditions:** Affinity chromatography allows for the use of mild elution conditions, which preserve the native structure and biological activity of the antibodies. This is particularly important for therapeutic antibodies, where maintaining functionality is critical.
- **Reusability of Columns:** The columns used in antibody purification can be regenerated and reused multiple times, making the process cost-effective and efficient, especially in large-scale production.

3. Methods of Antibody Purification
3.1 Protein A and Protein G Affinity Chromatography:

- **Protein A Affinity:** Protein A binds to the Fc region of IgG antibodies, particularly those of human, rabbit, and mouse origin. It is highly effective for purifying monoclonal and polyclonal IgG antibodies. The binding is pH-dependent, allowing for easy elution by lowering the pH to 3.0-4.0.
- **Protein G Affinity:** Protein G also binds to the Fc region of IgG, with a broader subclass specificity compared to Protein A. It is particularly useful for purifying IgG from species where Protein A binding is weak. Protein G is also effective for purifying antibodies from a variety of species, including rodents and livestock.

3.2 Antigen-Specific Affinity Chromatography:

- **Custom Ligand Design:** In this method, the antigen to which the antibody is specific is immobilized on the matrix. This allows for the purification of antibodies that bind to a specific epitope on the antigen. Antigen-specific affinity chromatography is particularly valuable for isolating monoclonal antibodies from hybridoma supernatants or for purifying antibodies from polyclonal sera that recognize a particular antigen.
- **High Specificity:** The use of the specific antigen as a ligand ensures that only the desired antibodies are purified, making this method extremely selective.

3.3 Immunoaffinity Chromatography:

- **Capture of Antigens:** In some cases, antibodies are used as ligands to capture and purify antigens from a mixture. This is known as immunoaffinity chromatography and is the reverse of antibody purification. It is particularly useful in the purification of low-abundance proteins or in the enrichment of specific antigens from complex biological samples.
- **Application in Diagnostics:** Immunoaffinity chromatography is widely used in diagnostic applications to purify and detect specific biomarkers or pathogens from clinical samples.

4. Applications of Purified Antibodies
4.1 Therapeutic Antibodies:

- **Monoclonal Antibody Production:** Affinity chromatography is the standard method for purifying monoclonal antibodies (mAbs) used in therapeutic applications. High purity and activity are essential for the efficacy and safety of mAb-based therapies, making affinity chromatography an indispensable tool in biopharmaceutical manufacturing.
- **Polyclonal Antibody Production:** Polyclonal antibodies, often used in diagnostic and research applications, are also purified using affinity chromatography to ensure specificity and reduce cross-reactivity.

4.2 Research Applications:

- **Western Blotting and ELISA:** Purified antibodies are widely used in immunoassays such as Western blotting, ELISA, and immunohistochemistry. High purity is crucial to reduce background noise and improve the sensitivity and specificity of these assays.
- **Immunoprecipitation:** In immunoprecipitation assays, purified antibodies are used to isolate and study specific proteins or protein complexes from cell lysates, aiding in the investigation of protein-protein interactions and signaling pathways.

4.3 Diagnostic Applications:

- **Diagnostic Kits:** Affinity-purified antibodies are used in various diagnostic kits for detecting specific antigens or biomarkers in clinical samples. The high specificity and sensitivity of these antibodies are essential for accurate diagnosis and monitoring of diseases.
- **Biosensors:** Purified antibodies are employed in biosensors designed to detect pathogens, toxins, or other analytes in environmental and clinical settings. The success of these sensors depends on the purity and specificity of the antibodies used.

5. Challenges and Considerations
5.1 pH Sensitivity:

- **Impact on Antibody Stability:** Some antibodies are sensitive to low pH, which is commonly used for elution in affinity chromatography. This can lead to denaturation or loss of activity. To address this, alternative elution strategies, such as using mild buffers or competitive elution, may be employed.

- **Buffer Optimization:** Careful optimization of the elution buffer is required to ensure that the antibodies are released from the column without compromising their structural integrity or function.

5.2 Ligand Leakage:

- **Ligand Leaching:** During the chromatography process, there is a risk of ligand leaching from the column, which can contaminate the purified antibody preparation. This is particularly concerning in therapeutic applications, where ligand contamination must be minimized.
- **Stabilizing Ligands:** Immobilizing the ligand through strong covalent bonds and using high-quality matrices can reduce the risk of ligand leakage and improve the stability of the affinity column.

5.3 Scale-Up Challenges:

- **Consistency and Reproducibility:** Scaling up the affinity chromatography process for industrial production of antibodies requires careful control of the conditions to maintain consistency and reproducibility. This includes ensuring uniform ligand immobilization, efficient column packing, and consistent flow rates.
- **Cost Considerations:** While affinity chromatography is highly effective, it can be costly, particularly at large scales. The cost of the ligands, matrices, and the need for regeneration of columns must be balanced against the benefits of high purity and yield.

16.3 Applications of Affinity Chromatography
Enzyme Isolation

Affinity chromatography is an essential technique for the isolation and purification of enzymes. The method relies on the specific interaction between an enzyme and a ligand that mimics its natural substrate, inhibitor, or cofactor. This specificity allows for the selective binding and purification of the enzyme from complex biological mixtures, such as cell lysates or fermentation broths, while preserving the enzyme's activity and native structure.

1. Principle of Enzyme Isolation Using Affinity Chromatography

1.1 Specific Binding:

- **Substrate Analogs as Ligands:** In enzyme isolation, the ligand immobilized on the chromatography matrix is often a substrate analog, inhibitor, or cofactor of the enzyme. This ligand binds specifically to the active site of the enzyme, mimicking the natural interaction that occurs during the enzyme's catalytic activity.
- **High Affinity:** The ligand-enzyme interaction is highly specific and typically exhibits a high affinity, ensuring that the enzyme is selectively retained on the column while other proteins and impurities are washed away.

1.2 Binding and Elution:

- **Sample Application:** The biological sample containing the enzyme of interest is passed through the affinity column. The enzyme binds specifically to the immobilized ligand, while non-specific proteins and other components flow through the column without binding.
- **Elution of the Enzyme:** The enzyme is eluted by introducing a solution that disrupts the ligand-enzyme interaction. This can be achieved by using a high concentration of the free substrate or inhibitor, altering the pH, or changing the ionic strength. The elution conditions are carefully optimized to release the enzyme in an active form.

2. Types of Ligands Used in Enzyme Isolation
2.1 Substrate Analogs:

- **Mimicking Natural Substrates:** Substrate analogs are compounds that resemble the natural substrates of the enzyme but are modified to facilitate binding without undergoing catalysis. These analogs bind to the enzyme's active site, effectively capturing the enzyme on the affinity matrix.
- **Example:** In the isolation of kinases, ATP analogs are commonly used as ligands because they mimic the enzyme's natural substrate, allowing for the selective capture of the kinase.

2.2 Inhibitors:

- **Competitive Inhibitors:** Competitive inhibitors that bind to the active site of the enzyme are often used as ligands in affinity chromatography. These inhibitors prevent the natural substrate from binding, ensuring that the enzyme remains bound to the column until elution.
- **Example:** Protease inhibitors can be used as ligands to isolate proteases from a complex mixture by binding specifically to the active site of the enzyme.

2.3 Cofactors:

- **Cofactor-Based Ligands:** Some enzymes require cofactors, such as metal ions or organic molecules, for their activity. These cofactors can be immobilized on the matrix to selectively bind enzymes that depend on them for catalysis.
- **Example:** NAD+ or NADP+ is often used as a ligand to isolate dehydrogenases, enzymes that require these cofactors for their activity.

2.4 Affinity Tags:

- **Tagged Enzymes:** In recombinant enzyme production, enzymes can be engineered with affinity tags (e.g., His-tag, GST-tag) that bind to specific ligands immobilized on the matrix. This allows for easy and selective purification of the tagged enzyme.
- **Example:** A His-tagged enzyme can be purified using a column with immobilized nickel ions, which bind specifically to the histidine residues in the tag.

3. Applications of Affinity Chromatography in Enzyme Isolation
3.1 Purification of Therapeutic Enzymes:

- **High Purity Requirement:** Therapeutic enzymes, such as those used in enzyme replacement therapies or as biocatalysts, require high purity and activity. Affinity chromatography is widely used to purify these enzymes to meet stringent regulatory standards for therapeutic use.
- **Preservation of Activity:** The mild conditions used in affinity chromatography help preserve the enzyme's native structure and catalytic activity, which is crucial for its therapeutic efficacy.

3.2 Enzyme Kinetics and Mechanistic Studies:

- **Isolation for Research:** Researchers often use affinity chromatography to isolate enzymes for kinetic and mechanistic studies. By obtaining highly pure and active enzymes, scientists can study the enzyme's catalytic properties, substrate specificity, and reaction mechanisms in detail.
- **Example:** The isolation of DNA polymerases using nucleotide analogs as ligands allows researchers to study the enzyme's role in DNA replication and repair.

3.3 Industrial Enzyme Production:

- **Large-Scale Purification:** In industrial biotechnology, enzymes are produced on a large scale for use in various processes, such as food production, biofuel generation, and pharmaceuticals. Affinity chromatography is employed to purify these enzymes efficiently, ensuring high yield and purity at an industrial scale.
- **Example:** The production of cellulases for biofuel production often involves affinity chromatography to purify the enzyme from fermentation broths.

3.4 Diagnostic and Analytical Enzymes:

- **Purification for Diagnostics:** Enzymes used in diagnostic assays, such as glucose oxidase or horseradish peroxidase, must be highly pure to ensure accurate and reliable results in clinical tests. Affinity chromatography provides the necessary purity and activity for these critical applications.
- **Example:** The purification of glucose oxidase using glucose analogs as ligands ensures that the enzyme retains its activity for use in glucose monitoring devices.

4. Advantages of Affinity Chromatography for Enzyme Isolation
4.1 High Specificity and Yield:

- **Selective Binding:** Affinity chromatography offers high specificity for the target enzyme, ensuring that only the enzyme of interest is retained on the column. This specificity leads to a high yield of purified enzyme with minimal contamination from other proteins.

- **Efficient Purification:** The strong and specific binding between the enzyme and the ligand allows for the purification of enzymes even from complex mixtures, such as crude cell extracts, in a single chromatographic step.

4.2 Preservation of Enzyme Activity:

- **Mild Elution Conditions:** The ability to elute the enzyme under mild conditions ensures that its catalytic activity is preserved. This is essential for applications where the enzyme's functionality is critical, such as in therapeutics or research.
- **Retention of Native Structure:** Affinity chromatography typically operates under conditions that maintain the enzyme's native conformation, preventing denaturation or loss of activity during the purification process.

4.3 Reusability of Columns:

- **Regeneration of Columns:** Affinity chromatography columns can be regenerated and reused multiple times without significant loss of binding capacity. This reusability is cost-effective and efficient, especially in large-scale or repetitive purification processes.

5. Challenges and Considerations
5.1 Ligand Leaching:

- **Potential Contamination:** One challenge in enzyme isolation using affinity chromatography is the potential leaching of the ligand from the column, which can contaminate the purified enzyme. This is particularly problematic in therapeutic or diagnostic applications.
- **Stable Immobilization:** To minimize ligand leaching, the ligand should be covalently immobilized on the matrix, ensuring that it remains bound to the column during the purification process.

5.2 pH and Buffer Sensitivity:

- **Impact on Enzyme Stability:** The pH and buffer conditions used during binding and elution must be carefully controlled to avoid denaturing the enzyme or affecting its activity. Enzymes can be sensitive to changes in pH, ionic strength, or the presence of certain ions or solvents.
- **Optimizing Conditions:** It is essential to optimize the buffer conditions to balance effective binding and elution with the preservation of enzyme activity.

5.3 Scale-Up Considerations:

- **Consistency and Reproducibility:** Scaling up the affinity chromatography process for large-scale enzyme production requires careful attention to ensure that the purification process remains consistent and reproducible. This includes maintaining uniform ligand density, consistent column packing, and stable flow rates.
- **Cost-Effectiveness:** While affinity chromatography is highly effective, it can be costly, particularly at large scales. The cost of the ligands, matrices, and the need for regeneration of columns must be balanced against the benefits of high purity and yield.

www.ingramcontent.com/pod-product-compliance
Lightning Source LLC
Chambersburg PA
CBHW051143130726
47988CB00005B/1972